A silver loving cup, presented to him by his employees in 1913 at the celebration of his town's tenth anniversary, became one of Milton S. Hershey's most treasured possessions. At the same celebration he heard "The Hershey Song," an anthem to his achievements.

MICHAEL D'ANTONIO

HERSHEY

MILTON S. HERSHEY'S EXTRAORDINARY LIFE OF WEALTH, EMPIRE, AND UTOPIAN DREAMS

———————

SIMON & SCHUSTER

NEW YORK   LONDON   TORONTO   SYDNEY

SIMON & SCHUSTER
Rockefeller Center
1230 Avenue of the Americas
New York, NY 10020

For information about special discounts for bulk purchases,
please contact Simon & Schuster Special Sales at
1-800-456-6798 or business@simonandschuster.com

Designed by Karolina Harris

Manufactured in the United States of America

10   9   8   7   6   5   4   3

Library of Congress Cataloging-in-Publication Data
D'Antonio, Michael.
   Hershey : Milton S. Hershey's extraordinary life of wealth, empire, and utopian dreams /
Michael D'Antonio.
     p.   cm.
   Includes bibliographical references and index.
   1. Hershey, Milton Snavely, 1857–1945. 2. Chocolate industry—United States—History—20th century. 3. Hershey Chocolate Corporation—History. 4. Businesspeople—United States—Biography. I. Title.

HD9200.U52H4715 2006
338.7'664153'092—dc22
[B]

                                                      2005051581

ISBN-13: 978-0-7432-6409-9
ISBN-10:   0-7432-6409-6

For Toni, who makes my life sweeter than chocolate.

CONTENTS

HERSHEY

INTRODUCTION

Tourists who travel by car—and more than four million come every year—often start at the landmark Hotel Hershey, which occupies a ridge that rises more than a hundred feet above the Lebanon Valley in central Pennsylvania. It's a Moorish-style fortress with ornamental towers and a green tile roof. The view from its veranda is the best one available. To the south a scene that looks like a model railroad display comes to life. Cars speed along smooth asphalt highways. Lush cornfields give way to a color-splashed amusement park with ten roller coasters, a Ferris wheel, and a snaking monorail. Beyond the neon and flapping pennants stand old factory buildings, church spires, and houses. Every once in a while a freight train will snake its way along the tracks that slice through the valley.

A drive into town on Sand Beach Road, which becomes Park Avenue, takes you along the east flank of the park. The double-track roller coaster—ninety feet high at its tallest point—is so close to the road that a falling cap could land on your car. Farther along, on a quieter, shady stretch of road waits a small zoo, which is set beside a pristine little creek. Park Avenue then takes a sharp turn and climbs up and over a bridge that crosses railroad tracks. On the other side you are suddenly deposited in another place and time.

In downtown Hershey, the streetlights are shaped like giant Kisses candies. A century-old factory made of soft red brick sprouts a pair of giant smokestacks decorated with the letters H-E-R-S-H-E-Y. The emerald fairways of a golf course stretch out from the factory lawn. Across the avenue, gracious old houses, some dating from 1905, occupy carefully manicured properties.

All of Hershey, including the zoo, the antique town, the amusement park, the playful streetlights, and even the factory, is clean and neat and cheerful. Even the names of the major streets—Chocolate Avenue and Cocoa Avenue—bring a smile to a visitor's face. And that's before he stops, gets out of the car, and realizes that the air in this Willy Wonka place smells like sweet cocoa. Hershey always smells like this. On a humid summer day when there is no breeze it's so strong you can taste it.

In this town of 13,000 souls, business people and civic boosters promote an image of kindhearted contentment. Squabbling is bad for business, and the main businesses in little Hershey—tourism and candy—rack up sales in excess of $5 billion per year. For this reason, the great howl of protest that erupted in Hershey in the summer of 2002 drew reporters and TV news crews from around the world.

It all started with small groups of worried citizens meeting in living rooms and kitchens. Then townspeople noticed handmade signs tacked to light poles, staked on lawns, and taped onto shop windows. Some said, "Derail the Sale." Others warned, "Wait 'til Mr. Hershey finds out!"

The object of these protests was the Milton Hershey School Trust, which held controlling interest in the famous chocolate company for the benefit of a residential school for needy children. The stock was worth as much as $10 billion and the trust was planning to sell it to the highest bidder. Fifty-seven years earlier, when founder Milton S. Hershey died, the trust guaranteed that local residents who shared a common sense of purpose and community would run the company and protect the economy of the town. If the stock was sold, the chocolate-making firm that had represented the playful and prosperous spirit of the community for a century would pass from local control.

Worried conversations about the sale quickly led to an organized opposition. Finally, on a scorching hot Friday in August, more than five hundred citizens marched through downtown waving placards and shouting while police looked on.

This being Hershey, when the people took to the streets they were careful to dress nicely and walk with care, avoiding damage to private lawns and public gardens. Younger protesters kept a kind eye on the elderly marchers to make sure they didn't suffer in the heat. Nobody cursed. Nobody threw a punch, a bottle, or a scrap of litter.

But as mild mannered as the demonstration was, it was also a sign of deeply felt worry. Never in the town's history had such a varied group united behind a single cause. The opposition included many retired Hershey company executives, including the silver-haired former chairman of the board, Richard Zimmerman, who stood to earn a fortune on his stock if the sale went forward. The retired executives were joined by union workers who stood with alumni of the Milton Hershey School. Men who once designed ad campaigns for Hershey bars developed antisale propaganda. Schoolchildren marched beside doctors, lawyers, and local politicians.

At a rally, alumni leader Ric Fouad shouted, "We're not here to mourn, we're here to mobilize!" Onlookers waved placards that read, "Power to the People!" and "Save Our Town!"[1]

The idea of selling the Hershey company was born of good intentions. Board members of the Milton Hershey School Trust, which held a controlling interest in what was formally called the Hershey Foods Corporation, had decided that the charity's dependence on the firm's stock was unwise. American securities markets were in the middle of a long steep decline. Some major companies—WorldCom, Enron, etc.—were collapsing in scandal and leaving investors with pennies on the dollar. Looking at the perilous markets, the board members secretly decided to sell the trust's stake in Hershey and invest the windfall in a more diverse portfolio.[2]

Although other charities held big stakes in corporations, the situation in Hershey was unusual. For one thing, the trust was devoted to a single enterprise: an eleven-hundred-pupil residential school for needy children. For another, the value of the trust was enormous. Estimated at $5 billion, it was already eight times larger than the endowment of Phillips Exeter Academy, the nation's next-richest school. Indeed, only six *universities* held larger endowments, which meant that the Milton Hershey School was richer than Cornell, Columbia, or the University of Pennsylvania.

But as big as it was, the trust was unusually vulnerable because a crash in one company's stock price would do enormous damage to its portfolio. The diversification that a sale would make possible would reduce this risk. It could also produce a onetime windfall. Bidders would recognize that Hershey's many brands, which included Reese's, York, and Jolly Ranchers candies, had been underexploited. Properly managed, which might mean breaking the company into pieces, the whole lot might be worth not $5 billion but closer to $10 billion.[3]

From a fiduciary standpoint, selling the company was in the interest of the trust and the Milton Hershey School. And the timing was right. The big global companies that dominated the candy business—Nestlé, Cadbury-Schweppes, Kraft—were in a buying mood. If the trust board didn't consider selling, it would fail to meet its duty to the institution and its students.

As much as the residents of Hershey cared about the needy children at the school, they had a hard time believing that a sale was necessary. Even without maximizing its investment, the trust's income far exceeded the board's ability to spend it every year. Not that they didn't try. They had built lavish facilities, expanded enrollment, and hired top-notch staff. With the cost of building maintenance factored in, they spent about $100,000 per year per child. And still the excess revenues piled up. How much more could the school need?

With the trust already rich, opponents of the sale thought the board was asking the community to make an unnecessary sacrifice. Roughly six thousand people held jobs in the company, including about three thousand unionized factory workers. A new owner was likely to see that bigger profits could be had if manufacturing were consolidated in other places, where wages, taxes, and other costs were lower. If the factories were moved, the jobs would be very difficult to replace. The change would also affect tourism and the very identity of the community. What's a chocolate town without a chocolate plant?

The town of Hershey had been created first in the imagination of the chocolate industrialist Milton S. Hershey, who then made it real in a place where there had been little more than a few farmhouses and acres of corn. The chocolate factory, the school, and the town were supposed to make up a self-perpetuating little utopia of capitalism and charity, and all three had thrived for ninety-nine years by adhering to his vision.

The idealism of Milton S. Hershey was cited over and over again by those who tried to stop the sale. With no real authority in the matter—private trusts are not required to answer to the public—they appealed to state officials and the court of public opinion. To do this, they put together a story that described the trustees as greedy and heartless outsiders who didn't understand the destruction they would visit on the town. They then welcomed the national media.

The reporters who came to Hershey saw a tableau of small-town America that was as appealing as the dream M.S., as he was known, held in his mind when he created his factory and his community. And like so many visitors before them, they agreed with the writer who, in the midst of the Great Depression, observed the town of Hershey's stubborn prosperity and isolation and declared it "a 10,000 acre world of its own."[4]

Not one journalist missed the opportunity to flavor the story with references to the town's peculiarities and charming asides about chocolate. By the time the press was through, the entire nation would understand that a uniquely benevolent and impossibly cute village, which called itself "the Sweetest Place on Earth," was being bullied out of its dreamy existence by coldhearted money managers.

"They're threatening to tear the soul out of this community," one community leader told *The Washington Post*.[5]

In the months-long struggle that took place after the Hershey Trust board acknowledged its plans to sell control of the company, most of the talk was focused on the future. Those who worried about the Hershey School and the children it served noted that other charities had recently lost billions of dollars as their stock holdings declined during the end of the bull market. The enormous David and Lucille Packard Foundation had seen half its money disappear as the price of Hewlett-Packard company shares fell. The Ford Foundation lost one-fifth of its value, and the Annie E. Casey trust fell 13 percent in the same bad market.

Opponents of the sale could argue using their own examples. When Tyco International bought AMP Manufacturing of nearby Harrisburg, it quickly laid off two thousand workers and shut its headquarters facility. Looking further afield, the Hershey sale opponents saw that in town after town where lumber companies, textile plants, and steel mills were sold, communities soon suffered enormous job losses. Smaller companies that supplied goods and services went bankrupt. Downtown business districts became ghost towns with plywood-covered storefronts, property values crumbled, and public services from schools to police withered for lack of tax dollars. Perhaps the best example of this pattern was Gary, Indiana, a prosperous center for steelmaking that became a nationally known symbol of urban blight when the mills shut down.[6]

In Hershey, the competing predictions raised by the trustees and their opponents—one side saw disaster, the other a smooth transition—left little middle ground and forced people to take a stand. Almost every person the opponents approached, from Milton Hershey School alumni to former company executives and even the governor of Pennsylvania, came out against the sale. Governor Mark Schweicker said that the sale would imperil the state's economy and announced that keeping the company independent was one of his top priorities.

The economic value of the candy company's presence was easy to grasp, but if one listened to what the most impassioned people on both sides had to say, other powerful concerns emerged. Time and again people spoke of the town as an idyllic, nearly perfect place where citizens felt happier, safer, and more secure than people on the outside. Beyond the issues of jobs and money, they were fighting about the concept of community, and the ultimate purpose of corporations, which, after all, are human enterprises that generate wealth through the efforts of flesh and blood people.

Bruce Hummel, business agent for the local union, spoke for many when he declared without a touch of irony that "Hershey is a utopia" worth fighting for. But the statement that was heard most often sounded an even more peculiar ring. Time and again people wondered aloud, "What would Mr. Hershey do?"

As the conflict over the town's future raged, former employee Monroe Stover, age 102, told the local paper that "Mr. Hershey would never have considered" the proposed sale.[7]

For their part, backers of the school trust's proposed sale reminded others that M.S. had himself considered selling the business before the stock market crash of 1929. Needy children were his first concern, they argued, and he would sell if it were in their best interest. For support, they cited Hershey's will in the way that fundamentalist preachers quote Scripture, pointing to a passage that invests in the trustees "full power and authority" to manage the vast fortune that M.S. left in their hands in any way they "may consider safe."[8]

At the height of the furor, an outsider who arrived in Hershey might have believed that M.S. Hershey, dead since 1945, had risen from the grave. The local papers published his picture on a regular basis. His name was spoken in coffee shops and in taverns, in schools and in offices. Everywhere people tried to put themselves in Milton Hershey's place, to imagine what would be in his heart and mind. Most of those who lived in the town of Hershey decided that the eccentric millionaire would favor keeping everything just as it was.

The most remarkable aspect of the great conversation that occurred around Milton Hershey's ideals was that it happened at all. In his life, which ran from before the Civil War, through the Gilded Age, the Great Depression, and World War II, Hershey's wealth, if not his fame, was exceeded by contemporaries such as Carnegie, Rockefeller, and Ford. Indeed, scores of men accumulated fortunes greater than Hershey's and built charities and institutions that became monuments to their achievements. But try to name a great person of Hershey's era who, in 2002, would preoccupy the imagination of an entire community, and thousands of people beyond it, as a great controversy raged. Where and when would anyone ask, "What would Andrew Carnegie (or Cornelius Vanderbilt or Henry Ford) do?"

M.S. Hershey inspired this kind of reverence because he had created not just a great business and an enormous charity, but a complete, prosperous, and self-sustaining community that reflected his idealistic attitudes about everything from commerce to education and architecture. And unlike other model towns of its era, Hershey succeeded and continued to grow long after its founder was gone. Indeed, even as they were fighting over the future, the people of Hershey were preparing to celebrate in 2003 the one hundredth anniversary of the town's founding and a full century of prosperity that was unbroken, even during the Great Depression. The plan envisioned a series of events, culminating in a parade on Milton's birthday, September 13.

The power of Hershey's legacy was plain to see in the ways that people rallied around his memory and his creations. Some people actually described the place as a little kingdom where the monarch's ideals continued to rule long after his demise. "If Milton Hershey were alive there's no way he'd want the Hershey Trust to sell the company," said Kathy Lewis, head of a local historical society. "He created a benevolent dictatorship. Selling Hershey is like selling the soul of a unique community."[9]

At first the quality of Hershey, Pennsylvania's devotion to its founder can strike a visitor as strange, almost cultlike. The American ideal doesn't generally offer room to the notion of a dictatorship on U.S. soil, even if it is a happy and benevolent one. Americans are more comfortable with an ethic that emphasizes individuality and autonomy. We prefer stories of utopias that failed because we believe that human nature abhors an egoist's grand designs.

But a close examination reveals that Milton S. Hershey's creations—the company, the town, and the school—were more a reflection of his values than his ego. Though he possessed a strong will and could be imperious, M.S. was often shy and sentimental. Despite his great wealth he lived in relative modesty, except when traveling abroad. And he held to common values, including respect for others, fair dealing, and honest effort. These were the values that were raised by those who protested the Hershey Trust's sale of the company.

Ultimately, the most compelling aspects of the Hershey story lay not in the immediate conflict but in the history that brought people together in support of an ideal personified by a man. From a modest beginning, M.S. created a model community powered by a highly successful corporation that was devoted to the welfare of its people. Alone among the special places built in an era of big dreams, Hershey has withstood every economic, social, and political challenge. At a time when many Americans feel isolated in their communities, insecure in their jobs, and confused about the nature and purpose of wealth, the Hershey story offers answers, cautions, and inspiration.

THE OAK AND THE VINE

1 Tall and lean with a lush black beard, Henry Hershey liked to dress in silk and often carried a gold-capped walking stick. He had a way with women. There was Mattie Snavely, whom he had courted for a moment. And there was a woman in Harrisburg, who had believed that Henry was going to be *her* husband. But finally he chose Mattie's sister. Veronica Snavely was a short, round-shouldered woman. Known as Fanny, on the surface at least, she was his opposite in almost every way.

Maybe that was the point. As the first true romantic Fanny ever met, Henry could express everything she repressed. Ambitious to a fault, he saw himself as a dramatic figure destined to do great things. He was so independent that he could walk away from the Mennonite faith and his community without showing a single sign of self-doubt. Lack of formal education prevented him from becoming a writer—his first and greatest ambition—but he still impressed others as a sophisticated, even artistic man. He dressed better than most, spoke more eloquently, and laughed more, too.

Fanny had been raised in a prominent but insular family of conservative preachers and hardworking farmers in Lancaster County, Pennsylvania. Her ancestors had been among the wealthier Swiss emigrants to flee religious persecution for the New World in the 1700s. They found in this patch of Pennsylvania a land with fertile green hills and mild weather that resembled the best farmland in their mother country.

Faith and family had molded Fanny in childhood. Her father was a bishop of the Reformed Mennonite Church, which had broken away from the main Mennonite Church because it had gone soft on such "carnal" behaviors as foolish talking, voting, and entertainments like county fairs and horse races. Members of the reformed church were more modest in their dress and quick to punish those who strayed with excommunication and shunning. According to doctrine, children were not automatically part of the church. The choice to join was theirs. Nevertheless, they were surrounded by believers and their lives were guided by church principles. Life in this community, and studies at a local finishing school, had prepared Fanny to be the practical and quiet wife of a steady, respectable man.

In Henry Hershey, Fanny found a dreamer of the first order. His independence touched something rebellious in her. In a quiet way, she was a freethinker, too. Like Henry, she had not joined the church. And she affirmed this break with her family as she agreed to stand beside Henry Hershey to be married at Holy Trinity Lutheran Church in the dead of winter, 1856. Henry, who arrived late to the ceremony, outshined his wife by wearing a frock coat, striped pants, a fancy vest, and a high silk hat.[1]

In 1856, the popular concept of marriage still revolved around the metaphor of "the oak and the vine" as described in Washington Irving's story "The Wife." As Irving and almost everyone else saw it, a proper wife entwined herself like English ivy around the oak that was her husband as he stood against the storms of modern life. He was expected to strive, and to endure inevitable setbacks. She was to accept these losses with grace and flexibility while guarding his dignity and maintaining a home. Eventually prosperity would arrive as God's reward for the resourceful husband and his steadfast spouse.

Fanny was accustomed to prosperity. Lancaster County was one of the richest farm regions in the world and her family had cultivated a fortune in both property and produce. The Snavelys were not alone in their wealth, thanks to the Lancaster Turnpike. One of the first stone-paved highways in America, the pike connected the county's farms to the growing city of Philadelphia and a half million hungry people. Each morning it was crowded with six-horse teams pulling locally built Conestoga wagons, the long-haul trucks of the day. Twelve feet high and sixteen feet long, the bow-shaped Conestogas left Lancaster creaking on oversized wooden wheels and laden with up to seven tons of meat, grain, vegetables, and dairy products. Every night they brought home both finished goods and cash.[2]

Farm revenues, deposited in local banks, financed the development of the elegant little city of Lancaster, with its many churches, markets, and a bustling commercial center. Beginning in the 1830s modern industries— iron furnaces, toolmaking shops, locomotive manufacturers—were built along the Conestoga River, bringing diversity to the local economy. In the 1850s there were times when the city grew so fast that brickyards couldn't keep up with the demand from builders. Carpenters and masons could charge premium rates. In 1857 the growing city's old water pumps were so overwhelmed by new development that city fathers approved construction of a new waterworks capable of producing a million gallons per day.

All the growth gave Lancaster a busy big-city feel. Trains bearing freight and passengers crossed through town at street level at all hours of the day and night, heaving soot, steam, and noise into the air. The nation's first commercial telegraph line, reaching to the nearby state capital of Harris- burg, originated in the city center. And local pride overflowed in 1856, when native son James Buchanan gained the presidency with a pro-slavery platform. Although many county citizens were abolitionists, Buchanan's rise to power, and the region's obvious wealth, contributed to the feeling that big things were possible.[3]

In Lancaster, Henry Hershey could see the magic that happened when ambitious men were armed with capital. Eventually he would confess that the Snavely wealth, and the possibilities it represented, had made a not quite beautiful young Fanny into an attractive bride. But in the first days of their marriage he made no play for her family's money. Instead the couple moved into the Hershey homestead twenty miles north in the Lebanon Valley, where Henry had lived as a boy. They leased land and Henry tried in his own distracted way to succeed as a tenant farmer. He and Fanny got along well enough that twenty months later Fanny was ready to give birth to their first child.

In the last weeks of the summer of 1857, Lancaster and its neighboring counties were settled in a comfortable and familiar routine. Farmers pre- pared for the nearby York County Fair, where they would show their pro- duce and livestock in competition. Best cow, best pig, best potato—they all got ribbons. A local entrepreneur was promoting corn syrup sweetener as an alternative to sugar and molasses. (Some said it tasted a little like rye whiskey.) And a big new mill in the city of Lancaster had begun to turn out iron rails for the North Central Railway. This was considered a sign of fu- ture prosperity.

But in fact the economic life of the region was about to be overwhelmed by faraway events. In New York a major investment house that had committed too heavily to overbuilt railroads was tumbling into bankruptcy. In cities across the Northeast, a dozen banks were reported "broken or suspended."[4]

As these events were taking place far away, Fanny labored in her bed to bring her first child into the world. On September 13, 1857, she gave her husband a son, Milton Snavely Hershey. It was a sign of Fanny's status that the boy was born with the help of a local physician.

On the day Milton arrived, news of a great and historic shipwreck in the Atlantic reached shore. Two hundred miles off the North Carolina coast a hurricane had swept across the sea and swamped a steamer called the S.S. *Central America*. The crew fired signal rockets, attracting a small brig that rescued the women and children on board. But there was no room for the men, and when the *Central America* finally sank, 425 were drowned and fifteen tons of California gold—valued at $400 per ounce in 2005 dollars—went with them into the Atlantic.

Joined with recent bank closings and other financial scandals, the loss of the gold, which was intended to back U.S. currency, destroyed the confidence of the investors who propped-up the nation's economy. In the Panic of 1857, as the crisis was called, investors raced to withdraw cash from their accounts. Half the brokerage houses on Wall Street went bankrupt. As the destructive waves rippled out from New York, banks and businesses throughout the eastern United States went under.

Commerce in Lancaster withered. Within months a local bank, the Lancaster Locomotive works, and an anthracite blast furnace run by Geiger and Company were forced to close. Many other companies contracted or canceled planned expansions. As industry hunkered down Henry Hershey, who chafed at farm life, inevitably looked into the distance for both an escape and a chance to make it big. He was a man of imagination. All he needed was a little inspiration. It appeared, oozing out of the ground, more than 250 miles northwest of Lancaster, in the small town of Titusville.[5]

In early 1860, the hopes of ambitious men across America were stoked by the tale of a former railroad conductor, sent by New Haven investors, who had struck oil in Titusville, Pennsylvania. A gaunt-looking man with deep-set eyes who wore a silk hat in the oil fields, the famous Edwin Drake would eventually be credited with a pivotal role in the greatest industrial transformation in history, moving the world into the age of petroleum.

But in the moment of his discovery, all Drake could have known for sure was that he had set off an explosion of speculation that rivaled the frenzy over gold at Sutter's Mill in 1848, when a half million people raced to the region north and east of San Francisco. After Drake's discovery, thousands of men armed with cash descended on northwest Pennsylvania like hungry grasshoppers. In a matter of months landowners had sold leases allowing prospectors to drill all along Oil Creek, where crude seeped from the ground and covered the water with a shiny coat.

Within a year, the Oil Creek Valley resembled a western gold rush town. Trees were stripped from the hillsides to supply lumber and open up drilling sites. A symphony of saws and hammers played every day as hotels, shops, boardinghouses, and derricks sprung up from the ground. Crowded between steep slopes, the narrow valley offered few truly flat building plots, so prospectors used dynamite to blast away rock and create level platforms for drilling. The steam-powered derricks erected on these sites were given whimsical names—Sleeping Beauty, the Vampire, Big Bologna—and colorful pennants flew from their peaks. After one of his visits to the oil fields, Andrew Carnegie would recall that the words "Hell or China" were written on a flag that fluttered over one oilman's shack.[6]

The heavy scent of petroleum hung like a permanent fog over the towns of the valley. Strikes became entertainment. People brought chairs to sit near wells, hoping to get caught in a sudden shower of oil when drillers passed the magic depth of seventy feet. Great fortunes were made as oil was pumped, loaded into barrels, and shipped to Cleveland for refining. Saloons where prostitution, gambling, and brawling were practiced day and night became temples of celebration.

Although failure was as common as mud in the oil fields, little was said about the men who borrowed more than they could afford to lose, and lost it anyway. Instead, tales of the wonders of Oil Creek Valley—oil spouting into the sky, men becoming rich overnight—were published in newspapers across America. Some of these reports were so wildly effusive that editors back home didn't themselves believe their correspondents. But they printed the dispatches anyway. Typical was an article reprinted in a small paper in New York state. The author warns, "I hardly dare record what I have actually witnessed" and then goes on to describe "men in very moderate circumstances" who had risked everything in a desperate gamble on oil leases. Their fears and anxieties mount until, on a Friday morning, "they had found oil, and in a moment, had stepped from *Poverty* to *Wealth*. . . . California never, in its palmiest days, offered as great inducements to men seeking fortunes."[7]

While the earth was gushing money in the northern part of the state, Henry Hershey tried in vain to pull profits from a small farm he purchased on April 2, 1860. Given the result, it's hard to imagine he made much of an effort. The young couple was so poor that Fanny sometimes "stripped" her neighbor's cows, milking them after their udders had been emptied, just to get the little that was left. And just two months and two days after he acquired the place, Henry gave the property back to the seller, and agreed to sell everything he owned to pay his creditors. On August 23, a public auction netted just over eleven hundred dollars. Within weeks the Hersheys were on their way to Oil City.[8]

Henry, Fanny, and their round-faced toddler, Milton, likely traveled to Pittsburgh by rail, where they then boarded a riverboat. In the autumn of 1860, the *Allegheny Belle* and other steamers that served the oil region from Pittsburgh were carrying hundreds of people per voyage. After transferring to smaller boats at Franklin—in a fit of boosterism one of these boats was renamed *Petrolia*—prospectors disembarked at Oil City, which a few months earlier had been known by the modest name of Cornplanter. Titusville, site of the Drake Well, lay twenty miles north, at the end of a road that was rutted and dusty on dry days, and as sticky as cake batter on wet ones.

The record of Henry Hershey's pursuit of petroleum offers few details, except for the fact that he had borrowed heavily to fund his adventure. Certainly he confronted the same everyday challenges that other prospectors faced. In 1860, the oil towns were so overrun by prospectors that basics like food, water, and shelter were wildly overpriced, if they could be had at all. Men gladly paid a dollar a night to sleep on a pool table and fights broke out over seats in boardinghouse kitchens where the food was barely edible. If Henry had been resourceful, and lucky, he would have rented a room for his family, or acquired one of the hundreds of shanties that had been thrown up by overworked carpenters. Fanny and Milton would have then been left to fend for themselves as Henry tromped through the valley to find a promising investment for his cash.

Between Oil City and Titusville, derricks rose like stalks of asparagus in a spring garden. Newcomers like Henry Hershey looked for prospectors who were running short of cash and would trade a share of their claim for the money to keep on drilling. Just what made one man's spot better than another was a matter for wild speculation. Some prospectors believed that oil ran downhill, so they favored low land. Others insisted that proximity to the running waters of Oil Creek was the key factor. Of course these notions were just guesses, and no more credible than the wild theories offered to explain the origins of petroleum. Some credited subterranean volcanoes while others said oil grew underground like perennial flowers. A retired sea captain, who had come to the oil fields from New Bedford, was sure that the oil came from whales stranded and buried when Noah's flood receded. He reasoned that the successful drillers had each managed to tap a rotten carcass.

No matter its source, it was easy for a man to imagine that great pools of precious fluid waited just below the earth's surface and all you had to do to get rich was bore enough holes. Shares in oil leases were traded casually. One teamster accepted 8 percent of a new hole from a prospector who couldn't pay the freight charges on the machinery and lumber he had delivered. The deal allowed the rig to go up. When oil was found the teamster made a fast $30,000 (more than $650,000 in 2005 dollars).[9]

The successes of men like the teamster kept the little Hershey family in the oil patch through the rest of 1860. Like many others, they were caught up in the peculiar dynamics of a mining fever. Whether it was gold in California, silver in Colorado, or oil in Pennsylvania, the scenario was the same. A big discovery drew hope-filled men to a desperate race for riches. While most were certain to fail, the real successes of the few kept hope alive for everyone else. It was hard to walk away when you believed that one more pan full of gravel, or hole in the ground, could make you rich.

In February 1861, while Henry Hershey still chased his dream of oil wealth, Abraham Lincoln stopped briefly in Lancaster on his way to his inauguration. Pennsylvania had gone strongly for him in the election, thanks to the votes of antislavery Amish, Mennonites, and Quakers. His visit was intended to express his gratitude and to calm a country on the eve of the Civil War. (He wouldn't return until the morning of April 22, 1865, when his body passed through Lancaster aboard the Lincoln Special on its mournful journey to Springfield, Illinois.)[10]

In Oil City, the threat of war only increased the speculative frenzy as prospectors anticipated the Union army's need for petroleum products. More than eight hundred wells were sunk in the summer of 1861. Construction began on a railroad that would assure safer, faster, more reliable shipment of crude. When the line was finished and trains began to run, the oil that surged out of the ground in the morning would arrive in Cleveland for refining in the afternoon.

Against the backdrop of excitement and the steadily increasing number of productive wells, Henry Hershey's failures were that much more painful. By January 1862, he was fast running out of cash and Fanny was six months pregnant with their second child. Worried about their sister, Fanny's brothers Abraham and Benjamin came to visit, and perhaps rescue, her.

To the Snavely men, Oil Creek Valley, which locals had begun calling "Sodden Gomorrah," must have seemed like hell on earth. Oil cast a slippery film on the ground, the walls of houses, even the people. The roads were jammed with wagons carrying heavy barrels of crude. Teamsters drove their horses hard. Those that were injured were shot and their carcasses were left in the ditch, where the flesh was eaten by the petrochemicals that spilled from broken and leaking barrels. The Allegheny River was so fouled by oil that it once caught fire, and the blaze destroyed a wooden bridge. On land, fires, explosions, and other accidents regularly claimed the lives of workers and their families.

Given what they saw, and mindful of the life of comfort their sister had enjoyed *before* she met Henry Hershey, the Snavely brothers made a quick decision. The oil adventure was over. They would pay to bring the entire family back to the Hershey homestead.

On some level Henry Hershey may have been grateful for the Snavely brothers' generosity, but he hated to return to the farm life. And he surely believed that in Oil City he was leaving behind the kind of opportunity that promised almost unlimited wealth to the right men. Indeed, as Hershey departed, John D. Rockefeller was beginning to consolidate his power in the oil region. Rockefeller had arrived in Oil City in the same year as Hershey, 1860. But unlike Henry, he was possessed of extraordinary energy, remarkable financial savvy, and an uncanny ability to remain focused on his goals. Soon he would dominate the flow of oil and its by-products nationwide, and the story of his rise to become the richest man in the world would be known by every American. Another oilman, whose firm was called the Dramatic Oil Company, would become just as famous as Rockefeller but for a different reason. His name was John Wilkes Booth.[11]

At the homestead, Henry Hershey found himself contained in the powerfully stable—he might say stifling—life of Mennonite farmers. In this community, self-denial and modesty were the highest virtues. Playfulness was met with scorn, and sensuality was greeted with shame. An oft told joke in the region poked fun at the farmer who fed wheat to his cow to get sweeter cream for his porridge. What kind of fool, wondered the pious, would dare such an indulgence?

Gone from Henry Hershey's life was the raucous, dirty excitement of Oil City, where soon oil would reach the astounding price of $12 ($168 in 2005) per barrel. In its place came terse conversations and the unchanging rhythm of chores that began at dawn and ended at dusk. At night Henry would have had trouble finding topics to discuss with his family and friends because they shared few common interests. Where Henry devoured news of the day and studied politics and business, the traditional Pennsylvania Dutch considered such things ridiculous. In fact they used a German dialect word for politics—*bolitisch*—as a synonym for absurd. In their eyes, almost everything about Henry and his marriage to Fanny would have seemed *bolitisch*, except perhaps for their efforts to make a family.[12]

Fanny gave birth to her second child, a daughter named Sarena, on April 12, 1862. Four-year-old Milton fell in love with the baby, and for a while the four Hersheys settled into a happy routine. Liberated from the dangers and filth of Oil City, Milton was introduced to fresh air and farm chores. He carried water, fed chickens, and collected their eggs. Every once in a while his parents would take him on a trip to Harrisburg, where they sold produce at a downtown market. Once he climbed into a Conestoga bound for Philadelphia, but he was discovered about three miles into the journey.

As a grown man, Milton would retain one vivid memory of those early days in the Lebanon Valley. The story begins in late June 1863, as the Confederate army under Robert E. Lee moved toward Pennsylvania and the battle at Gettysburg with the Union's Army of the Potomac led by George Meade.

On June 28, the people of York, which was about twenty-five miles from the Lebanon Valley, turned over their city to the Confederates without a shot being fired. That night a small band of Union soldiers used refined Titusville oil to set fire to the mile-long covered bridge that spanned the Susquehanna at Wrightsville. The glow from the fire was visible in the sky for miles in every direction. By morning the bridge, which linked the western shore near York with the east, was destroyed.

Relying on telegrams from correspondents, the *Lancaster Inquirer* reported on the massing of troops on both sides and predicted a great battle. "The danger to Pennsylvania and the North is still imminent," read one report. "Everything depends upon the encounter between Lee and General Meade. If our Army should be defeated we should have no hope, except in large armies to be raised in the North."

The paper supplied substantial details about the assembled artillery units, reconnaissance missions, and morale on both sides. Readers got more than enough information to make them feel threatened and vulnerable. For days the whole region was filled with fear and anxiety. By the night of June 30, the heated talk of war at the Hershey family supper table frightened five-year-old Milton into digging a hole in the garden and burying the few coins he possessed in a coffee can.

July 1 arrived cloudy, but dry. The air was almost still and the temperature hovered around seventy-five degrees. Milton heard the first rumble of cannon fire, more than fifty miles away at Gettysburg, shortly after dawn. As remarkable as this may seem, others reported hearing the same explosions. A preacher named Peter Nissley wrote, "We heard the cannon plain." Another local wrote that children heard the artillery reports "by lying with our ears to the ground."

Certain that the great battle to defend the North from invasion had begun, many terrified families took to the road, clattering northward and eastward in horse-pulled wagons. But rumors that Lee had crossed the Susquehanna and was headed to Philadelphia proved false. The Union army would prevail and within a week those who had fled were back in their homes. One of the few people in the Lebanon Valley to lose anything in the upheaval was little Milton. He dug holes for days, but never did recover the can he had hidden.[13]

In the autumn of 1863, with the dangers of the war an outgoing tide, Milton Hershey began attending a school in the settlement closest to the homestead, a crossroads called Derry Church. He didn't do well, and didn't enjoy going, but Henry Hershey insisted that his boy get an education. He already had plans for Milton to fulfill the dream he failed to achieve himself—becoming a writer. Fanny Hershey allowed the boy to attend, but she didn't share Henry's enthusiasm for education.

The couple suffered many other points of conflict. Henry's humor, his get-rich-quick schemes and his preference for talking about things rather than doing them, had ceased to be charming for Fanny. Even neighbors could see that the man was lazy. In a community where hard work on good land was the only reliable route to respectability, Henry Hershey was not likely to succeed. As time passed, Fanny grew to resent him more and more.

Henry, who was approaching forty, didn't seem to be settling down at all. After he failed at selling farm equipment, the Snavely family arranged for him to take ownership of a less than ideal tract of farmland they held at a crossroads called Nine Points. (Whether Henry actually paid for this land is in doubt.) Forty-four acres in a rock-strewn hollow with poor soil and a small cabin, Fanny called it the "little stony farm."

Because the property was miles from Fanny's family, and he was free from their oversight, Henry farmed in his own peculiar, halfhearted way. Since he enjoyed a drink, and the company of men, he must have been delighted too, to find McComsey's hotel and general store within walking distance of Nine Points.

It was a good time for a man to start a new venture. Huge federal expenditures for the war just ended had turned America into an industrial nation. At the same time, laborsaving iron and steel inventions—new plows, reapers, and mowers—were making farming more efficient and profitable. So much grain was being produced that farms had begun to export large quantities to Europe, creating a market that would absorb increasing production for decades to come.

In Lancaster city, the former Geiger and Company blast furnace was reopened, and new manufacturing plants spurred a population boom as workers came to fill new jobs. As hard as it worked, the city also learned to play again. In 1866, Lancaster's one real theater, the Fulton, got its first resident company of actors. It also hosted an opera company from Philadelphia and minstrel troupes from New York. One of the big hits of the year was Commodore Foote, the self-proclaimed "smallest man in the world" who with his equally tiny sister performed dance and comedy routines for packed houses. The more serious-minded in Lancaster frequented Hambright and Company, a small shop where they could gaze through a stereoscope at remarkably vivid pictures of Civil War battlefields or exotic landscapes.

All of society, high and low, turned out when the famous aeronaut John Wise, a local hero, brought one of his giant balloons to Centre Square and prepared for flight. Having experimented as a boy with a house cat tied to a parachute, Wise had grown up to become a famous daredevil, setting records for long-distance balloon flights and making the first airmail delivery in history. For a time he made Lancaster the home of American aviation and his achievements were a matter of great civic pride.

Each of Wise's flights was a form of aerial theater. While large crowds gathered Wise tapped a gas valve, which had been installed for his convenience, to fuel the flames that filled his balloon with so much hot air that it was as tall as the three story buildings that flanked the square. He then climbed into the car, ordered the tethers to be untied, and began to drift skyward. Sometimes he had trouble clearing the buildings on the square. A drawing from the time shows a young man reaching out a top-floor window to push Wise away from a façade.

Once he was aloft, Wise and his great balloon made a magnificent sight. With the people below shouting and waving their arms, the whole scene was as exhilarating as the wizard's departure from Oz in L. Frank Baum's 1900 novel.

Wise would continue to fly as a boisterous, white-haired old man. At age seventy-one he took off from Sterling, Illinois, disappeared over Lake Michigan, and was never seen again. The mystery of his disappearance was national news. After Wise's death, the U.S. Army would name its first flight school in his honor, and the John Wise Balloon Society would keep his memory alive into the twenty-first century. Author Baum, whose writing career was made possible by his own father's success in the Pennsylvania oil industry, was a twenty-three-year-old journalist at the time of Wise's disappearance.[14]

As a sociable, self-anointed intellectual who restlessly roamed the county, Henry Hershey almost certainly witnessed John Wise in flight as well as all the other wonders of Lancaster city. And given his penchant for conversation and impromptu lectures delivered to anyone standing near, he would have returned to the farm to share these experiences with Fanny, Sarena, and Milton.

By the time he lived at Nine Points, Milton Hershey was an extraordinarily experienced and well-traveled little boy. In an age when most people lived and died within a few miles of the spot where they were born, he had covered more than three hundred miles following his father to live in three different communities. At Nine Points he had more freedom to roam, and he met neighbors who were less conservative, less wealthy, and less established than his relatives. He encountered Christians who were comfortable voting, and he visited and picked cherries at the run-down farm owned by an African-American woman named Mary Salisbury. An outpost along the Underground Railroad, this Quaker-influenced corner of Pennsylvania had welcomed many runaway slaves and was known for racial harmony. An elderly widow, Mary Salisbury survived on the generosity of her neighbors.

But as much as Milton was enriched by his early life experience, he was also denied the kind of stability children need to feel secure. He had been moved from place to place, and he listened to his parents argue with increasing frequency and anger. As a bishop's daughter, Fanny was accustomed to a certain level of wealth, comfort, and status. Though Mennonites didn't embrace luxuries, they considered money and property to be a sign of God's grace, and because the Snavelys had plenty of both, Fanny had never wanted for anything. But with Henry she struggled to take care of herself and her children and she worried about the future. For his part, Henry refused to conform to her expectations and the norms of the community. He wasn't completely irresponsible, but he was unconventional and not the worrying type.

At Nine Points Henry established one of the strangest little farms in the county. First he invited neighbors to a party, called a frolic, where they helped him build a seven-foot-high dam to create a pond he would stock with fish. He then planted rows of specimen fruit trees, which he hoped to sell to farmers and to home owners in the city. Henry raised experimental breeds of poultry and cattle, planted berries, ornamental shrubs, and roses, and produced the first local crop of a new kind of hay called alfalfa. And as people might have expected, he coined a fanciful name for the place—Trout Brook Fruit and Nursery Farm.

But the novelty that Henry created on his forty-four acres was not enough to satisfy his restless mind. When he met a German immigrant who was tinkering with a design for a perpetual motion machine, he be-

came thoroughly enthralled. Conrad Wohlgast's machine was to be powered by a wheel equipped with weights that were supposed to slide on rods
and keep the whole thing spinning. For centuries crackpots and geniuses
had pursued the holy grail of a self-renewing source of energy. Henry possessed just the right combination of gall and ignorance to be sure that he
could help his friend succeed. The grandeur of this enterprise grew in his
mind to the point where he began telling anyone who would listen that
one day the names Wohlgast and Hershey "shall be on the tongues of all
civilized men." [15]

Young Milton was captivated by his father's playful schemes and big
ideas. But he was also a witness to his mother's struggle to compensate for
Henry's shortcoming. Fanny had to work hard to maintain the household.
She raised chickens and sold the eggs, churned butter and peddled what
she didn't use. She made corn brooms to sell to local homemakers. All of
this was proof of how far she had drifted from the comfortable life she had
known as a child.

Even with all of Fanny's efforts, there were times Milton went without
proper shoes and the little family didn't have enough to eat. The pain of
this life showed on his face. Neighbors saw Milton as an overly serious
child. [16]

The sober side of the Hersheys' only son was the product of what he saw
in his parents' marriage and what he learned from his mother. In the years
since she was married, Fanny had adopted an increasingly conservative religious outlook. In conversation she would stake out the high moral
ground, pressing on her son the Mennonite values of modesty and service
to community.

True to the model of motherhood in her time, which gave women the
duty of controlling the inherent wildness in growing boys, Fanny monitored her son's moral development very closely. She gave him a conscience
that would stay with him a lifetime. And through Fanny, and others, he
also learned to channel all of his energy and passions into a single outlet:
work.

Fanny's expectations for her son could also be seen as an attempt to save
him from following in his father's path. Henry showed no signs of settling
down. Fanny grew ever more resentful. She complained to her friend and
neighbor Anne Pownall, whose large, modern home was a two-story symbol of what Fanny had given up for her dreamer husband. Fanny grew
closer to her sister Mattie, the one Henry had courted first, inviting her to

spend more and more time at Nine Points. She also began to tell her husband that she would leave him if he didn't make a success of himself soon. (Divorce, like evil books and foolish questions, was to be avoided by Mennonites, so Fanny was just threatening to live apart from her husband.)

The Hersheys' marriage became one long argument. Conflicts over money led Fanny to start hiding the funds she received from her family. Milton's education again became a source of tension. He attended one country school after another. Typical was the one where the teacher had posted mottoes on the wall—"Knowledge Is Power" and "Do Your Best, Angels Do No More." Milton could barely read them. Henry was frustrated with his boy's slow progress. Fanny thought her husband put too much stock in what came from books. And she disagreed with Henry's design for their son's life. She imagined her son as a prosperous farmer or a successful Lancaster businessman—something solid and respectable—and he didn't need to go to college for that.

The winter of 1866–67 had been mild, especially compared with the previous year, which saw the coldest day on record in the region—eighteen below zero in Philadelphia. Nevertheless, the Hershey children were cooped up much of the time in the chilly cabin at Nine Points. Whenever Milton managed to get to school, he encountered classmates with the usual coughs and sniffles. When Sarena, not yet five years old, came down with a sore throat and a mild fever, Fanny may have been worried but she would have hoped that it would pass like any other cold.

It didn't pass. After a couple of days Sarena began to shiver and a faint red rash emerged on her neck, then spread down her chest and across her body. She felt sick to her stomach and had trouble keeping food down. Along with the rash, she probably developed darker red lines in the creases of her armpits. Her tongue swelled and turned a frightening shade of crimson. By this point anyone would have been able to diagnose the child's illness. It was scarlet fever, an often fatal illness that was especially dangerous in children between the ages of four and eight. Scarlet fever epidemics were common in nineteenth-century America, and it killed more children than any other disease.

Willow bark tea, which contained the key ingredients in modern aspirin, was available to ease pain and fever, and a wide assortment of very popular patent medicines—most alcohol based—was sold in Lancaster city. But medical care in that time and place involved nothing more than a physician's words and some vile-tasting potion. Milton so hated the medicines the family doctor brought that he once jumped out of a second-story window, and broke his leg, in an attempt to evade him.

If her illness followed the normal course, Sarena improved after a couple of weeks as the rash subsided. But any hope that Fanny and Henry felt would have been short-lived. Roughly three weeks after the onset of the illness, Sarena took a turn for the worse.

No record exists to show exactly how Sarena finally died. In the age before antibiotics, some scarlet fever victims developed meningitis or suffered liver or kidney failure. Most often, the original sickness would temporarily abate, only to be followed by a more ferocious disease: rheumatic fever. If this happened to Sarena, her temperature would have soared high enough to make her delirious and perhaps, comatose. Chest pain would have been followed by heart failure. Sarena died on March 31, 1867, just as spring was beginning to warm the pastures and orchards at Trout Brook Fruit and Nursery Farm.

Roughly one in every six American children born in 1860 died before the age of five. (In 2005, this figure was less than one per hundred). But the fact that death in childhood was so common didn't ease the grief of mothers, fathers, and siblings. Milton Hershey would count his sister's death as one of the great tragedies of his life.

It was around the time of Sarena's illness that Fanny fully embraced the Reformed Mennonite Church. The conversion process had been gradual. But by 1867, when her daughter died, Fanny was dressing like a Reformed Mennonite lady of her time, in black and gray, with her head covered at all times. Though she was not a regular churchgoer, she had adopted a way of speaking, and a way of looking at the world, that would be best described as biblical.

Not long after her daughter was buried, Fanny ceased talking about her. She also rejected Henry for good. As his wife turned away from him, Henry also suffered a big setback on the farm. The dam that created his fishpond burst, spilling water and trout everywhere. The few that survived to inhabit the brook would later die in a drought. One of the lasting pictures in Milton's memories from that place would be of the bloated, gasping fish that littered the streambed.

• • •

Milton finished school for good in 1870, at age twelve. He had learned how to read and write, and to do simple math and he was eager to get on with life. Still hoping his son would become a man of letters, Henry arranged for him to be an apprentice for a printer who published a paper in the small town of Gap, about seven miles from Nine Points. Henry had enjoyed a long-running, mostly amicable debate with the printer Samuel Ernst, who refused to publish his articles because they weren't fit for his highly religious readers. Ernst had a temper, and Milton didn't like the print shop at all. After a few months he purposely let his hat fall into the press and got himself fired.

Fanny, who felt Henry had forced the job on their son, was happy to see Milton leave the print shop. Her unmarried sister Mattie agreed that the boy's failure was not his fault, but Henry's. (At this time Aunt Mattie was becoming a stronger and more constant presence in both Fanny and Milton's lives.) Milton's next job would be one Fanny preferred, at a Lancaster confectionery named Royer's Ice Cream Parlor and Garden. Located on busy West King Street, Royer's was a pretty place with a candy counter and a shaded terrace where customers enjoyed a popular dessert of ice cream and lemon pastry on Saturday afternoons.

Henry considered the candy shop "women's work" and never approved, but by this time his word meant little to Fanny. Not long after Milton had settled into a routine in Lancaster, he and his mother moved into a little house in the city. From this point on, Fanny and Henry would live separately. One neighbor would recall that Henry still loved his wife and that eventually "he would have made a good husband, if she had let him." But it was too late for that.

Although Fanny was through playing the vine to Henry's oak, she did not abandon her own desires for comfort, wealth, and a life that reflected religious virtue and the Pennsylvania Dutch commitment to work and thrift. Unable or unwilling to divorce Henry, she would devote her time, energy, intellect, and labor to the only other male who might help her realize all her unexpressed ambition and pride: her son.[17]

HEROIC BOYS AND MEN OF INDUSTRY

If you had been a fifteen-year-old boy in Lancaster, Pennsylvania in 1872, you would have wanted to work at Joseph C. Royer's Ice Cream Parlor and Garden. It wasn't just the obvious benefits that come with a job where your mistakes melt sweetly in your mouth. More important was the fact that there was no better place to see pretty girls, ambitious men, and prominent visitors. Nestled in the center of the town, the shop was half a block away from City Hall and close to the main market where farmers sold their produce and meat. It was also convenient for performers and patrons of the Fulton Opera House, who had only to walk around the corner to visit Royer's after a show.

As the hub of Lancaster culture, the Fulton hosted a series of talks by various luminaries billed as the Home Course. Inspired by the nationwide lyceum movement, which promoted adult education, such courses were considered essential to life in any cultured community. Before the Civil War, lyceum speakers were primarily educators and serious writers such as Emerson and Thoreau, but by the 1870s entertainment was also valued and programs tended to include more humor and storytelling.

In the year when Milton began work at Royer's, the biggest event in the Fulton lecture series filled all fifteen hundred seats in the auditorium and every inch of standing room. On a Friday evening in January when sleet pelted the city and slowed the carriages that brought people to the theater, Mark Twain walked onto the stage, paused to glare at his audience for a long, uncomfortable moment, and then delivered a monologue called "Roughing It," which he had debuted in Chicago just a month earlier.

Although his major works—*Tom Sawyer*, *Huckleberry Finn*, and the rest—still lay in the future, the thirty-six-year-old Twain offered his Lancaster audience the wit and wordplay that were already his trademarks. "Roughing It" was constructed around his recent adventures in the West, and in the course of the lecture he described the folly of hunting mountain sheep, the curative powers of Lake Tahoe, and the perils of editing a newspaper in Virginia City, Nevada—"I edited that paper six days and then I had five duels on my hands."

A wiry man with bushy red hair, overgrown eyebrows, and a thick mustache, Twain was a master of timing and comic surprise. Sometimes he would pause for dramatic effect, drawing the silence out for such a long time that the audience would start to giggle under the strain of anticipation. Then, when he reached the most exciting moment of a story, he would contort his face and body so dramatically that physicians in the audience became alarmed. His voice was alternately reedy and flat and then booming with authority. All of the adventures he described became parodies of various frontier myths, and all of the people in these stories were ridiculous. Most ridiculous of all was Twain himself. Consider, for example, his recollection of his brief career as the most fastidious employee of a silver mine:

> Whenever I had a lot of that sand to shovel I was so particular that I would sit down for an hour and a half and think about the best way to shovel that sand. And if I could not cipher it out in my mind just so, I would not go shoveling it around heedless. I would leave it alone to the next day.[1]

A year after he strode the stage at the Fulton, Mark Twain and Charles Dudley Warner would publish *The Gilded Age*, a book that not only named but defined the era of industrialization, growth, excess, and concentrated wealth that the nation was entering. Twain and his co-author recognized the money-grab mentality that gripped much of society as railroads and other technologies began to meld hundreds of local economies into one big national market. One of their characters made the phrase "There's millions in it!" part of the national vernacular.

Twain and Warner saw how aggressive new businesses were able to exploit and corrupt the government and dominate labor. And they carefully depicted the rise of a new elite—self-worshipping industrialists—along with the decline of public morality. Eventually the conditions that Twain and Warner described in *The Gilded Age* would aid Milton Hershey's pursuit of great fortunes. Of course, as a shopkeeper's apprentice, he would hardly have been aware of society's workings as they were described in the novel. But even in Lancaster he encountered people who could have been characters in its pages.

On busy nights at Royer's, Milton was often assigned to handle the horses that pulled the carriages of the shop's customers. He loved the animals and enjoyed interacting with their owners.

John Coyle, a flamboyant young attorney who came to Royer's with a different date almost every night, was especially fond of Milton and appreciated the way the slight, wavy-haired boy tended to his horse. Joseph Royer was determined to please his regular customers, and whenever he saw Coyle pull up outside, he would bark for Milton to hustle out there to take the reins. Milton would stay with the horse for as long as the man and his date were inside. When he returned Coyle would flip Milton a dime (worth more than $2 in 2005) for his trouble.

People visited Royer's to have a good time, and the mix of city sophisticates and farm folk who came over from the market made for amusing moments. As an old man Milton would still laugh as he recalled an incident involving an Amish woman who had never seen herself in a full-length mirror until she glanced at her reflection inside the candy store.

"As you know these women dress somberly and look much alike. On one side of the store was a row of large mirrors that extended down to the floor, and before I could wait on her she had walked to that part of the store. Seeing her reflection in the glass she exclaimed, 'Ach, Fanny, I didn't know you were in town, too!' She was amazed to learn that what she saw wasn't her friend Fanny, but her own reflection. I couldn't help laughing at her, and she laughed too after I had explained it to her."

When he wasn't serving Amish women, young people on dates, or theatergoers, Milton worked in Royer's kitchen, making both ice cream and a variety of candies. Although Royer's product list does not survive, the most common candies of the day were all made of boiled sugar, including taffies, rock candy, lemon drops, lollipops, and soft candies. Since he was a fancy confectioner, Royer probably made marshmallows, a French invention of the 1850s, along with candied fruits and nuts. If the store offered any kind of chocolate beyond hot cocoa, it would have been used to coat sugar candies or to make individual chocolates, which were expensive, grainy, and somewhat bitter in taste. (As of 1872, the Swiss confectioner Daniel Peter and pharmacist Henri Nestlé had yet to figure out how to smooth the flavor and texture of chocolate with milk.)

Most of Royer's candies began life in large cauldrons filled with water and sugar that gradually thickened under high heat. Although water boils at 212 degrees Fahrenheit, when sugar is added the boiling point rises to 330 degrees. This meant that Royer had to use special gas jets to produce adequate heat. Milton and his fellow apprentices would have to stir the scalding mixture to keep it fluid, and watch for the moment when it was about to solidify. At that second they would take the liquid off the heat and pour it out. If the semisolid sugar was destined to be taffy, they would let it cool, then throw it onto hooks and pull it to make it soft and airy. This job, which had to be performed over and over until the consistency was just right, could leave a young man panting and exhausted.

Physical strength was important for candy makers, but a good sense of timing was even more valuable. The best confectioners were able to anticipate the "crack"—the moment when the gooey mixture in the pot was about to reach the perfect consistency—almost every time. Given that the whole process was accomplished without sensitive thermometers or timers, experimentation was the only way to develop this instinct. Milton, who had watched his father live his entire life as an experiment based on feel, was a natural at the kettles.

Joseph Royer was able to teach Milton much of what he knew, and the boy became both reliable and competent. He soaked in his employer's always-please-the-customer philosophy, and learned about buying ingredients, managing inventory, pricing goods, and handling employees.

But Milton was still a teenager and subject to distraction. One evening he and another boy forgot to switch off the fan that cooled a batch of peanuts they had placed in a large roaster. While the boys were at the Fulton watching a show, the fan blew peanut shells up a flue and into the sky over the shop. When they came back, the boys saw thousands of peanut shells fluttering down to the street. Royer turned out to be more patient than Ernst the printer. He kept Milton on even after he found out about this incident.[2]

• • •

At the start of Milton's apprenticeship, Lancaster was still riding the national economic boom that was fueled by federal spending for the Civil War and the Reconstruction. Railroads had led the way, building more than 35,000 miles of new track—doubling the existing miles of railway—in seven years. In Lancaster work was begun on a new line called the Lancaster and Reading Narrow Gauge, which was supposed to serve the demand for both passenger service and the shipment of goods from new factories.

Growth in the city was so strong that demand for gas to power lights and new industries was pressing the limits of the supply. Local taverns and oyster houses—where six fried oysters cost ten cents—were crowded with customers. In better neighborhoods the newly wealthy built beautiful mansions—Italianate architecture was in style—to reflect their status. In downtown Lancaster, shopkeepers expanded their stores and competed fiercely for the flood of new cash.

While many merchants and tradesmen worked hard to publicize their businesses and serve the newly rich, none could match the showmanship of Dr. Benjamin Mishler, manufacturer of Mishler's Bitters. In 1873 Mishler said he would build a complete home on an empty lot in ten hours. The announcement generated plenty of free publicity and guaranteed that Mishler's name would be printed and spoken for days, if not weeks, on end.

Before dawn on the morning of August 1, a crowd began to gather in front of the vacant lot at 553 South Prince Street, about ten blocks from Royer's confectionary. Building materials had already been deposited at the site, and a foundation had been laid. At six o'clock more than a hundred workers dashed to the piles of brick and wood and began building. As the day wore on, police were summoned to manage the crowd, which had grown to several hundred. Brick walls rose. Windows were set in the openings left by masons. A tin roof was nailed to the rafters and a wide front door with four panes of glass was set on sturdy hinges. At 4:30 P.M. the final nail was driven. Mishler's ten-hour house—two stories and eight rooms— was completed. His son Benjamin moved in that night.[3]

Sadly, the kind of lighthearted excitement reflected in Mishler's project wouldn't be seen again in Lancaster for years. That fall the nation's leading investment house, Jay Cooke and Company of Philadelphia, suddenly declared bankruptcy. The firm, which had grown powerful by financing the Union army's prosecution of the Civil War, had sold securities to finance the Northern Pacific Railroad's construction of the nation's second transcontinental route. Jay Cooke had raised a hundred million dollars from thousands of investors. When the Cooke Company announced it lacked the cash to repay them, it sparked a run on banks and securities houses nationwide. As investors rushed to sell, prices for railroad stocks, which had been wildly inflated, plummeted. Thousands of paper millionaires lost everything, and many banks went under as depositors withdrew their cash. Those lenders who survived simply stopped giving credit, which made it impossible for firms to buy supplies or finance expansion and new equipment. Nearly ninety railroad companies disappeared. More than eighteen thousand other businesses, many of which depended on the railroads, went bankrupt. Unemployment surged to 14 percent.[4]

With so many people out of work, industry demanded more from labor and paid less. The economy entered a period of deflation, with new efficient technologies driving down the price of finished goods and prompting fierce competition, especially among manufacturers. The men who owned the more successful companies built fortunes on a scale never before seen while workers struggled to adapt to new demanding jobs. In factories, foundries, and mines, they worked ten-hour days in conditions that were often dehumanizing and dangerous. In the last two decades of the nineteenth century, roughly seven hundred thousand workers would die on the job.

A well-read man of his time, Henry Hershey saw that conditions were set for decades of bitter conflicts between owners and workers. The disparities between labor and capital became a recurrent theme in the soliloquies he loved to deliver on front porches and at dinner tables. "The rich man has champagne," he said, "and the poor man can't even get beer."

In Lancaster, the Panic of 1873 dried up lending and cast a pall over business. Construction of the Lancaster and Reading Narrow Gauge Railroad was stopped literally in its tracks. Out in the country, at Nine Points, Henry Hershey finally ran out of ideas, money, and time. In seven years his fanciful Trout Brook Fruit and Nursery Farm had failed to become profitable and he was forced to give it up.

As they had before, the most successful Lancaster farm families, including the Snavelys, would ride out the recession on their accumulated wealth, picking up the business left behind when weaker competitors went under. After his farm was lost, Henry Hershey found shelter in the city home occupied by his estranged wife, her sister Mattie, and his son, Milton.

In 1873, a forty-four-year-old American man had an average life expectancy of sixty-one. By these figures, Henry was well into middle age and having to start over one more time. Although he believed that one should never dwell on failure or regret, Henry had seen his last best chance to create the life of his dreams at Nine Points. With that dream gone, he took to the city streets and the country turnpikes to sell frames and a few of his own pictures. He must have been a good salesman, because a number of Amish and Mennonite homemakers, who typically rejected frivolous decorations, nevertheless bought pictures from Henry. But door-to-door sales, conducted via horse and buggy, were hardly the way to get rich.

Even with the sour economy, wealth was the subject of a growing national obsession and the image of America as a land of opportunity dominated the press and popular literature. Tales of a new breed of millionaire, such as Henry Hershey's old oil-field competitor John D. Rockefeller, filled the newspapers. Many of these men, including Andrew Carnegie, built their empires on Pennsylvania coal, iron, and steel. But others, like George Westinghouse of Pittsburgh, were regarded as models for that new iconic figure—the American inventor. In 1869 Westinghouse gained international fame and began to accumulate a huge fortune with his air brakes for trains. Invention, steel, oil, and railroads made Pennsylvania a business powerhouse that nearly equaled New York in manufacturing and finance. The state also led the way in building the nineteenth-century cult of wealth.[5]

For those who preferred to get their inspiration not from newspapers but from pulp novels, Horatio Alger supplied rags-to-riches fantasies that became a genre all their own. Although they would eventually become the object of parody, Alger's relentlessly optimistic stories of poor country boys (and a few girls) who triumph over adversity were wildly popular. Alger's novels reflected real trends of the time. Americans had begun a steady migration from small towns and farms to cities where, like Alger's protagonists, young men hoped to find fortune and excitement. These books also contributed to the archetypal myth of the day, making the struggling young man into a heroic model.[6]

If these twin American archetypes—heroic boy and great man of industry—weren't enough to make Milton Hershey chafe at the limits of apprenticeship, he also felt his mother's ambition. Early in his training Fanny saw that candy, which had a long shelf life and came in many varieties, was the most promising of Royer's products. She visited the shop and paid Royer to excuse her son from his ice cream duties. He needed to learn all he could about the confections that would yield the greatest profit.

When Milton had gone about as far as he could go under the older man's instruction, it was his mother and her family who guided the next step. Now a young man of eighteen, Milton was going to the big city to make his name and fortune. But unlike Horatio Alger's heroes, he would enjoy some advantages. First, he knew a trade—confectionery—and its secrets. Second, he would have the financial backing of his mother, his Aunt Mattie, and the extended Snavely family. Third, he would pursue his success in the one American city where, in 1876, a tremendous opportunity awaited despite the recession that had ruined business and destroyed jobs across the continent—Philadelphia.

Ten years earlier, when Milton was still a child chasing hop toads at Nine Points, a few of the nation's leading businessmen and politicians had begun to discuss ways to commemorate the centennial of the American Revolution. Paris was putting the final touches on its Universal Exposition, and a commission was dispatched to study the fair. On their return one commissioner proposed that America's exposition be held in New York's Central Park, which was then under construction. When this idea foundered, groups in Washington and later Philadelphia made their own proposals. The capital's oppressive summer climate and Philadelphia's superior financing settled the contest. Federal, state, and city officials immediately began planning a massive exhibition that would cover nearly three hundred acres on a site overlooking the Schuylkill River from an elevation of 120 feet.

At the time when Philadelphia was awarded the exhibition, the world's great cities were locked in a fierce and costly competition over international fairs and conventions and the prestige they conferred. London's Great Exposition of 1851 had set the standard, attracting more than six million visitors to the Crystal Palace, a breathtakingly beautiful hall built entirely of glass and cast iron. In London thirty-two nations exhibited wonders of art, technology, and nature, including the first life-size re-creations of dinosaurs. After the Crystal Palace, countries around the world tried to outdo one another with ever larger and more spectacular attractions. America had not been a serious player in this competition—one newspaper deemed a 1853 fair in New York "a wretched failure"—until the centennial, and the nation's rise as an industrial power, offered both the means and the moment.

Before the Panic of 1873, business owners and political leaders in Philadelphia were excited by the prospect of hosting the fair. But after the depression hit, it became even more important. As unemployment persisted in other cities, thousands of workers were hired in Philadelphia to clear land and construct five main exhibit halls and nearly two hundred smaller buildings providing seventy acres of covered space. They also laid out gardens, roadways, and water and sewage systems. Decorative artists installed statuary and fountains throughout the grounds. Just beyond the border of the park, in West Philadelphia, thousands of additional workers erected an entire new neighborhood of hotels, shops, and eateries.

The pre-exhibition fever infected even those who operated businesses far from Fairmount Park. The most audacious among them, clothier John Wanamaker, spent half a million dollars on a former railroad depot at Thirteenth and Market Streets, where he built the first true department store in America. Opened just in time for the centennial, Wanamaker's emporium was filled to overflowing with every item imaginable. It included a men's smoking room, an in-house restaurant—another first—and more than 120 "departments" staffed by the most attractive, mannered, and well-spoken young women Wanamaker could find. The store was not just a retail hub. It was an emblem of the changing times. One day Wanamaker and his innovations would be credited by historian William Leach with leading the transformation of America from a pastoral "land of comfort," where the farm met every need, to a "land of desire" marked by accumulation and consumer fads.

When the Centennial Exposition opened on May 10, 1876, it was the biggest and most varied display of culture, art, industry, and agriculture ever presented in the world. But it was hardly an aesthetic triumph. Future critics would describe the sprawling collection of buildings and fountains as garish and vulgar. In his 1954 work *The Tastemakers*, the critic Russell Lynes declared that the centennial was "the epitome of the accumulated bad taste of the era that was called The Gilded Age, the Dreadful Decade or the Pragmatic Acquiescence, depending on which epithet you thought most searing."

But while historians would note its vulgarities, the people who attended the centennial thought the exposition to be, in the words of one contemporary reviewer, "a fairyland, an incantation scene, something that we wish would never pass away."

In excess of 180,000 people came to see the opening of the exhibition. Most entered the grounds at a gate in front of the enormous Main Exhibition Building. A quarter mile long and 464 feet wide, this hall was at the time the single biggest structure on earth. Inside, fifty countries from Great Britain to Siam displayed everything from delicate lace to massive artillery pieces along eight miles of crisscrossing aisles.

But as grand as the main hall was, the biggest mechanical attraction of the centennial was housed next door in Machinery Hall. There, George Corliss of Providence, Rhode Island, had built a seventy-foot-high, two-cylinder steam engine capable of turning a fifty-six-ton flywheel and producing 1400 horsepower. It would be used to run hundreds of machines on exhibit.

On opening day President Ulysses S. Grant noted that the fair would be a source of "unalloyed pleasure" and an inspiration for national progress. Then he and Brazil's Emperor Dom Pedro turned a control that set the giant Corliss engine in motion. The energy it produced was distributed by an elaborate system of gears and shafts totaling 10,000 feet in length to power more than 800 machines. A visitor to the hall would have seen the towering Corliss and heard the clatter and clank of sewing machines, presses, dental drills, mowers, mechanical calculators, and diamond-tipped saws. The hall was also home to new inventions that relied on other sources of energy, including electric lights, a gasoline-fired combustion engine, and an electric-powered telephone.

The exhibition overwhelmed the senses of many who came to see it. According to one account, seventy-three-year-old Ralph Waldo Emerson was "dazzled and dumfounded" by what he saw. A correspondent for *The Atlantic* described "triumphs of ingenuity" and "marvels of skill." Many of the innovations first displayed at the centennial would quickly find their way to everyday use across the world. The sizzling arc light, for example, was soon installed in stores and city streets in New York. In 1879, a group of businessmen would form a company that brought telephone service to Lancaster.

With early attendees reporting on the wonders they saw, the centennial fair attracted visitors from around the globe. In the six months that it was open, almost 10 million people—in a country of just 46 million—paid fifty cents to spend a day amid the wonders that had been brought to Philadelphia from around the world. But a day was hardly enough to view all the exhibits in Machinery Hall, let alone the hundreds of other wonders displayed in other buildings. If you wanted also to see Ben Franklin's postmaster's account book, George Washington's trousers, or statues made entirely of butter, you would need much more time. Most visitors allowed themselves several days to take in the fair and other sights, including historic Independence Hall near the city center.

In the evenings, when the fairgrounds were closed, tens of thousands of visitors crowded Philadelphia's restaurants, theaters, shops, and saloons, spending the money they had saved to finance a once-in-a-lifetime adventure. Waiting to receive them was nineteen-year-old Milton S. Hershey, proprietor of the Spring Garden Confectionery Works.

Young Milton Hershey could not have chosen a better time and place to put what he had learned from Joe Royer into a business of his own. In all, the centennial would bring nearly $38 million ($700 million in 2005 dollars) to Philadelphia, a flood of cash so huge that even a novice shopkeeper would have had to really try in order to fail. This was especially true for Milton, since a great deal of that money rested in the pockets and purses of people who passed his shop on Spring Garden Street on their way from the fairgrounds to Independence Hall and the city center.[7]

Financed by his Aunt Mattie, who also chose its location, the Spring Garden shop was furnished with tables and chairs brought by wagon from Lancaster. In the kitchen Milton installed a stove, a large copper kettle, and hooks for pulling taffy. Eager to associate his shop with the excitement of the exposition, and perhaps suggest that his company owned a giant factory, Milton had the image of the Machinery Hall engraved on his business cards. Bigness was obviously on the young man's mind. Beneath the picture were the words "Length 1402 feet. Width 360 feet [sic]."

The Spring Garden shop opened on June 1. It was a beautiful late-spring day. The temperature stayed in the low seventies and the evening light lingered well past eight o'clock. A week of similar weather passed, providing the perfect setting for fairgoers who strolled the streets looking for lighter fare after a full day of education and exhibits. On Spring Garden Street they could follow their noses to Milton Hershey's candy shop, where a pipe that Milton had installed in the coal chute carried the sweet aromas of his basement kitchen into the neighborhood air.

Milton Hershey sold the centennial crowds so much sugary stuff that he soon needed extra help just to keep up with demand. He was ready to serve even larger crowds on July 4, when troops from around the nation came to parade and fireworks lighted the night sky over Fairmount Park. Local businesses got another big boost on Pennsylvania Day, September 28, when a record 274,000 visitors went to the centennial. The following month was the busiest at the fair, with 2.6 million tickets sold. Attendance tapered off after that, but even in the exhibition's final month, November, Philadelphia Day attracted almost 200,000 people, who were treated to another fireworks show to mark the closing of the exhibition on November 10.

After so much hype, excitement, and activity, November 11 felt desolate and cold to those who came to dismantle the exhibits and empty the buildings. In the weeks immediately after the closing, forty-two freight cars were loaded with items that exhibitors had donated to the Smithsonian Institution in Washington. On December 1 hundreds of buildings were auctioned to buyers, who moved them off the grounds and turned them into private homes, train stations, and even hotels. Statuary was sent to parks and government sites around the country. An observation tower was moved to Coney Island. And in a bid for additional sales, the Krupp armaments company of Germany donated the cannons it had put on display in Philadelphia to the Sultan of the Ottoman Empire.

Depressing as the postcentennial scene may have been, commerce in the city did not crash. Milton Hershey's business kept growing. He opened a wholesale shop in another part of town and moved the retail store a few doors down the street to larger space. In 1877 his mother and his aunt arrived to add their unpaid labor to their boy's promising new business.

With Henry back in the taverns of Lancaster County buying drinks to celebrate the impending success of his perpetual motion machine, Fanny, Mattie, and Milton worked long hours making and wrapping candies that were sold wholesale to other shops and retail by the young women who worked the front counter.

In 1878, Philadelphia was slowly coming down from the high of the exposition and returning to business as normal. In the daily papers, articles about famous fairgoers and the size of the crowds had been replaced by more standard news of the day about accidents, fires, and violent crimes. A look at the press from the time makes it seem as if every day brought another calamity. In August pirates—real pirates—attacked a schooner anchored in the Delaware River. In October a hurricane swamped a district of low-lying houses, killing ten people.

All the mayhem must have made the security of a bustling little candy business even more attractive to Milton, Fanny, and Mattie, who worked hard to increase sales and contain costs. The boy entrepreneur loved to experiment with recipes and eventually came up with a type of soft, chewy caramel that customers found irresistible. More help was hired to wrap the candies that Milton made from the large shipment of sugar he received from a nearby wholesaler and fresh milk from Lancaster County.

Things began to go awry in late 1879 and early 1880. Milton's meager education may have played a role, making it hard for him to manage his accounts. At the same time he faced intense competition from literally hundreds of other candy retailers and wholesalers in the city. Whatever the cause, in October 1880 Milton sent to Lancaster for a man named William H. "Harry" Lebkicher, who accepted a job managing the books. A Civil War veteran, Lebkicher was closer to Henry Hershey in age and was known in Lancaster for being a tough businessman. Lebkicher let his young boss know just how bad things were. Beginning in December, Milton sent a series of pleading letters to relatives in Lancaster County. Mattie and Fanny had run out of ready cash, and the once thriving business on Spring Garden Street was about to go under.

Dear Uncle
I am sorry to bother You but cannot well do without as it takes so much money. Just Now aunt Martha wishes You to send 600 dollar . . . and she will stand good for it. She just want it till the first of the Year, so you will greatly oblige Me by send it as sune as possible on Monday and do not fail as it will save us some trouble.

Respet Nephew
Milt
Martha Snavely

[In Martha's hand] I will write Some othr time

The letter was addressed to Abraham Snavely, the same uncle who had traveled to Oil City to rescue Milton and his mother from Henry's misadventure in petroleum. Now, though Milton and his aunt had obviously struggled with spelling and syntax, Abraham was called on again. Only a large sum of cash—$600 was almost twice what a typical worker earned in a year—would see the confectionery through the coming Christmas season. Abraham sent the money, but it didn't solve the crisis. Four months later Milton wrote again, asking for nearly as much, and invoking his aunt's position in the family.

"Aunt Mattie says that you and Uncle Ben are to send it to us at once," he wrote. He went on to explain that his store would be moved into a larger space "so that we can increase our output of candies" and also noted that Mattie, who had freed up some funds, was making a new, large investment in the shop.

The larger space that Milton found for his shop on Beech Street came at a lower rent than he was paying on Spring Garden. To further cut costs, he listened to his new accountant's advice and stopped selling cakes, which were more perishable than candy and had never produced much profit. These moves may have stabilized the business for a time. At least Milton and Mattie stopped writing to Lancaster for more cash. Then in August 1881, after a string of days hot enough to melt all but the hardest sugar candy, Henry Hershey drove his buggy up to the hitching post out front. He got out and retrieved a wood and glass cabinet from his rig, and hauled it inside.

Built to sit atop a shopkeeper's display case, the glass and wood cabinet with shiny brass fittings was a beautiful thing. The front was divided into individual panes, and behind each of these panes were displayed different candies. They were held in place by a board that slid down from the top. To serve a customer, a clerk could open the cabinet from behind to remove various items. What made this cabinet special was that even as pieces were sold, the display continued to look freshly filled.

Henry was certain that Milton could use his special cabinets to sell caramels. And he had other ideas. He wanted to load them with his own brand of cough drops and give them to retailers around the city. He talked about pouring the profits into a scheme for turning the wire fences of farms into telephone lines. And then there was his plan for packaging dry cereals and canning vegetables.[8]

Mattie Snavely tried to warn Milton about his father. As his first lender, and most dedicated co-worker, she had the standing to give this kind of advice. No one, not even his mother, worked harder to support Milton's efforts. Mattie was the one who had first pushed him to go to Philadelphia and she had found the Spring Garden Street storefront.

Few women of her time and place would have become so involved in a business venture. Women of the late nineteenth century, especially those from rural counties, were supposed to marry and devote themselves to home and family. According to this model, American woman were to be both self-sacrificing and moral exemplars, calling their husbands to a more wholesome life. The ideal ignored women who never married, but this neglect had a good side. Maiden aunts were able to choose unusual outlets for their energies. Mattie chose her sister's son, Milton, and the two would develop a close relationship.[9]

But Milton was also his father's loyal son. Over Mattie's protests Henry was welcomed into the business, cabinets and all. Milton changed his stationery to add pictures of the cabinet and the line "Sole Manufacturer of the Celebrated HH Cough Drops." He also let Henry experiment in the basement kitchen of the Beech Street shop. Some of his trials worked out well. He did make a passable cough drop. But others were costly failures. Most notable were the canned tomatoes that fermented and exploded in the basement of the store. After cleaning up, Henry brought the mess to a municipal dump. But that was not the end of the story. The police caught Henry dumping without a permit and made him remove the whole lot and find some other place to put it.

The mild success Henry had with cough drops wasn't enough to make up for his failures. As Milton's aunt had warned, Henry's patented cabinets didn't sell well, even though Henry continued to insist they would. He eventually asked Milton to buy out his interest in the cabinets. Though he couldn't afford it, Milton paid the price, $350. After he got his money, Henry headed to Colorado intending to get rich in the silver mines.

With his father gone, Milton depended even more on his aunt. Mattie even replaced his mother as the dominant woman in his life. Fanny said as much in her letters home, noting, "I don't know what Milton would do if he didn't have her to fall back on." Harry Lebkicher found much to appreciate in Mattie, too. Fanny wrote that the trusted old accountant "would ask her to marry him" if he got the chance, but Mattie was not interested.

Although she took the time to gossip about her sister, most of what Fanny reported to her relatives had to do with business and how "money seems to disappear like magic with us." On January 3, 1881, Milton again wrote to his uncle to plead for money. When he heard nothing, he wrote on the seventh, and once more on the tenth. The last of these letters was the most desperate. Milton made it clear that he could no longer pay his bills and was about to lose his credit with suppliers. Again he invoked his aunt, telling Abraham that the loan was as much for her as for him, writing that Mattie "thought you would do this much for her this time."

The money eventually came, but business did not get much better. Caught in the web of family animosities, and burdened with the pressures of a failing business, Milton fell ill. He spent most of a month in bed while Mattie and Harry Lebkicher tried to keep the confectionery going. At one point a doctor warned that Milton might not survive. But by spring he was well enough to go back to work, if only to oversee his shop's final months.

No matter how hard Milton Hershey worked, he couldn't balance the expense of making his products with the slow pace of payments from his wholesale customers and the tight credit terms demanded by his main supplier, the Franklin Sugar Company. (Unfortunately for Milton, sweeping changes in the international sugar market, most notably the switch to beet sugar in Europe, were still two or three years away. When they took effect, prices would fall by more than half.)

All through 1881 Milton kept borrowing from his uncle. Finally, in early 1882, his aunt returned from a visit to Lancaster to report that her brothers Abraham and Benjamin would send no more cash. According to a family member's account, the Snavely brothers had tied up their wealth in mortgages, a tannery, and the Conestoga Cotton Mills. They said they had nothing left to help their nephew and advised him to close shop and salvage whatever equipment was worth keeping, so that he might try again in some other place. Milton suspected that his uncles had finally lost faith.

The same family history reports that in March 1882 two of Milton's country cousins arrived at his shop in a big wagon pulled by two giant Percherons, the French-bred draft horses that were the favorite of Lancaster farmers and teamsters. They dismantled Milton's kitchen, piled the copper candy kettles and other equipment in the wagon, and then let their cousin join them on the driver's seat for the long haul back to Lancaster County.

At twenty-four, Milton Hershey had invested the first six years of his adult life in a business that failed. By all accounts, he had driven himself mercilessly, trying to prove he deserved the faith and financial backing he

had received from Mattie, his mother, and their brothers. He had practically ignored the young women of Philadelphia, and enjoyed little of what
the vibrant city—America's second largest—had to offer. With sixty miles
to travel, and the Percherons moving at just a few miles per hour, he would
have time to reflect on the experience.[10]

WANDERING

3 The West was synonymous with opportunity long before Horace Greeley instructed the youth of the nineteenth century to pursue their fortune in the land of silver and gold. By 1881, it was lodged so firmly in the nation's imagination as the setting for the great American odyssey that an adventure in the wilderness that lay beyond the Mississippi was considered the all-purpose method for turning boys into men.

In that year, no place represented the West better than Leadville, Colorado, which was in the middle of a historic boom. Twenty years earlier the area had been the site of a brief gold rush. The prospecting had been difficult. Miners had to work through vast quantities of lead ore to find any precious metal. When the gold petered out, the town's population fell from a high of 10,000 in 1861 to 200 in 1874. Leadville was just a grocery store, two saloons, and a scattering of houses that year, when a trained metallurgist named A.B. Wood visited and discovered that the "heavy rock" pushed aside by gold miners contained high levels of silver.

Seven years later, Leadville teemed with 15,000 inhabitants. The city had twenty-four miles of improved streets and five miles of underground water pipes. Each day thousands of men took to the hills, desperate to dig up their fortunes. More came every day. In the summer of 1881, one of the new arrivals was Henry Hershey. Having never really grown up, it probably never occurred to him that he was, at age fifty-one, too old to heed Greeley's advice.

As he had in Oil City, Henry ignored the odds—most prospectors failed—and joined the tide of dreamers who traveled on the recently completed railroad to the burgeoning city of Denver, where he was outfitted for Leadville and the wilderness beyond.[1]

Although it was already bigger than Lancaster, Denver was still straining to acquire eastern-style culture and polish. In 1882 travelers arrived in the city at the new Union Station, a Romanesque palace built to imitate the great railroad halls in the East. Denver boasted electric lights, streetcars, and an opera house that drew the major players of the day. Just prior to Henry's arrival in Colorado, Oscar Wilde had appeared at the city's opera house to lecture on interior decoration.[2]

If either Wilde or Henry Hershey had expected to encounter hostile Indians and gunslingers in Colorado, he would have been disappointed. Between 1875 and 1880 the state had been the scene of just three recorded gunfights. In 1879, the army fought its last war with Indians in Colorado, and in 1880 the Ute tribe was forced to leave the state for a reservation in Utah.

The main threats a newcomer to Denver faced were similar to those found in every city of the time: con men, thieves, and communicable disease. At about the time of Henry's arrival, William "Buffalo Bill" Cody reported the theft of $2,000 worth of jewelry from his hotel room in the city. On street corners tricksters operating shell games relieved gullible men of their money, and in the well-used rooms above most local saloons adventurers risked receiving a long-lived infection along with their purchase of pleasure.

The mining regions were more rowdy than Denver, and Henry was older than most of his competitors. The few sources available suggest that his prospecting time in Leadville was brief. Soon he took to the Colorado countryside to peddle livestock remedies. He also painted pictures, which he sold to city people in Denver, and there's some evidence that he worked for a time as a junk dealer. Even with all these activities he couldn't support himself well enough in the West to become financially independent. He continued to ask his son for cash, and Milton supplied it whenever possible.

The family legend, which flows from Fanny's branch of the clan, has it that Milton S. Hershey resented his father's interference and requests for money so intensely that in the months before his shop in Philadelphia went bankrupt, he had shunned Henry and berated him on the streets. The two would never again enjoy a loving relationship, or so this version of the story goes.

But if Milton was ever truly angry with Henry—given Fanny's dim view of Henry, this is in doubt—the feeling was short-lived. After receiving a letter from his father, which painted a vivid picture of the opportunities in the West, Milton boarded a train for Denver to reunite with him. This move was also encouraged by a doctor who thought the climate would do Milton good. At the time, thousands of people with respiratory disease—called "lungers" in the slang of the day—were going west for a dry-air cure.

Unlike his starry-eyed father, when Milton reached Colorado he resisted the lure of prospecting and immediately sought more reliable work in the city. Denver banks were flush with profits from the nearby mines. They were using it to finance growing industries, sprawling Victorian-style houses, and entire new commercial districts. Milton found a job in a most familiar place, a candy shop. The store's specialty was caramels, but instead of using paraffin to give the candy "chew," the confectioner used milk, which was blended with vanilla and sugar. As the mixture was heated, the water in the milk evaporated and the natural bacteria was killed. After cooling, he had a softer, smoother, sweeter candy that could be kept on the shelf for many weeks without spoiling.[3]

In a few months Milton learned the recipe and practiced it enough to have both the proper mix of ingredients and the step-by-step manufacturing process committed to memory. Unimpressed with Denver, and presumably cured of his breathing problems, he left for the East in the summer of 1882 with Henry by his side. They stopped first in Chicago, then a city of half a million people, where they briefly made candies for the wholesale trade in a basement on State Street.[4]

At the time, no big city in North America was more rough and dangerous than Chicago. After his visit there, Rudyard Kipling described it as a place where "the air is dirt" that is inhabited by "savages" and "a collection of miserables." Even at church on Sunday, Kipling found "a revelation of barbarism complete." Having seen much of the city and felt true "horror," he finally declared, "I urgently desire never to see it again."

In Chicago the Hershey men didn't fare much better than Kipling. After a brief period of struggle they dissolved the little enterprise they had run on State Street, and Milton left for Lancaster County with the idea of persuading the Snavelys to back him in New York. More worldly than his son, Henry stayed in Chicago working as a business agent of some sort. He listed the grand and gilded Palmer House as his address, but the hotel's records do not support this claim. Instead he likely stayed at one of the many flophouses nearby.[5]

• • •

If a man of the 1880s couldn't return from the West with a fortune, he could at least bring back some valuable new knowledge and a few good stories. Milton S. Hershey was no richer when he got home, but he could tell a tale about his brush with danger.

In Milton's adventure story, before he began working for the candy maker in Denver he had walked the city in search of a job. In one alleyway he opened the door to a nondescript shack where he had seen a "Help Wanted" sign. An old coot splayed on a couch pointed to another door. "Go in that back room, with the other boys," he growled.

"Hershey walked back and saw several young fellows and didn't like their appearance," recalled Paul Witmer, a business associate who had heard this story from Milton Hershey himself. "He went back and asked the old man what the job was. The old man would not say. Mr. Hershey got suspicious."

Rumors had recently spread in the city about labor contractors who tricked or abducted young men and made them work at slave wages tending livestock hundreds of miles from the city. Milton had one hundred dollars in his pocket, and was hardly desperate for work. But when he went for the door, he found it locked.

"Mr. Hershey said to me, 'In those days we carried a gun.' He pulled out the gun and said, 'You let me out the door.' The old man pulled a string or something that unlocked the door, and Hershey went out."[6]

Flashing a gun, and living to tell the tale, firmed up Milton's otherwise soft image. But as much as it may have done for his sense of manhood, the experience in that back alley had almost no real value when compared with what he had learned while working in that Colorado candy shop. The Denver recipe for caramels, which yielded a vastly superior candy, was not under any copyright or patent. It would be his advantage in a new business that he planned to open in the biggest, most competitive market in the country. Fortunately for Milton, the Snavely family still had cash in hand. Aunt Mattie was so well fixed that she was about to invest in three adjoining house lots in downtown Lancaster. Still optimistic about Milton's energy, character, and intelligence, she agreed to back her sister's son once more. In October he took a train to New York.

With the glimpse of Chicago he got on the way home from Denver, Milton Hershey should have been forewarned about what he would find in

New York. In the 1880s big American cities were places of stark and startling contrasts, where the super-rich of the Gilded Age were surrounded, but mostly untouched by, vast numbers of desperately poor immigrants.

The two groups represented distinct commercial markets. The wealthy elite had an insatiable appetite for luxury and excess. They filled their mansions with antiques from French estates and dressed their babies in diamond-studded gowns. The other marketplace was inhabited by huge numbers of working people who were poised to buy low-cost, mass-produced products. Business had begun to respond to them with canned foods and other staples such as Ivory soap, delivered in a new kind of packaging, developed in Brooklyn, called the cardboard box.

The mass-market strategy—high-volume sales at low prices—was a revolutionary idea. Until the mid-nineteenth century, the production and sale of basic goods was an adversarial sport and the seller's main goal was to wring the maximum profit from each item sold. Shoddy workmanship was the norm, and shopkeepers did their best to hide the flaws in the items they offered. One booklet on retailing actually advised that stores be kept small, dark, and overcrowded to prevent customers from inspecting their purchases before they handed over their money. It's no wonder that Americans generally preferred to grow or craft what they needed themselves, and avoided merchants as much as possible.

After the Civil War, the rise of modern department stores signaled the end of dark and dirty retailing and the transformation of the shopping-and-buying experience. Bright airy stores displayed goods in attractive ways and clerks behaved more like servants and less like hustlers. Manufacturers also began to change, with the advantage shifting toward those who stressed quality and efficiency. Until this period, making stuff, even the most basic items, was a difficult and risky business fraught with failure. But steam, steel, and other innovations made the process of producing everyday objects far easier. Instead of a single worker laboriously stitching a shirt or forging a tool, new technologies and systems allowed for quicker and more precise manufacturing on a large scale.

With better offerings and fairer prices, merchants began to shed their negative image and rise in social status. For generations Americans had placed a high moral value on farming and regarded industry and its middlemen as suspect. (Thomas Jefferson, who declared farmers to be "the chosen people of God" was the best-known evangelist of this agri-ideal.) Now, as the marketplace won the public's trust, men who strayed from the farm to enter business could keep their heads high. Manufacturers, whole-salers, and retailers were becoming respectable.[7]

In time, national brands and the high value their trademarks guaranteed would rule the consumer economy. But this process was just beginning in 1883. This was especially true for food products, which tended to be per-ishable. Campbell, Heinz, and a few other companies were learning how to prepare and package goods so they would stay safely fresh for weeks and months. But for the time being, almost everything people ate was pro-duced, sold, and consumed in the same region or locale.[8]

Nothing in Milton S. Hershey's New York adventure suggests he ever intended to join the mass-market pioneers. Though his father had always recommended thinking big, Milton intended to start small, making candy to sell retail and wholesale on the island of Manhattan. But rather than immediately jump into a new business in a new city, as he had in Philadel-phia, he would work for someone else for a while, learning about local suppliers and the tastes of New Yorkers.

At the time Manhattan had roughly fifty candy wholesalers and hun-dreds of retailers. Much of the business operated on a neighborhood basis, and this meant that the quality of the offerings varied widely. Candy kitchens, which held most of the trade, sold sugar-based sweets that ranged from pedestrian to dangerous. Shortly after Milton Hershey got to New York, the Society for the Prevention of Cruelty to Children forced health officials to crack down on a Brooklyn candy maker who sold "rye and rocks" candy to neighborhood kids. It turned out that half a pound of these candies would make a child drunk. Two pounds contained enough alco-hol to kill a twelve-year-old.

The only solid chocolate candy in New York was offered by high-end confectioners in the toniest Manhattan neighborhoods. Despite its high price, this chocolate was brittle and often gritty, and it melted in summer heat. No one in New York—or, for that matter, all of America—could offer customers the most treasured candy of the time at any price: real milk chocolate. In 1883, only Daniel Peter of Vevey, Switzerland, whose secret ingredient was pharmacist Henri Nestlé's dehydrated "milk flour" was mak-ing this mellow, silky treat.

As Milton Hershey looked for work he found reputable confectioners doing their best to imitate the Europeans. The Runkel Brothers sold "Vi-enna sweet chocolate" on Seventh Avenue. Humbert's shop, which was a bit north of City Hall, specialized in chocolate cream "drops." Hershey got a job with one of the largest companies, Huyler's Candies. Jacob Huyler, who advertised that he sold "bon bons and chocolates," owned two busy shops. One was at 863 Broadway, just north of Union Square. The other was at 35 Nassau Street, in the heart of the booming financial district.[9]

The two locations were Huyler's greatest advantage in business. On Nassau Street he was convenient to businessmen inclined toward luxuries big and small. On Broadway he was handy for wealthy women who shopped the fashionable Ladies' Mile, a retail paradise that stretched from Union Square to Twenty-sixth Street.

Thirty years earlier, the neighborhood north of the Ladies' Mile had been the "country" to most New Yorkers. Houses there occupied large plots and livestock still grazed on the land. In the time since, builders and real estate speculators had pushed the urban border steadily northward. By the early 1880s, the edge of the city was around Seventieth Street, where a huge and beautiful modern apartment building—nicknamed the Dakota because it was so remote—was rising on a slope overlooking Central Park.

As he looked for a place to start his own business, Milton Hershey avoided the hinterlands around the Dakota, where squatters still occupied illegal shacks, and searched for an affordable location close to a well-settled area. Eventually he was drawn to a fast-growing neighborhood bounded roughly by Fortieth and Fifty-ninth Streets. Eventually called Midtown, this area would become the busiest commercial district in the entire United States. In 1883 new businesses were opening on every block. One of the largest was William Vanderbilt's American Horse Exchange, which occupied the future site of Times Square.

The best spot Hershey could find was a little store with a basement kitchen in a three-story building on the west side of Sixth Avenue between Forty-second and Forty-third Streets. Nearby homes and apartments were occupied by a wide range of social classes, from his former boss Huyler, who lived on West Forty-second, to the poor children who attended Colored School No. 3 one block to the south, between Seventh and Eighth Avenues.

By spring of 1884, Hershey was making and selling candy seven days a week at 742 Sixth Avenue. His shop stood in the shadow of a new elevated railroad. The elevated's small-scale locomotives—with names such as the *Aristotle* and the *Jay Gould*—burned soft coal and showered the streets with cinders and ash. They brought families and courting couples to a park across the avenue from Hershey's store. The main feature of that park was the Croton Reservoir, which held 20 million gallons of drinking water for the growing city. Designed to resemble an Egyptian temple, the structure was so large that the top of each wall was a wide walkway, which was used for promenades. A bit of candy, bought from Hershey, was a perfect treat for New Yorkers who spent an afternoon in the park or taking in the view from atop the reservoir walls.[10]

In the evening Hershey could sell to the travelers lodged at the area's big new hotels, including the 250-room Rossmore and the St. Cloud, a monstrous creation of bright red brick, which one critic described as a hulking "Gulliver among Lilliputians." Hershey could also serve the crowds who came to the new theaters that were making the neighborhood Manhattan's latest entertainment center.

The biggest of the new performance halls was the Casino Theater, which had opened a year before Hershey got to New York. Nine stories high and built in a distinctly arabesque style, the Casino's exterior included a round tower that resembled a minaret. Inside, the main auditorium seated nearly one thousand people. The top of the building was occupied by a roof garden café, where theatergoers could drink and dance into the night after seeing the American debut of the latest operetta from London. When Hershey opened his business on Sixth Avenue, the Casino was offering *The Beggar Student*, a love story set in Naples.

The Casino Theater, and the crowds it brought to his neighborhood, may have reminded Milton Hershey of the Fulton Opera House and his days at Royer's. It certainly contributed to local foot traffic, and Hershey's business went well.

But even as he turned a profit, Milton was confronted by the darker side of New York. His store was just two blocks from the edge of Hell's Kitchen, a neighborhood that police were afraid to patrol, where gangs firebombed businesses when owners refused to pay for protection. Even in New York's middle-class neighborhoods, swindlers and drunks carried concealed pistols, and thieves used chloral hydrate—later called knockout drops—to separate tavern customers from their wallets.[11]

Tough as life was for working adults in 1880s New York, the poor and especially their children suffered more. In some neighborhoods, where one-third of all the babies born died before reaching their first birthdays, the corpses of infants were left on the streets. More fortunate babies were left at charity houses. One, run by Roman Catholics, accepted any mother's baby, as long as she stayed to nurse her child and one other baby who lived at the orphanage before she departed for good.

In this time, abused and neglected children became a major concern for some prominent men, who felt a duty to promote the greater good and recognized the danger represented by large numbers of delinquent children. For a short while, groups formed to protect animals from abuse took up the cause of children, too. The first such case involved a child named Mary Ellen Wilson, who was abused by foster parents. A social worker who discovered that no law protected children from violent stepparents persuaded the New York Society for the Prevention of Cruelty to Animals to intervene on her behalf. Mary Ellen's story was trumpeted in the press, and it spurred changes in the way communities responded to the needs of poor, neglected, and abused boys and girls.

By 1880, a separate New York Society for the Prevention of Cruelty to Children was in the child-saving business and it soon had imitators across the country. A network of orphanages, which tripled in number between 1860 and 1890, arose to shelter the children who were taken off the streets. (In light of the Mary Ellen Wilson case, many believed these institutions were safer than foster homes.) By 1890, the country had more than 550 "asylums for dependent children," housing nearly fifty thousand children.

Public support for the cause of needy children was stoked by the press. Journalist Jacob Riis wrote about children forced to work as forgers and thieves. And he described the slums where more than half the city's one million people lived, as squalid breeding grounds for disease, crime, and exploitation. An estimated forty thousand New York children were categorized as "vagrants" and one thousand underage girls worked in saloons.[12]

Milton S. Hershey passed through the places Riis revealed in his columns as he made wholesale deliveries to pushcart vendors and small stores. The experience would affect him for the rest of his life, and contribute to his eventual decision to found one of the nation's great charities. It also formed the foundation of a critique of urban life he expressed later on. "Cities never seemed natural to me," he said, "and I never learned to like them."

Like it or not, the biggest city in America was the place where Milton would begin to get his business right. In New York the quality of Hershey's products and the scale of his operation were well matched to the market. In 1884, his mother and Aunt Mattie came to New York to join him again in the kitchen, where they wrapped the candies and put them in boxes. Sales were so good that Hershey was soon able to hire some young women from the neighborhood. He also brought his trusted old ally Harry Lebkicher up from Philadelphia, where he had been working as a trolley conductor. With all the paid helpers Milton had hired, his mother and his aunt could concentrate on making a nearby house he had rented into a proper home.

Henry Hershey had a proven knack for showing up whenever his son had a few dollars, and New York was no exception. The exact date of his arrival was never recorded, but a clue may lie in a new line of products Milton began to produce after he had been in the city for a little more than a year. Hershey's cough drops—his father had pushed cough drops when the two were together in Philadelphia—were supposed to tap the enormous winter market for sore throat lozenges. The problem was, New Yorkers already had a favorite brand.

Simple black or red sugar lozenges, Smith Brothers Cough Drops were one of the first trademarked products in America. William and Andrew Smith had begun making them in Poughkeepsie in 1847. The eccentric, bearded brothers, who used their profile portraits as a trademark, developed an early method for mass production. The drops were made from huge batches of syrupy liquid that was boiled, cooled into a solid, and then cut. The cut pieces were then dumped into five-gallon milk pails. Wagons took the pails to homes, apartments, and farms, where families worked to put the drops in paper boxes. At the height of winter production, some people in Poughkeepsie might have gotten the impression that half the population was up nights boxing cough drops. Church Street, site of the factory, was nicknamed "Cough Drop Street" by local citizens.

By paying low wages and manufacturing their product in a low-cost area—a strategy Milton Hershey would one day copy—the Smith Brothers defeated all their competitors, including imitators such as the Smythe Brothers, the Smith Sisters, and the Schmidt Brothers. They would also overpower Milton and Henry Hershey, who were not able to mount a credible challenge to the Smiths, even when the harsh winter of 1884–85 brought a sore throat to almost every man, woman, and child in the city. Father and son split around this time, and some evidence exists to suggest that Henry actually competed with his son for while, selling candy under the Hershey name in lower Manhattan.

Even though the cough drops had not taken off and his father was com-

peting with him, Milton believed business would be good enough to justify another move to a larger space, just around the corner on West Forty-
second Street. In the new quarters he would no longer be dependent on a
landlord to supply steam (in the old place, the man in charge of the boiler
was unreliable), and he had space to accommodate a larger staff. Unfortunately, the bet he had made on cough drops was more costly than he could
have anticipated. By the summer of 1886, he was unable to pay $10,000 he
owed to the company that had supplied him with equipment he had
bought to make Henry's drops. Then the landlord for his original space
sued to enforce the lease that Milton broke when he moved.

With a large debt that he couldn't or wouldn't ask his mother's family to
refinance, Milton closed the shop, crated his machinery and other belongings, and sent his mother and Aunt Mattie home to Lancaster. He shipped
his belongings, including sugar, molasses, kettles and other equipment
from his shop to Lancaster, where it would be held by the stationmaster
until the freight was paid.

Left behind in New York, Henry Hershey chose to live in the notorious
Bowery district. The neighborhood was a raucous destination for poor immigrants—Italian, Chinese, and German—as well as petty crooks and Sal-
vation Army missionaries. Taverns offered gambling and free newspapers to
go with a man's five-cent glass of beer, and for another seven cents he
could sleep on a rope hammock strung between timbers in the basement.
At many of the saloons young women were employed to serve customers
whatever they wanted, but Henry preferred places like Vokes Beer Garden,
where German was spoken and food and drink were the only items for
sale.

Still tall, elegant, and opinionated, Henry had plenty of stories to tell
the Vokes Beer Garden crowd—there were his adventures in the West and
his Oil City days—and he stayed in the Bowery for years. Once again he
took up painting, and sold some pictures. He made pretty oils of fish and
vegetables. But the record of his life in this period is sketchy, becoming
clearer again only in the early 1890s, which would find him back in Colorado, surviving on a monthly check sent by his son.[13]

EDIBLE MUD

4 It was not a glorious homecoming.

In the summer of 1886 Milton Hershey arrived in Lancaster just ahead of a lawyer for the machinery agent who would file a court claim for the $10,000 still owed on the equipment Milton had bought in New York. Hershey was so broke he had to turn to his old friend Harry Lebkicher to pay the railroad to release the crates he had shipped home, and he had to ask the teamster who picked up the load for credit on the fifty cents he charged to haul the stuff from the depot to a small room he arranged to rent in a warehouse.

Though he was only twenty-eight, Milton's bushy mustache and the stress of two big failures made him look older. Soon strands of gray would start to appear in the mustache. But he was still slim, as he was in youth, and photos show that his left eyebrow was always a little raised—a trait he inherited from his mother—which gave his face a sly, knowing appearance.

Fourteen years since he became Royer's apprentice confectioner, Milton Hershey was still infected with his mother's high expectations and his father's dreamy ambition. And he carried both these burdens as he walked the five miles from the city of Lancaster to the Snavely family's big farm in rural New Danville.

Given family ties, the Snavely wealth, and their past support, Milton would set aside his embarrassment and ask for one more loan. If failure is the best instructor, he could argue that he had earned a doctorate in Philadelphia, Denver, and New York. He intended to make a candy no one else produced in the East—Denver-style caramels. And he had reason to believe that in Lancaster, where he could do business on a more personal basis with folks he knew, he would finally succeed. Hershey's uncles and his aunt, Mattie, heard him out, and then turned him down. They had finally decided that Fanny's boy was too much Henry Hershey's son, and they wouldn't risk any more money on his dreams.

For the first time in his life, Milton Hershey was without the support of his mother's family. His father, who had never been much help before, was lost in the life of the Bowery. But as much as he may have felt adrift and alone, Milton had been liberated, too. Years later he would say, with a hint of pride, that he realized he had become, like his father, a "black sheep" in the eyes of his Snavely uncles. This rejection was a great motivator.

Alone in the rented room at the warehouse, Milton began to make candy. He sold it himself, from a handbasket, on the streets of Lancaster. He did well enough to buy a pushcart and move to a larger space in a red-brick factory on Church Street, where the other tenants included a manu-facturer of horse-drawn carriages. Soon his mother and Aunt Mattie were adding their hands to the work again, wrapping the sweets that Milton cooked, cooled, and cut.

In the new space Hershey had the room to make his special caramels on a large scale. But before he could start he needed $700 to buy a big copper boiling pot and other equipment. At first the city's bankers turned him down. But then he persuaded Aunt Mattie to lend him her good name and credit, if not the cash. She pledged a small row house she owned on South Queen Street, and the Lancaster County National Bank, which had done substantial business with the Snavelys in the past, gave Milton Hershey a ninety-day loan.

After a little experimenting, Milton solved a small problem that bothered most people who bought ordinary caramels: they were often too sticky and dif-ficult to chew. By raising the amount of milk he used, and therefore the fat content, he was able to make a caramel that wouldn't stick to the teeth. The extra fat also gave the caramels a distinctly smooth, sweet, buttery taste.

The advantages of fresh milk went beyond taste and stickiness. It also gave Hershey's caramels a certain cachet with people concerned about health. In two decades, pasteurization had transformed cow's milk from a potentially dangerous drink—a bowl of cherries and bad milk were the likely cause of President Zachary Taylor's death in 1850—into a symbol of pure nutrition. Lancaster County milk assured consumers that Hershey's caramels, flavored with vanilla, cocoa, and other ingredients, were good, healthy food, and their fresh mellow taste was instantly recognized as superior.

But as good as the caramels were, a city of roughly 30,000 people can consume only so much candy, even if customers could buy a handful of pieces for just a penny. Milton would need a bigger market, and perhaps a wholesale buyer, to make his business work. This time, he got lucky. A British importer passing through Lancaster found Hershey's candy kitchen. The Englishman tasted the caramels and learned they would keep fresh for weeks and perhaps months. He ordered a huge shipment, promising to pay if the candy arrived in London in good condition. Once this arrangement was working smoothly, he said, he would place bigger orders.

The British buyer had appeared at just the right time. Milton's ninety days were up, and his bank loan was due. With the wholesale contract in hand, he went to the bank to ask for more time to repay the $700. He also requested an additional $1,000 to fill the big order. As it turned out, Hershey didn't deal that day with the senior officers, whose stubbornly conservative approach had seen Lancaster National through sixty-five years of boom and panics that had ruined other local banks. Instead he spoke with a junior officer named Frank Brenneman. Decades later, John McLain, a Hershey company executive, would tell the story he had heard from Brenneman about this fateful encounter:

> Hershey came down and said, "I can't pay. I want you to come up and see. I have material and merchandise. Let me show you what I have." Brenneman went up. Afterwards he told me, "It was not imposing—the dust, the dirt and racket in the wagon-maker's shed. His mother and aunt, his only employees, were sitting there wrapping caramels." Brenneman went on to say, "I don't know what to do."

Brenneman was impressed by Hershey's honesty. He hadn't tried to exaggerate his little firm's potential, and he had made it clear that his future depended on the success of that single export contract.

> Mr. Brenneman told me, "I told Hershey to come back the next day. I walked the floor debating whether I would take the chance. He had told me all. He didn't conceal the bad part. He made no excuses for it. He was honest. I decided I would lend him the money. But I was afraid to present to the bank that note with that story. To avoid trouble, I put my own name on the note."

Hershey would need to fill the London order quickly enough for it to spend seven days crossing the Atlantic by steamship, and for the customer's check to travel back to Lancaster before the due date on the loan. (That was assuming, of course, that the buyer could be trusted to pay him at all.) To get the work done, he added a small number of real employees to the little unpaid family workforce and invested in additional equipment. Working day and night, he met his deadline, saw the shipment off, and waited.

With just days left before he would face foreclosure on the note, Milton Hershey received an envelope from London. Inside was a check, drawn on the Bank of England, that would cover all of his debt. Hershey told the story of this moment to John McLain, who retold it in 1955.

> Hershey told me this: "When I opened that mail and saw that, I just went round in circles. The first thing I did was reach for my coat and hat and I started down the street, and was gone some blocks before I realized I had on my spattered caramel apron." He had on an overcoat, so he tucked the apron under the coat, went into the bank and said, "I want my note."

A check written in British pounds was something unusual for the Lancaster bank. Hershey agreed to pay $1.50 to send a cable to London to verify the draft. He and Brenneman were both pleased when word came back that the check, for £500, was good. (The draft from London would be worth close to $50,000 in 2005.)[1]

After so much struggle it was strange that one big break—an order from an importer who happened to pass through town—would make Milton Hershey a success. The classic script would call for, at the very least, some minor setbacks and skirmishes with tough competitors. But none of those things happened. Instead, Hershey's sales abroad increased steadily, giving him a secure base for his business. He also exploited his recipe, and the advantages of his location, to build his business at home.

Lancaster provided Hershey with a nearly perfect environment for growing a wholesale candy company. Close to New York, Philadelphia, Baltimore, and Washington, it occupied the heart of the Mid-Atlantic states, a region that dominated American business, finance, invention, and commerce. Although constituting just 10 percent of the nation's landmass, this territory contained more than half the country's industry and possessed the infrastructure to support it. In Lancaster, the Pennsylvania Railroad provided transportation in all directions. A new gasworks assured a steady supply of fuel, and an Edison power plant had begun to transform electricity from a novelty into a source of light and energy that meant factories could operate twenty-four hours per day. Finally, the Pennsylvania Dutch influence made local labor honest, hardworking, and compliant.

High quality and a fair price won Hershey repeat business from shops in an ever widening circle from downtown Lancaster. Using what he had learned from the Smith Brothers about branding, Milton protected his place in the market by labeling his caramels with the name Crystal A and urging his customers to accept no imitations. Eager to accommodate a tenant who paid on time, Hershey's landlord allowed him to take over more and more space in the factory building.

Steady growth over the next five years pushed the number of workers at the Hershey factory past seven hundred. M.S. named his firm the Lancaster Caramel Company and offered an enormous variety of flavored caramels in different sizes, shapes, and price ranges. The dour but loyal Harry Lebkicher, veteran of Hershey's two previous candy campaigns, was again brought in to help manage accounts.

With a trusted man watching the books, Milton was free to indulge his passion for experimentation. Candy making depends on precise heat, pure ingredients, proper timing, and careful mixing. The primary chemical event in this process occurs when sugar is dissolved in water and heat is used to break it into individual molecules. Soft candies like caramel and fudge require constant mixing as the liquefied sugar cools. Without the stirring action, boiled sugar will tend to recrystallize into hard candy. Texture and flavor depend on when other ingredients are added—before, during, or after boiling—and on other factors such as cooking time and whether a fan is used to accelerate cooling. The best hard candy was made by furious boiling, or "cooking it high."

In time, candy companies would employ chemists to perfect production, but in the nineteenth century confectioners depended on old recipes and experiments with new ingredients. Hershey spent days at the kettles, tinkering with his caramels. He added nuts to some, and covered others with sugar icing. He found that a little corn syrup—the sweetener that was introduced at county fairs the year he was born—improved the "chew."

Gradually he added new premium brands—named Lotus, Paradox, and Cocoanut Ices—to the Crystal A line. For less wealthy customers he produced Uniques, which were made with skim milk and priced at eight for a penny.

By the early 1890s, Lancaster Caramel occupied all 450,000 square feet of the redbrick factory building on Church Street. The cooking was done in enormous steam-heated kettles—some as big as five barrels—where hundreds of pounds of sugar were mixed in each batch. The kettles were lined up in long rows, and testers would walk from kettle to kettle making sure the heat was reduced at exactly the right moment. The molten caramel would then be poured out on marble slabs cooled by blowers. When it had cooled enough to handle, workers would heave ten-pound globs onto hooks positioned two feet above the tables where they worked. They would pull on the caramel until it nearly came off the hook, then throw the mess back on and pull some more. Eventually the pulling made the caramel soft and pliable enough to be sent on for cutting, icing, wrapping, and boxing. At the loading dock the boxes would be piled into horse-drawn wagons, which lined Church Street throughout the day. As the teamsters waited to take their turns at the dock, they breathed in the scent of caramel and horse manure, a combination that must have smelled like money to Milton Hershey.

Although competitors could battle Hershey on price, they couldn't match his quality, and this advantage allowed Lancaster Caramel to expand its market every year. When freight charges made it hard for him to compete in the Midwest with National Caramel of St. Louis, Hershey opened a second plant on West Harrison Street in Chicago, which soon employed four hundred people. (In two years this facility would be moved to the small city of Bloomington, Illinois, which was closer to dairies.) Two more factories were opened, in Mount Joy and Reading, Pennsylvania, so that new contracts with customers as far away as Australia and Japan could be satisfied. The company's payroll exceeded fourteen hundred.

The caramel houses, as they were called, operated twenty-four hours per day and were early models for the production line methods that would eventually be perfected by Henry Ford. They were organized so that raw materials were efficiently transformed into finished, packaged goods. But as much as Hershey and his managers tried to make the process into a smooth routine, it wasn't perfect. And it could be dangerous.

In one case a young man feeding a cooled batch of candy through the metal rollers of a machine suffered an injury that was serious enough to make him unfit for work. His father sued because just before the accident, M.S. had removed a safety guard that he had rigged up himself. Hershey lost at trial, and the father won $1,000. But an appeals court overturned the verdict, finding that machine, without the custom-made guard, was widely used and removing it did not constitute negligence.

Painful as it may have been, one worker's smashed fingers couldn't compare with the mishap that later occurred during a routine overnight shift at the Reading factory. Workers in the boiling room were following Hershey's standing order—"cook it high"—to produce a batch of hard candy. The heat on the kettles was turned as high as the valves allowed. The sugar water began to boil and the pressure in the kettles rose. At about 3:15 A.M., as an inspector walked up to one of the big copper vessels, it suddenly exploded. Parts of the kettle flew straight up into the ceiling while a fire broke out on the factory floor. A hundred workers, most of them young women, ran to the exits as the fire spread.

Although the fire department responded with pumpers and several companies of men, the Reading caramel house was completely destroyed. A few workers were injured, but miraculously, none were killed. Even the inspector survived, though he was so dazed he couldn't explain how he wound up walking shoeless in the street. He quipped, "I guess that damn batch went high enough for him this time."[2]

Milton S. Hershey had become one of Pennsylvania's more prominent men, and there seemed to be no limit on how big his company could grow. Some of this success was due to his intelligence and determination. Then there was the quality of his product and the special advantages he enjoyed in Lancaster. But Hershey was also blessed to have started his business at a unique moment in the nation's economic history.

In 1870 America had begun an immigration boom that would last fifty years and triple both the country's population and the number of potential customers for products like Hershey's caramels. In this half century, one new breakthrough technology after another—in communications, energy, transportation, and manufacturing—transformed a collection of isolated communities into an integrated industrial nation and the world's largest marketplace. By 1900, the United States, led by Pennsylvania and the other Mid-Atlantic states, would be responsible for a third of the world's industrial wealth, producing more than the manufacturers of Germany, France, and Great Britain put together.[3]

More phenomenal change was yet to come. The rise of electricity and oil as power sources would boost American energy consumption by 400 percent and increase productivity from the farm to the factory, driving down the price of most commodities. For example, the dairies that supplied Hershey benefited enormously from the development of the automatic cream separator, which allowed them to produce more milk and cream at much lower costs.

Less obvious, but just as important in the long term, was the gradual emergence of national consumer product companies that would use mass-marketing techniques to insinuate themselves into daily life. It was no coincidence that Coca-Cola was founded in the same year that Hershey started up in Lancaster. Dozens of powerful national food brands emerged in this era, including Pillsbury flour, Log Cabin syrup, Lipton tea, Good & Plenty candy, and Juicy Fruit gum. All were new tastes that could be enjoyed by a growing middle class that discovered fresh novelties on a monthly basis.

Americans were eager to buy cheap, quality goods of all sorts. But as early as the 1880s they noted with some anxiety the passing of a slower, traditional way of life that could be viewed with dreamy hindsight. People understood they were living in an extraordinary time. Politicians, clergy, and social commentators debated whether they were witnessing the demise of humanity or a burst of creativity equal to the Renaissance. At the same time, inventors, entrepreneurs, and big-money investors raced to profit from everything that was new.

Understandably, public attention was focused primarily on the marvelous inventions that improved everyday life, and the industrial behemoths—in oil, steel, and railroading—that were growing to astonishing size. In 1891, just one of these companies—the Pennsylvania Railroad—employed 110,000 people, roughly three times the number of all those serving in the U.S. armed forces.

The industrial giants and newly devised monopolies exerted enormous influence on American life and politics. By the late 1880s money from the biggest industries had corrupted much of politics. Certain members of Congress, for example, were known to represent steel, railroads, oil, or sugar trusts. Typical was Representative J.N. Camden of West Virginia, who secretly worked for Standard Oil and killed legislation that would have helped its competitors to ship their oil at lower cost. At the same time, the term "robber baron" became part of the vernacular and the horrific conditions in foundries, steel mills, and other workplaces were widely documented by the press.

So much was written and said about the ruthlessness of the biggest corporations and their founders that they were often depicted in editorial columns and cartoons as plundering feudal lords. This image wasn't helped by the overhonest statements that sometimes poured from the mouths of the new capitalists. Meat packer Philip Armour once explained, "I do not love the money; what I do love is the getting of it, the making of it. . . . I do not read, I do not take any part in politics . . . but in my counting house I am in my element."

With men like Armour exhibiting such raw ambition, a national debate arose over the moral aspects of great wealth, the tension between capital and labor, and the role of corporations in society. Americans still tended to favor the idea of all men being created equal. The appearance of a class of super-rich, super-powerful citizens who enjoyed enormous advantages that they passed to their children provoked resentment, especially among organized workers and farmers.[4]

In 1888 Edward Bellamy published *Looking Backward, 2000–1887,* which imagined a twentieth-century utopia in which wealth was shared equally, national identity was the core social value, and industry served the state. This novel offered a socialist vision of a future America without slums, suffering, and profiteers. It quickly became the second biggest-selling book of the century, behind *Uncle Tom's Cabin.*

Bellamy tapped widely held fears about the rapid rise of powerful corporations, the industrial transformation of society, and the excesses of the Gilded Age. Within months of the book's publication, Bellamy Nationalist Clubs were formed across the country. Members hoped to make real his vision of a classless society. Some also founded short-lived communes based on Bellamy's ideas. These were the first American utopian communities based on political ideas, rather than religious ones, and some evolved to embrace both socialism and "free love."

While the Nationalist Clubs and others responded dramatically to the social and economic tumult of the age, the lions of industry and commerce fought against unions, government regulation, and every other effort to rein in their power. The archetype was John D. Rockefeller, who held the Calvinist view that wealth, his included, represented God's grace.

While many abhorred the oil trust he built to dominate the world market, they were also fascinated by his power.

The moral challenge of great wealth was addressed in 1889 by the steel magnate Andrew Carnegie in an essay called "The Gospel of Wealth," which argued that the rich must serve as generous stewards of society. Carnegie described surplus wealth as "trust funds" that were to be given away for the benefit of "poorer brethren." He put his argument in religious terms that reflected his upbringing among anti-Calvinist Scots, and he concluded, "The man who dies thus rich, dies disgraced."

Carnegie was a contradictory man. He spoke of social responsibility, but conditions at his steel mills were nothing short of hell on earth. He continually squeezed workers to produce more at lower costs. He followed an inconsistent approach to labor, defending unions and settling one strike amicably while allowing Pinkerton men to put down another with intimidation and violence. But ultimately Carnegie would sell off his holdings and give away 90 percent of his money to support research, libraries, public parks, education, and world peace. The example of his life would inspire a century of American philanthropy.[5]

While Bellamy, Carnegie, and others called on Americans to find a response to the excesses of their time, science and industry were producing wonders that would inevitably distract them from moral issues. The pace of invention was breathtaking, with new machines, new foods, and new ideas coming so fast that people had trouble keeping up. Practical versions of the telephone, the phonograph, moving picture machines, and electric trains were all produced in the late 1880s and early 1890s and they were among the most popular marvels displayed for the public in Chicago at the World's Columbian Exposition of 1893.

Timed to commemorate the voyage of Christopher Columbus, the Chicago fair was the first world exposition on American soil since the centennial of 1876. Boosters hoped it would show the world their city had become a more civilized and appealing place. But the exposition was troubled from the start. Violent storms and labor problems plagued the construction of the huge halls. Then on May 3, two days into the fair's run, an investor crisis on Wall Street began the great Panic of 1893. Thousands of businesses were ruined and millions lost their job as the economy was plunged into a depression that would last for four years.

Attendance at the Columbian Exposition plummeted at the start of the panic. On some days the White City, as the gleaming collection of buildings was called, looked almost empty. But gradually the journalists and visitors who did attend from faraway places went home to describe a place of unmatched beauty and wonder. People began to think about going to see it for themselves.

Built at a cost of $27 million, the main buildings of the White City looked like they were made of alabaster marble and evoked the temples of ancient Rome and Athens. The columns of Electricity Hall soared forty-eight feet high. The Administration Building was crowned by a golden dome, and a statue of Diana stood atop Agriculture Hall. The sight of these buildings made some literally weep with admiration.

Along with the imposing architecture, visitors discovered 633 manicured acres divided by man-made pools, ponds, and lagoons, which were served by electric launches that glided so quietly that they seemed to swim like dolphins across the water. Fountains shot water a hundred feet in the air and nearly two hundred thousand bulbs lit the site at night. The brave-hearted could ride a balloon a thousand feet into the sky or hop aboard the world's first Ferris wheel. Two hundred and fifty feet in diameter, built to rival the Eiffel Tower, the wheel made by bridge builder George W.G. Ferris carried as many as fourteen hundred people at maximum capacity. Once it began turning on June 16, it rarely stopped for very long. At food concessions Americans also got their first taste of Pabst beer, Cracker Jack, Shredded Wheat, and a new sandwich called a hamburger.

The indoor exhibitions in the White City were devoted to categories such as machinery, transportation, women, and electricity. The largest collection was presented in the Hall of Manufacturers and Liberal Arts, which covered more than thirty acres, making it the biggest structure in the world. Visitors wandered through a large display of American goods and separate exhibits of items from various countries around the world. The largest of these were sent by France, Great Britain, and Germany. You could see anything produced anywhere, from some of the most expensive jewelry to textiles and household appliances. Nearby, in a building all its own, German arms manufacturer Fritz Krupp, who had sent his cannons to the American centennial in 1876, displayed the largest gun in the world, a 250,000-pound "pet monster" that could fire a one-ton shell.[6]

With all there was to see and do, it's hard to imagine anyone getting bored by the Columbian Exposition. But visitors who became overwhelmed by the scale of the fair and its dazzling sights could always take a break and visit another local landmark, the new town created by the railroad car manufacturer George Pullman. Heralded as America's greatest large-scale, planned industrial town, Pullman, Illinois, was a modern community of twelve thousand people, well built and well kept, with a commercial arcade—forerunner to the modern shopping mall—and other big city amenities. Every home had indoor plumbing and gas service. It was widely promoted as an ideal place and a model for future communities.

But with row upon row of look-alike brick houses and the autocratic style of its founder, Pullman had a distinct dark side. Many workers resented George Pullman's efforts to promote their community as a village of well-paid and contented citizens. Unable to buy their homes—Pullman only allowed for rentals—workers often felt trapped in the model town. They also understood that almost every aspect of their domestic lives was subject to the rules set by the very same bosses who controlled them at work. This may be why a typical resident stayed in Pullman for just four years.

Outside critics saw trouble in Pullman, too. Jane Addams, the famous social reformer, called the founder "a modern Lear" who had become a dictator. *Harper's Weekly* said that the power exercised by Bismarck in Germany was "utterly insignificant" compared with the rule the car company exercised over the citizens of Pullman. "Nobody regards Pullman as a real home," noted the magazine.

Residents couldn't help but notice that George Pullman tried to make them pay as much as possible for everything. For example the public library, which was run by the founder's cousin, charged such a high membership fee that it never had more than two hundred members. Rents in the company town were higher than they were in neighboring Kensington and Roseland and consumed as much as 30 percent of a worker's pay. Pullman even expected the lone church building in the community to return 6 percent per year by renting its space to various denominations.[7]

As early as September 1893, the economic conditions that made Pullman's success possible were starting to unravel. With railroads no longer buying so many cars, the company was beginning layoffs that would eventually reduce its workforce from 5,500 to 3,300. Those who still had jobs faced wage cuts that would total 25 percent. Rents on Pullman homes remained unchanged however, and this set the stage for future conflict.

• • •

As a very young man in Philadelphia, Milton Hershey had been enchanted by the Centennial Exposition, so it was natural that he was attracted to the fair in Chicago. If he needed some justification for taking so much time away from Lancaster, he could go visit his factory in Bloomington.

Hershey spent enough time at the fair to enjoy everything it offered and many of the attractions set up outside the fairground, including Buffalo Bill's Wild West Show and Congress of Rough Riders of the World. Among the official exhibits was a Lancaster-built Conestoga wagon, presented as a symbol of the past, which stood close to the New York Central Railroad's Engine Number 999, which had recently hit a record speed of 112 miles per hour.

Although the Wild West show and Engine 999 were impressive, Hershey was touched more directly by an exhibit in the agriculture building, where foodstuffs from around the world filled a huge pavilion topped by a glass dome that was 130 feet high. There, among the smoked meats, barrels of grain, bundles of lambs wool, and piles of tobacco leaves was hidden a little temple, thirty-eight feet tall, built entirely of chocolate produced by one of Europe's largest confectioners, the Stollwerck brothers of Cologne.

The thirty-thousand-pound Stollwerck temple was a masterpiece of edible architecture. From a foundation made of dark chocolate blocks rose columns topped by Teutonic eagles. The columns were made with swirls of white cocoa butter—a by-product of cocoa manufacturing—to make them resemble marble. They supported a dome with a crown at its highest point. Inside the temple was a larger-than-life chocolate statue of the mythological Germania, complete with sword, standing on a pedestal that was decorated with relief images of Bismarck, Kaiser Wilhelm I, and historical figures.

The temple was just one of several chocolate-related exhibits at the fair. In another part of the Agriculture Hall, the French built a little house out of small paper wrappers from chocolate makers. And in the Machinery Building, where dynamos and turbines whirled to the delight of thousands, J.M. Lehmann of Dresden, Germany, operated a small factory that turned raw cocoa beans into chocolate bars.

Lehmann's factory was not a model or miniature display. It was a full-size working production line. It had an oven for roasting the beans, which were cooled, hulled, and ground. The beans then spent hours in special mixers equipped with marble rollers that went back and forth to produce a smooth chocolate paste. (Named conches because they were shaped like giant seashells, these machines had been invented in 1879 by Swiss confectioner Rudolph Lindt.) Once the conching was done, presses squeezed moisture from the product, and sugar, vanilla, and cocoa butter were added to create an edible mud that could be poured into molds. When the chocolate was cooled and removed from the molds, Lehmann had chocolate bars.

In a hall where so many exhibits smelled of grease and oil, the warm sweet fragrance of Lehmann's chocolate factory was intoxicating. Some of the American fairgoers may have savored the smell of chocolate before, at a neighborhood candy kitchen, but few of them would have ever tasted hard chocolate candy that was as rich and smooth in texture as the bars that Lehmann distributed in the Palace of Mechanic Arts.

Manufacturers in other European countries, especially Great Britain, were well on their way to creating a big market for so-called eating chocolate. Improved quality, mass production, and lower prices were creating a chocolate craze in Europe, which was encouraged by the product's association with goodness and even virtue. British temperance groups promoted chocolate as an alternative to alcohol. Industrial experts recommended a dose of chocolate to keep factory workers performing at their best, and some government authorities prescribed it as a nutritional essential for orphan children. Such a claim was a step down from the eighteenth-century use of cocoa as a medicine, but it would turn out to have some basis in fact. Over the years science has found some evidence that, along with calories and a little jolt of caffeine, a dose of chocolate can improve your mood and may inhibit blood clotting. While this is good news for chocolate eaters, modern science provides even better news for companies that make it. Some neuroscientists believe that chocolate, which stimulates the same areas of the brain activated by cocaine—the orbital frontal cortex and the midbrain—is addictive.[8]

The idea that chocolate could make people sober, healthy, and productive helps to explain why, in Great Britain, Quaker families such as the Cadburys, Frys, and Rowntrees were drawn to the business and rose to dominate it. Many Quakers, including the founders of Cadbury, were involved in the temperance movement. John Cadbury believed alcohol contributed to poverty and illness. Chocolate was a wholesome alternative. It was also a new business, which meant it hadn't become dominated by others.

Chocolate wasn't the only nineteenth-century food linked to religious, social, and health concerns. In the United States all of the most popular brands of soft drinks, including Coca-Cola, Hires root beer, and Dr Pepper, began as medicinal products. (The soft drink Moxie was made by the Moxie Nerve Food Company of Boston.) Similarly, the enormous dry cereal industry was begun by Seventh Day Adventists who, as vegetarians, promoted grains as a boon to health. The famous Battle Creek Sanitarium, which inspired a cereal-based health craze, was founded by Adventists as the Western Health Reform Institute. For decades it was run by members of the Kellogg family, religionists who also built the great cereal company.

Like the Seventh Day Adventists, and American Mennonites, Quakers in Britain suffered from discrimination and found it difficult to enter many trades. In some cases the discrimination was informal. No one would take on a Quaker as an apprentice or partner. But in other instances the prejudice was official policy. For more than a century Quakers were barred from attending university and thus prevented from becoming lawyers, doctors, or clergy. However, they could start up a business based on a new product like eating chocolate. And like Mennonites, the Quakers stressed harmony, community, and moderation in all things. They considered themselves stewards of the world's blessings and were serious about this role. For them, chocolate was the perfect do-good-while-doing-well product.

Great Britain's thriving chocolate industry was known by Milton Hershey, who had begun to travel regularly to the British Isles and the Continent. There he visited cities that were safer, more beautiful, and more appealing than any he had seen in the United States.

In England he also noticed how companies such as Rowntree, Fry, and Cadbury were creating a big new industry serving low-cost chocolate to the masses. He learned that George and Richard Cadbury, sons of the founder, had moved their factory out of smoky, slum-filled Birmingham to a rural site where they had put up a new chocolate works and were considering building a company town to go with it.[9]

At the Columbian Exposition, Milton Hershey visited Lehmann's chocolate machines over and over again to study them in action, inhale the scented air, and taste its sweet product. He recognized the superior technology on display and understood the commercial potential for European-style chocolate in America. According to a manuscript written years later by one of his relatives, Hershey often brought his cousin Frank Snavely, manager of the Chicago caramel plant, to see the chocolate works.

"The caramel business is a fad," said Hershey, as Snavely stood beside him. "It is not a staple business. But chocolate is something we will always have."

Other businessmen visited the Columbian Exposition hoping to experience this kind of "aha!" moment. The fair was not just entertainment or amusement. It was intended to celebrate human progress, promote innovation, and stimulate the exchange of ideas and, ultimately, the sale of new technologies. Krupp, for example, hoped to sell his great gun to armies around the world, and J.M. Lehmann didn't spend six months making chocolate just to please the exposition crowds. He was there to sell his machines, and in the end he had at least one big success.

Before leaving Chicago, Milton Hershey placed an order to buy every single piece of Lehmann equipment he had seen in the Palace of Mechanic Arts. He didn't want new machines shipped from Dresden. He wanted the specific pieces he had studied in operation. The last of the exhibition's 26 million visitors attended on closing day, October 30, 1893. Soon afterward, the chocolate works was crated and put on rail cars, bound for Lancaster.[10]

CATHERINE

5 J.M. Lehmann sent an engineer named Wunderlich to help Milton Hershey set up his equipment in the Lancaster caramel house and teach the Americans how to operate each device. The centerpieces were the conches, which mixed ingredients for hours on end, and the melanger. Together, they cost $20,000 (about $400,000 in 2005).

Weighing ten tons, the melanger was a huge, round, polished steel tub with a smooth granite bottom, which was heated from below by metal coils carrying steam. Ground cacao, sugar, and flavoring were poured into the tub which slowly turned as heavy granite rollers spun round and round inside it to produce liquefied chocolate.

According to the *New Era*, a Lancaster newspaper, the melanger's rollers weighed more than one thousand pounds each. The whole setup, one of just three in the world, could make five thousand pounds of chocolate per day. According to the paper, this was just the beginning. Milton Hershey intended to become the largest chocolate maker in the world.

By New Year's Day 1894, Milton Hershey was making cocoa powder for drinking, baking chocolate, and sweet chocolate coatings that could be poured over caramels. Two years would pass before solid chocolate candy labeled with the name Hershey would be sold to the public. A hands-on learner, Milton would use this time to experiment with roasting, grinding, pressing, and mixing. According to the tales handed down over the years, Milton set his removable shirt cuffs on a counter in the factory and plunged into the task for hours, and sometimes days, on end.

Admirers credited these endless experiments with the development of Hershey's first quality chocolate, but in fact Milton, whom people had begun to call M.S., had hedged his bets. According to one source, he brought workers from Daniel Peter's milk chocolate factory in Switzerland to work for him in Lancaster. In 1894 he recruited a chocolate maker named Smith from a small firm in Chicago. And in 1895 he raided the Walter Baker & Company in Massachusetts for two more experienced men who were named Reed and Davis.

The Baker Company, which began operating the first successful chocolate mill in America in 1765, was the nation's oldest and largest producer and wouldn't have missed the two defectors. But with the Swiss makers as well as Smith, Reed, and Davis on the job, Hershey had experts who could fill in the gaps in his education.

With his Lancaster Caramel Company doing $1 million in annual sales (equal to $21 million in 2005), and chocolate looming as his next big thing, M.S. searched for experienced managers who could help him steer his enterprises. The idea that talented executives could use certain basic principles to guide a company to success was gaining in currency. The latter decades of the nineteenth century had seen the rise of both a new profession—business management—and an entire class of polished and highly paid corporate commanders who kept track of affairs in large complex companies. This new discipline was led by Frederick Winslow Taylor, the creator of what he termed "scientific management."

Taylor almost certainly suffered from obsessive-compulsive disorder. As a child he habitually counted his own footsteps, timed his daily activities, and included the note "make lists" in his daily logs. In adulthood he employed his pathology to pioneer intricate studies in time and motion. He used a stopwatch to break down a worker's actions, adjusted the design of tools, and then choreographed routines to make labor more productive. In one of the earliest tests of his scientific management, he used his methods to triple the productivity of steelworkers.

At first Taylor's new science, which rejected initiative in favor of simple organized tasks, was considered radical and even threatening by some workers. But as a Pennsylvania Quaker and a leading progressive, he spread his message with an evangelist's zeal, preaching that individual workers should serve a system of production that would create so much wealth that a perfect society would emerge to the benefit of all. In the end, he said, workers would earn more as they did more. He even equated efficiency with morality and a glowing future society. As Taylor once explained to a congressional committee, "This, gentlemen, is the beginning of a great mental revolution."

Eventually so-called Taylorism was widely accepted and became so in-grained in American business that its basic tenets—more, better, faster—became universal norms. Workers accepted his principles because employers tended to raise wages as they adopted the Taylor plan. Overseas, his thinking would be studied by Lenin and revered as America's greatest contribution to human progress. "The Taylor gift to Europe is not only an American lesson, it is *the* American lesson," said one Finnish academic.[1]

Industry's need for experts who might provide a competitive advantage became ever more acute as the nineteenth century wound to an end. In this age of innovation, the development of a product or technology was usually followed by a ferocious competition as entrepreneurs rushed to grab pieces of the new business. (A hundred years later the same dynamic emerged as new technologies made the Internet accessible and hundreds of companies were formed to capitalize on it.) The classic example from the Gilded Age involved the battle for the cookie and cracker market.

Until about 1890, cookies and crackers were labor-intensive items pro-duced by neighborhood bakers. Then new machines were developed to allow large-scale production of everything from sugar wafers to saltines. With the right packaging and transport system, a single brand could be sold across a huge region. By mid-decade, two large firms, the New York Biscuit Company and the United States Baking Company, controlled the cookie and cracker business. After a ruinous price war they were saved from bankruptcy in 1898 by merging to create the National Biscuit Com-pany. The new conglomerate had more than a hundred bakeries, an an-nual output of 360 million pounds of crackers, and no real rival.

The National Biscuit Company was created by business executives, not bakers, and its success was considered proof of the value of modern man-agement. According to one study, the ranks of professional managers would grow from roughly 120,000 in 1870 to nearly 900,000 in 1910. Those at the highest rank came from universities where newly developed departments of business and management prepared young men to be lead-ers of industry.[2]

But while executives helped companies grow, they also posed chal-lenges to the egos of entrepreneurs who viewed their companies as exten-sions of themselves. This kind of conflict arose in the mid-1890s, when Milton Hershey turned to his cousin William Blair to manage the caramel company. Blair was a competent but bull-headed man who resisted many of his boss's suggestions. He was sarcastic and had a way of speaking that made M.S. Hershey lose his temper. People could see this happening when Blair went to Hershey's office in a glassed-in corner of the caramel factory. After one particularly heated argument, Blair quit. Soon he was vacationing in France with his family.

Not long after Blair resigned, M.S. traveled to New York, where he had dinner with a sugar salesman. The man ordered a house specialty, a big slab of beef served on an oiled piece of hardwood. With a flourish he demonstrated how a "planked steak" should be carved. Impressed by the man's sophistication, Hershey hired him on the spot to replace Blair.

Unlike Blair, the new fellow was willing to innovate. But his decision to use more cheap corn syrup and cut back on the amount of cane sugar in Lancaster caramels backfired. Customers could taste the lesser-quality sweetener and soon the wagons that carried freshly made candy to the railroad depot were coming back fully loaded with caramels returned by unhappy retailers. Hershey lost $60,000. The man from New York was fired. Blair was rehired. And M.S. came to understand the risk of emotional decisions. At one dinner meeting with his top men, M.S. ordered a planked steak and as he started to carve instructed his men to watch closely because "it cost me $60,000 to learn this."

Along with Blair, Hershey came to rely on a sales manager named William F.R. Murrie, whom he hired away from a Pittsburgh confectioner called Weaver and Costello in 1895. Murrie was the opposite of Hershey in many ways. Where Hershey was short, polite, and spoke in a soft voice, Murrie was a big, profane man with striking red hair and a loud voice he used to both charm and intimidate. He told stories about adventures he'd enjoyed as a barnstorming baseball player and traveling salesman. In one, a dead-drunk friend of Murrie awakened in a customer's warehouse nestled inside a coffin with a lily in his hand. Murrie spoke often of the time when he worked as a telegrapher and sent a garbled message that caused a train wreck. Another famous Murrie tale involved a swan let loose in a saloon.

Besides tall tales and jokes, Murrie knew enough parlor tricks to amuse any audience. One of his favorites, mastered during hundreds of stays at inns and hotels, was signing his name upside down, so a clerk wouldn't have to turn the register.

Hired to serve Hershey as a salesman, Murrie promised to write more orders than the factories could fill. When he succeeded, Hershey put him in charge of a force of salesmen that was as big as one hundred in the busiest times. At the head office in Lancaster, Murrie was a commanding presence whether barking orders or mingling with the seven hundred caramel house workers.

Although Murrie's big sales contracts increased the demand for production, and therefore raised the pace of activity in the caramel house, employees found the factory a good place to work. The pay was better than they would have received at many other local manufacturing plants, and the mood was pleasant. They were even allowed to hold dances in the building.[3]

With Blair, Murrie, and other managers in place, Milton Hershey had the time and energy to focus on other concerns, including family. On April 14, 1894, his Aunt Mattie died of pneumonia after a few days' illness. At sixty-two, just three years older than Milton's mother, the never married Martha Snavely had poured her heart, her money, and her labor into her nephew Milton. She was prominent enough that her death was noted in Lancaster's paper, the New Era. On the same day the paper reported that Jacob Coxey's army of populist protesters was camped outside Washington and the nation's chewing gum craze had reached the point where "no amount of preaching seems to have the slightest influence on suppressing it."

Mattie had never joined the Reformed Church, because she couldn't accept its goal of uniting all denominations under its banner. But to honor her father, the second bishop ever to serve the church in Lancaster County, members of the Reformed Mennonite congregation in New Danville allowed a funeral to be conducted in their meetinghouse. A generous donation from nephew Milton persuaded the church to bend its rules to allow flowers at the service.

Absent from Mattie's funeral was Henry Hershey. Though sixty-four years old, Henry had not given up his wandering. Fortified with cash from his son, Henry was off on another Colorado adventure. This time he lived for a while in Greeley, a commune and utopian experiment started by Nathan Meeker and named for the famous newspaper editor. Meeker had worked for Greeley's New York Tribune, and his boss had supported other communes where the ideas of early French socialism were put into practice.[4]

Worried about what his father and his money were doing in Colorado, Milton made a plan to get control of both. First he spent more than

$10,000 to reclaim the homestead in Derry Church, which had passed from the Hershey family's hands in 1877 following his grandfather's death. The large two-story house with open porches came with a barn and other outbuildings and between thirty and forty acres of land.

Once the farmhouse was cleaned up, Milton hired a manager named Daniel Schlesser, who moved in with his family and began to return the place to productive farming. M.S. warned the Schlessers that his father would soon join them. Mindful of the conservative outlook shared by the people of Lebanon Valley, he added, "Don't be alarmed. He very likely will come wearing a silk hat, carrying a cane, and wearing a frock coat. But that don't mean a thing."

Henry arrived in Derry Church wearing his fancy clothes but with few possessions except for enough books to fill shelves seven feet high and twelve feet long. His dark hair had begun to turn gray and when he removed his silk hat you could see a bald spot on the back of his head. He had lost most of his teeth and often refused to wear his dentures.

But Henry's mind remained young. He was still able to speak at length on almost any subject—a future of horseless carriages and flying machines was a favorite topic—and he rarely shrank from the opportunity to do so. At the kitchen table he would lecture anyone who would listen on the conflict between workers and corporate bosses and the inconsistencies of the Christian faith.

"Getting into arguments about the Bible was his hobby," one woman recalled about Henry. A preacher might stop by once to argue a point of Scripture, she said, but few ever returned for a second debate. This earned Henry a reputation as "an infidel." His status as a sinner wasn't enough to frighten people away, however. Local schoolteachers often invited him to speak, and he'd grace their students with impromptu lectures on the Greek gods or recent fossil discoveries.

Soon after he settled at the homestead, Henry had a large greenhouse built, where he experimented with various crops. None were ever put into production. Ever restless, Henry liked to drive his buggy—a model named the Jenny Lind—to nearby Erb's General Store, where he would sit and talk for hours.

People who didn't like Henry Hershey pointed out that he often drank to excess. Those who liked him said he enjoyed his whiskey but was seldom if ever drunk. No one disputed that he loved children and pretty women. And whenever he could, he would goad a farm boy into a wagon race. Invariably he held back his own horse, a chestnut gelding named George, allowing the boy to win.

"I had a spring wagon and an old mare," recalled John Moyer. "He would say, 'How about racing?' I would get the stick out and lay it on the old mare. He would hold his horse in a little and let me beat him. He liked the fun of seeing me drive."

Henry Hershey brought color and amusement to the Lebanon Valley. He made people laugh, made them think, and gave them someone to gossip about. Those who took his side in the community assessment of his marriage thought that Fanny Hershey had been cruel to treat him as if he were dead. Henry was a genius who would have thrived with a woman's support, they believed. Others, who may have feared his independent mind, said Henry was a scoundrel who had taken advantage of his wife and her family.

The truth lay somewhere between these two views. As a father, Henry was typical for his generation. Most men left the duty of raising children entirely to their wives, getting involved only when called upon. This was a generally accepted approach. But as a husband he had failed to meet his primary responsibility to support his family, and among the Pennsylvania Dutch this was a shame he could not escape.

In buying the homestead and bringing his father to live in it, Milton may have been scheming to reunite his family. (Several sources suggest this was the case.) But his mother would not live with a husband whom she had resented enough to declare dead. Instead, Henry was eventually joined at the homestead by his sister Elizabeth, who was considered nearly as rebellious as her brother. Disabled to the point where she needed crutches to get around, Elizabeth had committed an offense so sinful that the Reformed Mennonites had excommunicated her. (Although no record of her transgression survives, the way she was treated suggests a sexual scandal.) Members of the congregation, including some people in her own family, partially shunned her. She wasn't allowed to share the dinner table with them when they visited, and they would not shake her hand.[5]

The coterie at the farm was finally filled out by Harry Lebkicher, who had come to Milton's aid in Philadelphia. M.S. would support Harry for the rest of his life. It was an odd group: hard-drinking, loquacious Henry, the disgraced Elizabeth, and the laconic Lebkicher. But because of Milton's generosity, each of them found comfort and security at the homestead.[6]

• • •

Milton could be generous with himself, too. With his caramel profits he bought a big, beautiful home with wraparound porches at 222 South Queen Street in Lancaster; his next-door neighbor was the local congressman. After purchasing it in 1891, he outfitted the house in style, including a $700 Swiss music box among the furnishings. He bought peacocks for the yard and a pet dog for companionship. Until the Gilded Age, dogs were rarely welcomed in city homes. But in the 1890s a dog was a sign that you had both the money and time to care for it. Milton's first pet was identified as a St. Bernard by a boy who recalled it chasing him, but later Milton would favor German shepherds. M.S. also treated himself to vacations in this country and in Europe. Upon returning from one long stay on the Continent, he was dressed in a loud checked suit and wore diamond jewelry.

Along with new clothes and trinkets, Milton acquired a more sophisticated approach to life. Somewhere in the world beyond Lancaster he learned to gamble—on cards, casino games, and horses—and it became a lifelong interest. He also developed a taste for fine food of the sort that never graced the table at the homestead or any other Pennsylvania Dutch farmhouse. A record of his appetite is offered by the menu for a banquet held to honor him at Lancaster's Hamilton Club—its president was also the powerful head of Milton Hershey's bank—in June 1894. The evening's fare, written in gold script on custom-made plates, included:

Little neck clams—Sauterne
Green turtle soup—Sherry
Brook trout and cucumbers—Sauterne
Sweet breads larded
Asparagus tips
Roman punch in ices
Snipe water cress—Burgundy
Pigs in blanket—Champagne
Crab salad, cheese and wafers
Ices and fancy cake
Strawberries
Cigars, Coffee, Cognac

Among those at the table were prominent lawyers and tobacco dealers. The banquet chef, William G. Payne, had been born a slave but rose to prominence in Lancaster preparing meals for the rich and powerful at this club for white Christian men. Although Payne's menu for the Hershey banquet may seem extensive, and it was by Lancaster standards, it was not overly fancy for a man of Hershey's wealth and position.[6]

As Thorstein Veblen reported in *The Theory of the Leisure Class* (1899), by the time everyone sat down at the Hamilton Club to enjoy chef Payne's little neck clams, the rich of the Gilded Age had embarked on an era of "conspicuous consumption." Men of means competed to see who could buy and possess the most extravagant items, from houses to hats. As Veblen noted, even "choice articles of food" became symbols of power, status, and sophistication. This was especially true when it came to alcohol. For the poor and middle class, drinking was a sin. For those who could afford cognac and champagne, it indicated social superiority.

The rules of conspicuous consumption affected the way men related to people as well as things. Wealthy bachelors who could seek and savor the very best for their table were also inclined to delay marriage until they had shopped for and found precisely the right woman. The care attached to the selection reflected sweeping changes in the way society regarded marriage. A century before, men and women were married in austere civil ceremonies. Romantic church weddings didn't become popular until 1830. This new tradition emphasized the sacredness of the bond. Sophisticated men and women sought, as one author wrote in 1852, "a blending of two souls in mutual holy affection." By the 1890s, the ideal was a lifelong partnership of truly sympathetic, compatible, and complementary people.

With such a high standard for marriage, it's no surprise that many men had trouble ending their bachelor days. In 1890s America the percentage of unmarried men was larger than at any time in history. Fraternal organizations, saloons, sports clubs, and prostitution flourished as many enjoyed the lifestyle of what historian Howard Chudakoff called *The Age of the Bachelor*. This was especially true in major cities, which afford men a greater opportunity to make the kind of money these diversions required.

Although big cities were magnets for happily single men, and M.S. Hershey visited them often, smaller communities also offered plenty of distractions. In the 1890s Lancaster was home to a long list of social clubs and athletic teams, dozens of bars and saloons, several gambling houses, and many bordellos. (The one available report on the trade in Lancaster notes that about forty-five "houses of prostitution" operated there in 1914, serv-ing three to five thousand customers per week.)

As a successful businessman, who was both unattached and quite worldly, M.S. Hershey would have risked little if he indulged in all that Lancaster had to offer. But no record or testimony survive to tell us if he did. In his hometown he was not regarded as a man's man. Instead, one contemporary recalled him as somewhat "peculiar," the sort who might enjoy a beer at the pool hall but couldn't play the game. In fact, "there was not a game he *could* play," added John McLain, who knew Hershey in those days.

When he turned forty in 1897, M.S. Hershey was a wealthy, accom-plished man who lacked the warm relationships that bring peace, comfort, and balance to life. Not entirely comfortable in the man's world of sports and clubs, he was not the type to bring good cheer to a tavern or laughs to the crowd on a street corner. And where romance or marriage were con-cerned, his slate was essentially blank.

Not that Lancaster women weren't interested. One pair of sisters named Riley, for example, competed for Milton's attention for years. But almost everyone who knew M.S. Hershey well had concluded he would live his entire life unmarried, sharing his home with his mother and pouring all of his energies into business. Of course, few people in Lancaster knew much about what M.S. actually did on his many trips to New York, Chicago, and the major cities of Europe. One exception was William Murrie, who sometimes traveled with the boss to visit important customers.[7]

In the official story of the meeting that would end M.S. Hershey's loneli-ness—the story recorded in company-approved documents—William Murrie and his boss were on a sales trip when they stopped in Jamestown in western New York state. Located about halfway between Buffalo and Cleveland, Jamestown was home to a thriving confectionery and soda fountain called A.D. Works. Like so many candy and soda shops, Works's was as much a social center as a place of business. Young men and women lingered beside the glass cabinets, hoping to find something more than candy inside the sweet shop. One, Catherine Sweeney, caught M.S. Hershey's eye.

A head taller than Milton, Catherine was the twenty-five-year-old daughter of Irish immigrants. She was slim and had long auburn hair that she usually wore pinned up. Often sick as a child, she had the tender, fair complexion of a young woman who had spent little time out of doors. She was witty and a flirt, but her wide-set, soft gray eyes, long lashes, and full cheeks gave her a look of childlike innocence. She played the piano, loved the theater, and in the words of one relative, "was not a woman to be bored." Friends and family called her Kitty.

A Catholic whose father had immigrated when he was a teenager, Catherine was everything that Reformed Mennonite women were not. She immediately became Milton's reason to return to upstate New York again and again. Courtship got easier when, months after they met, Kitty moved to New York City and found work at the ribbon counter in Altman's department store, which was at Sixth Avenue and Eighteenth Street, in a district called Fashion Row. Benjamin Altman was one of the most enlightened employers of his day. He shortened work hours, built rest rooms and a cafeteria for his employees, and even subsidized their education. His mammoth store was not just a good place to work, it was advertised as "one of the greatest department stores in the world." It was just a few steps away from the elevated rail line, and just a few hours, by train, from Lancaster.

One who made the trip often was M.S. Hershey, who had fallen in love, but not in a way that anyone in Lancaster noticed. Then in May 1898, when his mother complained that he hadn't spent a Sunday at home "in two years" he shocked her with the news that he was going to be married on his next trip to New York, after which he would likely spend "every Sunday" at home.

On Wednesday, May 25, 1898, roughly a year after they met, Milton S. Hershey and Catherine Sweeney traveled up Fifth Avenue to St. Patrick's Cathedral, a towering white marble landmark of gothic spires and stained glass that was the symbol of the papacy in America. In a chapel in the rectory they stood before a Roman Catholic priest and two witnesses drafted for the duty and were married. No Sweeneys, Hersheys, or Snavelys attended.

Two days after the wedding, the news was published on the front page of the *Lancaster Intelligencer Journal*. Workers at the caramel factory were surprised when they read the report in the paper. It was the first they had heard of Catherine Sweeney. "Dumbfounded," was the way John McLain described his reaction. The news sparked gossip all over town, and it only got worse after Milton brought Catherine home.

"The women wanted to see the wife," recalled Charles Ziegler, a young office man. They considered Catherine to be "a very over-dressed woman, probably not too well educated. The question between the housewives was, 'How could a Mennonite possibly live with a Catholic?' I remember the people there would gather on somebody's stoop in the morning and discuss Mr. Hershey's wife." One of the main topics for this talk was the charge, later proved true, that Catherine couldn't cook. Other sour observations—that Kitty was after Milton's money and had known a string of wealthy men in New York—would be repeated for years to come.

If anyone should have understood the match, it was Milton's mother, who had also made a surprising, even exciting choice when she got married. But Fanny Hershey was no longer the risk-taking young woman who had waited at the Lutheran church for her fiancé to arrive in his fancy suit of clothes. Fanny was now a committed Reformed Mennonite and she was accustomed to being the dominant female figure in her wealthy son's life. While helping Catherine unpack her extensive wardrobe, which had been purchased from the fashionable Fox Sisters in New York, Fanny knew just the right way to communicate her disdain.

"Tell me, Kitty," she asked, "have you ever been on the stage?"

In September M.S. Hershey bought a small house on South Duke Street, and his mother soon moved there. At the big home on South Queen Street, with its verandas and striped awnings, Catherine slowly developed a social circle and won over at least a part of Lancaster society.

Though no longer the only woman associated with the celebrated M.S. Hershey, Fanny retained the clucking support of those who couldn't accept the beautiful, stylish, Irish Catholic woman Milton brought home in May 1898. For them, the former Catherine Sweeney would always be the subject of gossip and suspicion. Kitty gave them plenty of ammunition. For example, when she attended the Mennonite funeral for Milton's uncle Abraham, the one who had helped M.S. with his first attempts at business, Kitty teased one little girl named Lila Snavely with her foot until she started giggling. The girl's father "gave me the Dickens," Lila Snavely would recall, "but I could not help it. Mrs. Hershey was jolly. She was lots of fun."

Children liked the new Mrs. Hershey. To them she represented a world and a way of being that was lighter and brighter. Neighborhood girls such as Katherine Shippen were so fascinated by this new lady that they would spy on her for hours.

"I used to stand there looking through the fence waiting for her to come out," Shippen recalled when she was herself an old woman. "The swing was toward the back of the house, and she would stroll out to the swing in her lovely gown and red slippers, which I shall never forget, and I thought she was the most beautiful lady I had ever seen."

Men in the Lancaster area agreed. Henry Hershey was especially fond of Kitty, who visited him often at the homestead. They had much in common. They were both religiously open-minded and intellectually independent in a community that rewarded conformity. They both loved clothes. They both liked to laugh. They both approached the world with a sense of adventure.

When they were at home, Kitty and Milton enjoyed entertaining and were active in the Tally Ho Club. Formally the Lancaster Road Drivers, it was a social organization that brought wealthy people together for Sunday parades of fancy carriages and fine horses. The larger carriages, called tallyhos, carried as many as a dozen women in fine dresses and men in bowlers and derbies.

The Hersheys also began vacationing together—in Europe, the American West, even exotic Coney Island—soon after they were married. In part this was to escape the gossip in Lancaster, which Milton hated. But the trips also gave them a chance to spend time together, which was more difficult at home, where business dominated Milton's time. At home, he almost always welcomed a phone call from the office or a visit from his key men. Catherine was frustrated with this policy. Once she playfully pressed two pillows on her husband's ears so he couldn't hear his lawyer ring the doorbell. The tricked worked, at least that one time.

Catherine didn't need to use any pillows to keep Milton's attention when they traveled. She also didn't have to worry about who might be watching her when she went out to shop. She loved to discover whatever was new and beautiful in the world. She didn't just buy for herself. Wherever she went, she sent things back to her two younger sisters and, later, to her nieces. And when he allowed it, she bought finer things for Milton to wear, too.[8]

Milton Hershey was not as interested in Europe's clothiers as he was in its confectioners. While his wife was collecting beautiful things, M.S. Hershey gathered ideas for business. Anyone who went to Europe in the 1890s with his eyes open would have seen that chocolate was fast overtaking every other sweet treat, and that the business of making it and selling it was becoming very big. Hershey knew all this before he left Lancaster, because orders for caramels from Great Britain were declining. When he met with Alexander Champion, one of his importers in London, he confirmed the cause: chocolate was quickly eroding the market for Crystal A caramels.

"When the sale of your caramels began to drop, you went to England for ideas," noted F. Bevill Champion, Alexander's son, in a 1937 letter to M.S. Hershey. "My father suggested the manufacture of Swiss Milk Chocolate in America. You saw the importance of this idea at once, secured samples from my father, and his advice."

Although everyone considered the Swiss product superior, Great Britain had fallen in love with all kinds of chocolate, and the three Quaker-founded companies were making bars and small candies on a truly industrial scale.

Leading the field was the Cadbury family and their company, which had escaped industrial Birmingham for a "factory in a garden" in the West Midlands. Between 1893 and 1899 the Cadbury workforce grew from about 800 to 2,600. In that time the firm developed a lab to experiment on new products and production methods and an advertising department that churned out posters and print layouts to promote sales and make the Cadbury name a brand that signified wholesome quality. All of these activities reflected the most modern approach to business.

But the Cadburys were more than commercial pioneers. They wanted to use their corporation, and their money, to make over the world, one small bit at a time, according to Quaker principles. They had already been at it for some time. Founder John Cadbury had campaigned to prevent young boys from being used as chimney sweeps, and helped create the Animals Friend Society, which became the Royal Society for Prevention of Cruelty to Animals. The family was deeply involved in adult education programs and concerned about human rights. When offered a cacao plantation on São Tomé, they rejected the deal because slave labor was used on the island. (They also refused to buy cacao from anyone who used slaves.) Instead they bought an estate in Ghana, where growing conditions were less favorable but slavery was outlawed.

As much as they worried about the poor abroad, the Cadburys were most concerned with the welfare of the wage earners in their own factory. They were among the first to institute half days on Saturday and to close entirely on legal holidays. Cadbury workers got medical and dental care at the factory. The owners also provided them with discount train fares so they could afford to commute from Birmingham, hot meals in company dining rooms, and sports leagues for their exercise and diversion.

As the end of the century approached, and their fortunes increased, the Cadburys became even more ambitious in both business and social engineering. They made their first *milk* chocolate—the use of milk was a major improvement—in 1897. But it was inferior to what the Swiss were producing. George Cadbury went to Vevey to find out why, and soon after he returned his company began building a plant for condensing milk. For years to come Cadbury would experiment with various recipes and manufacturing techniques, trying to match the smooth, sweet taste of the competing product from the Continent. While the Cadburys would need eight more years to develop a superior grade bar called Dairy Milk, which they first sold in 1905, they moved more quickly when it came to their bigger ambition—the creation of an ideal community.

From their beginnings in gritty Birmingham, the Cadburys had long been troubled by the squalor of the slums occupied by industrial workers and their families. In these communities crime, malnutrition, and disease were rampant and one of every five children died in the first year of life. This was not just bad for the people who lived in these places. It was bad for business. After all, the sick, the injured, and the bereaved made for poor workers and even worse customers.

By the 1890s British intellectuals and academics were looking for ways to solve the problems of the slums. One group, organized under the banner of the garden city movement, envisioned modern, planned communities of cottages where people could have urban amenities and conveniences in a setting that would be as healthy and clean as the countryside. A leading proponent of this idea, Sir Ebenezer Howard described this utopia in 1898 in his book *Tomorrow: A Peaceful Path to Real Reform*.

"Tomorrow" was too late for the Cadburys. Even as Sir Ebenezer was writing out his plan for the garden city, they had begun trying to create the kind of place that the movement imagined. The site was alongside their factory, where the Quaker industrialists had previously built sixteen homes for their highest-ranking employees, so they could live comfortably next to the chocolate works. In 1895 they purchased Bournbrook Hall, a 120-acre estate, and began constructing a community of cottages set back from tree-lined roads, each with its own garden. The homes would be occupied mainly by Cadbury workers, but the place, which they named Bournville, was open to anyone who appreciated its modern houses, quiet parks, clubs, and other amenities.

Unlike other utopian experiments, Bournville was not a sectarian religious community. Quaker values required it be receptive to all faiths, even as it promoted communal values. But there was more than a hint of paternalism in the Cadbury way. Committed to temperance, the family forbade the sale of alcohol in Bournville, and they did whatever they could to promote traditional family life. Women workers who married received gifts of carnations and Bibles and were then sent home to raise their families.

Such heavy-handed policies were noted by outside critics who thought the Cadbury's idealism was a cover for self-interest. George Cadbury was so angered by this suggestion that he offered to pay £1,000 to anyone who could prove that he made a penny from his philanthropy. No one ever collected on the offer. And in the meantime residents expressed great admiration for the company and the town. No wonder. Every year brought new programs and benefits made possible by steadily increasing profits. The Cadburys reduced the workweek from 53 1/2 hours to 48. Then they opened saving accounts for each worker, with the corporation making the first deposits. By 1900, as the number of Bournville cottages reached 313, the company would divest itself of all the real estate, turning it over to a trust. The deed establishing the trust said its purpose was to "ameliorate the condition of the working-class and laboring population."

Consider all the Cadburys accomplished by the start of the twentieth century. Bournville was the ideal English village. The company's product, chocolate, was a delight that anyone could afford. And the corporation's founders were perpetual do-gooders who stood up for cats and dogs and the working class. As these ingredients came together, and were mixed with constant positive publicity, Cadbury became one of the most valuable and perhaps the single most beloved brand in Great Britain. It was practically synonymous with happiness, goodness, and progress.[9]

The Cadbury family's success in building its business, its reputation, and its social influence was obvious to anyone who lived in Great Britain or who, like the candy-industrialist M.S. Hershey, visited often. But people didn't have to travel to Europe to encounter the Cadbury story. The corporation and Bournville received regular fawning attention in the American press, too. (New York's *Cosmopolitan* magazine described it as an ideal garden city.) The Cadburys set an example for a whole class of reformers in the United States, loosely called progressives, who shared their idealism and desire to make the world a better place.

American progressives, who were mostly from the middle and upper classes, also worried about the problems of big city slums, poor families, and dissatisfied workers. Many saw programs to enhance the education, health, and welfare of the poor and working classes as a matter of morality. They were also a way to diffuse social tensions that might increase along with the disparities between the very rich and everyone else.

A huge gap had opened between the wealthy and the rest of America. Between 1878 and 1890, the holdings of the wealthiest families had roughly doubled, while the net worth of the median household had gone from $500 to $540. Overall, 1 percent of the population controlled half of the nation's assets. At the same time, the working class was growing more militant. A strike by Pullman workers in 1894 had disrupted rail traffic nationwide, destroyed the reputation of the company's model town, and ended only when the U.S. Army intervened. More troubling labor protests followed, including the infamous 1897 strike by coal miners in Lattimer, Pennsylvania. The strike, which occurred just fifty miles from Lancaster, was especially bitter and was broken when sheriff's deputies opened fire on the marching workers. Estimates vary, but the most reliable reports suggest that about twenty strikers were killed and forty were wounded.

Like the squalor and disease in urban ghettos, the rising labor unrest worried those who benefited from a stable social environment. How long, they wondered, could the resentments of the poor and working classes be contained? What could the powerful do? The progressives responded with ideas that promised to ease the suffering and preserve the peace.

The wealthiest among the progressives—Andrew Carnegie was the leading example—established foundations that funded good works across the nation and, eventually, around the globe. But benevolence in the cause of conscience or idealism was not confined to big cities and the super-rich. In small communities, men of means created charities and civic improvement organizations. And even the middle class got involved, through do-good groups such as Rotary, Goodwill, Eagles, and the National Civic League, which saw their memberships peak in the years between 1890 and 1910.[10]

In Lancaster, Milton S. Hershey was ready to take part in the progressive crusade. He had a strong sense of morality and responsibility, as well as a mind inclined toward practical solutions. His comments about big cities leave no doubt that he shared the anxieties others felt about festering social problems. Soon he would have the money he needed to embark on an adventure that would allow him to use everything he had learned about business, everything he knew about human nature, and everything he believed about the purpose of wealth and the promise of American life.

EGO, ECCENTRICITY,
AND SCREWBALLS

6 Once M.S. Hershey had done it, entrepreneurs around the country realized there was money to be made turning sugar, flavorings, and milk into sweet caramels. By the mid-1890s, competitors had arisen across the country, offering essentially the same product at the same price. One, Daniel LaFean, was so bold an imitator that he operated a factory just twenty-five miles west of Lancaster in the city of York. He too used milk from the region's famous farmers and benefited from the area's reputation for producing pure and wholesome food.

LaFean was a blustery and ambitious man who would go to Congress in 1904 and make a name for himself protecting veterans' pensions and bringing federal money to his district. He was stout, with a bushy mustache, and locals said that he "never did things by halves." He got into banking and the telephone business. And once, for his birthday, he hosted a banquet for more than one hundred newsboys, treating them to beef tenderloin and stuffed turkey and getting his name in the next day's editions. (Though charming, this was hardly an original stunt. Many politicians of the day paid special attention to newsboys. For example, in New York the denizens of Tammany Hall sent thousands of them on picnics to Coney Island every summer and bought them dinner at Christmas.)

In 1898 LaFean joined with partners from the Northeast to create American Caramel, with factories in Philadelphia and York. The new firm, which would sell candy nationwide, was capitalized with the sale of $1 million in stock.

In that year the stock market was up almost 25 percent. (This was the midpoint in a five-year rally that would see the average share double in value.) Investors had recognized the stupendous growth in consumer brands and were eager to buy into companies that might build loyal national followings like Coca-Cola and Kodak. For this reason, shares in American Caramel were an easy buy for some. But if they had studied the candy market a little closer, they might have kept their wallets closed.

The caramel business was getting crowded with competitors who, like the cracker companies, might chew up one another in a price war. At the same time, America's appetite for chocolate, an alternative candy treat, was growing. Cocoa imports had more than doubled, from 9 million pounds in 1883 to 24 million pounds in 1893, and the trend was continuing.

Then there was Europe to consider. Trends in food and fashion still began on the other side of the Atlantic and the chocolate fad there was enormous. Anyone who had ever tasted the Swiss-made candy would have understood the value of mass-produced, and therefore affordable, quality chocolate. Few sensual experiences can compare with eating chocolate. Buttery, sweet, and musky, the taste of good chocolate is at once soothing and exciting. It is earthy and refined, substantial and fleeting. But the experience of chocolate is not just about taste. It is also about feel. First there's the soft snap as it yields to the teeth. Then the solid pieces dissolve into satisfying syrup. The thick liquid clings gently to the tongue, melting over the taste buds to deliver intense and then fading shades of flavor.

M.S. Hershey had experienced chocolate at its best and noticed that "everybody likes it from the first taste." In the mid-1890s he told his cousin Frank Snavely, "Caramels are too rich to eat every day. I am going to concentrate more and more on making chocolate because I believe it will be a more permanent business in the long run."

The king of caramel had already decided to bring milk chocolate to America, and make it his only business, when Daniel LaFean first offered to buy Lancaster Caramel. In negotiating the sale, the two men would play roles that were archetypes of modern business. LaFean, a latecomer to the industry, had faith that sales would continue to grow and thought his company must grow if it was to survive. Hershey believed he had ridden the market to the crest, and from that vantage point could see its decline. He had his eye on the next big wave.[1]

At their first meeting with the Lancaster crowd, LaFean and his partners suggested a straight merger. Hershey turned them down. Then LaFean offered to buy Lancaster Caramel outright for $500,000. Hershey's lawyer, John Snyder, advised him to reject the offer. He did, and LaFean briefly lost his temper, threatening to drop the whole idea and devote himself to driving Hershey out of business.

When both sides had cooled, LaFean returned to Snyder's office on King Street in Lancaster to try one last time. He began by offering $500,000 cash and $500,000 worth of stock in the new company. Determined to squeeze as much cash out of the deal as possible, Snyder turned down the offer, as well as a series of additional ones. With Hershey anxiously watching, Snyder got LaFean up to $900,000 in cash and $100,000 in stock but continued to say no.

"Hershey thought Snyder was stupid not to take it," recalled John H. Myers, who was Snyder's stenographer during the negotiation. "Hershey had left it to Mr. Snyder because he trusted him with anything at all. But when Snyder refused that last offer, Mr. Hershey became quite upset. They made the offers in the front office, and Mr. Snyder and Mr. Hershey went into a private office to talk it over at each offer." When the lawyer rejected the $900,000 in cash, "Mr. Hershey was prancing up and down, giving him hell."

Myers would recall that LaFean eventually agreed to make an all-cash deal for $1 million. Why he paid this premium price would forever be a mystery. But decades later, one source would suggest that Lancaster Caramel's accounts may have been jiggered in a way that made the price seem right. "There was padding," explained Ruth Hershey Beddoe, a distant relative who was Milton and Kitty's frequent traveling companion. "I got it from the highest legal authority in Dauphin County. I am only saying the books were padded."

In Myers's telling of the story, the sale was concluded when a telegraph message outlining the terms of the sale was sent to LaFean's financier, the Industrial Trust Company of Providence, Rhode Island, and the bankers gave their approval. But in fact the sale was more complicated. The Industrial Trust Company had imposed restrictions. Milton Hershey would have to travel to Rhode Island to receive a check for $1 million dollars. He also agreed to immediately use much of the money to buy American Caramel Company stock. In this way, Snyder would be able to say he got his boss a nice fat sum, but the financier in Providence would not be forced to put so much money at risk. At 11:00 A.M. on August 10, 1900—a day when East Coast temperatures topped 100 degrees—the deal was made final in Providence. M.S. Hershey had his million-dollar check for a fleeting moment, and Daniel LaFean's company took control of its main rival. With a phone call to Lancaster, the transfer of property was recorded with city officials before noon.

When Hershey returned to Lancaster, attorney John Snyder got a big commission check and the stenographer, Myers, received a box of cigars. Days after the sale, Hershey handed one of his office workers a $150,000 check for deposit in a company account and announced he was going to New York to negotiate a big purchase of cocoa beans and sugar "to make this chocolate business roll."[2]

The sale of Milton S. Hershey's factory was important enough to make the papers locally and in Philadelphia. Under the headline A BIG BUSINESS DEAL The *Lancaster Daily New Era* noted that LaFean had "found it very difficult to compete" with Hershey. The new management planned to double the output of the big Lancaster factory, which would make American Caramel the largest producer in the world. The firm would be run by William Blair, the Hershey cousin who had played a big role in the success of Lancaster Caramel.

As an aside, the *Daily New Era* noted that M.S. Hershey would, for a while, lease some space in the caramel factory so that he could continue to make his chocolate. "Mr. Hershey's chocolate business ranks second in extent in this country," the paper concluded. "Now that his entire attention can be devoted to it, it will be his ambition to place it in the lead, and, judging from the past, the question of his success seems already assured." Snyder, it was later noted, actually advised M.S. to get out of business entirely and enjoy his million-dollar windfall.

Just what was meant when the paper called Hershey's chocolate company "second in extent" is difficult to tell. When sales of all chocolate products were combined, Walter Baker & Company in New England was still far ahead, and there were many regional suppliers larger than Hershey. Ghirardelli in San Francisco, for example, was selling a million pounds of cocoa a year. The only way Hershey might be considered a significant player was if the paper was counting only hard chocolate candy.

Hershey certainly produced a huge *variety* of chocolate items. He made extracts for cooks and bakers, coatings for confectioners, and dozens of kinds of chocolate candies, from wafers and Easter eggs to chocolate cigarettes and chocolate dominoes. For a brief time he challenged Baker's mainstay with a product called Hershey's Baker's Bitter-sweet.

The play on the Baker name was just part of Hershey's sales strategy. Although company legend would hold that he succeeded with quality and without marketing tricks, from the very beginning Milton Hershey used up-to-date sales techniques. He copied the gold and maroon packaging used by Daniel Peter in Europe. And like Levi Strauss, who stamped his signature on work pants, Milton S. Hershey put his signature on his labels to guarantee customers they were getting the genuine article. Hershey advertised heavily in journals sent to candy retailers and gave away thousands of postcards illustrated with patriotic images. America's victory in its 1898 war with Spain, which left the United States in control of Cuba and the Philippines, was a favorite topic.

"Thing about making good chocolate is to use HERSHEY'S" was the message on a card that also declared "Remember the Maine" and featured a picture of the famous battleship. (An explosion aboard the *Maine*, which then sank in Havana harbor, had been the immediate justification for the war.) Another card, engraved with a portrait of Admiral George Dewey, whose fleet defeated a Spanish squadron in Manila Bay, advertised "Flora Fina Chocolate Segars, Hershey Chocolate Co. Lancaster PA."

In the years after the Rough Riders took San Juan Hill and Dewey sailed into Manila Bay, almost everyone who sold anything tried to tie his product to symbols of American power and triumph. Hershey was part of the crowd, but he also tried to create a unique identity for his trademark. To this end, he began putting a whimsical drawing of a baby in a cocoa pod (she looks a little like a tiny bobsledder) on all of his chocolate products.

The baby in the cocoa pod would remain a Hershey icon for decades, but in 1900 locals in Lancaster would have paid closer attention to one of Hershey's other eye-grabbing devices—the automobile he used to deliver cocoa to retailers. Either the first or second car ever seen in the city (a local doctor was the other early motorist), Hershey's Riker electric vehicle was basically a metal box set on four bicycle wheels, powered by an electric motor and steered by a brass-handled tiller. A professional driver from Baltimore was hired to make deliveries as far away as Scranton. As he careened around Pennsylvania at speeds up to nine miles per hour, everyone he passed saw the Hershey name painted on the Riker's side panels.[3]

After the sale of the caramel business, Mr. and Mrs. Hershey took a postsale trip to France, Austria, Germany, and Egypt. While they intended to take in many tourist sights, they also went abroad primarily to get medical treatment for Catherine.

For years Catherine had suffered from a progressive illness that periodically struck her with pain and debilitating fatigue and affected her coordination. Some in her family said that in her youth she had been diagnosed with an enlarged heart. But the definitive diagnosis mentioned throughout her life was locomotor ataxia.

Although it was not a subject for polite company, and many laymen didn't know it at all, physicians of the time used the term "locomotor ataxia" to describe nerve damage caused by the latter stages of syphilis. In the age before antibiotics, this disease, which can be passed from mother to child but is generally sexually transmitted, was not well understood. Untreated infections ran an unpredictable course. Initial skin lesions subsided quickly and might be followed two or three months later by a rash and fever. All patients recovered from this illness and ceased to be infectious, and some would never get sick again. But roughly one-third would one day, after years or even decades of health, develop late-stage symptoms, which would lead to death by organ failure.

In Catherine's case, no historical source mentions syphilis directly and people in Hershey and elsewhere have maintained a polite silence on the subject for a century. However, the weight of the medical evidence leaves little doubt about her illness. And at least one close family friend allowed herself to hint at the cause of Catherine's suffering when she was interviewed in 1954 by a biographer who had been authorized by the Hershey company to write a book about M.S.

In transcripts of Paul Wallace's interview with Mrs. Thomas Chambers, she contradicts much of what was commonly believed about how Catherine and Milton met and fell in love. In her version of events. Catherine was not a blushing innocent in a Jamestown candy store when she met Milton, but rather a mature and experienced woman living in the city of Buffalo.

Where did Catherine Sweeney and Milton Hershey meet?
They met in Buffalo. She went to Buffalo to work. It was awful. . . . He
    was crazy about her.
Did M.S. Hershey often come to Jamestown?
Hershey never came to Jamestown.
What did Catherine Hershey do in Buffalo?

I would not tell. Her mother didn't complain because her mother wanted the money. Mrs. Sweeney, she was awful for money.

Further evidence for the cause of Catherine's symptoms is found in the trips she made to Germany, where she was a patient of a world-famous neurologist named Wilhelm Erb. Author of many articles on syphilis/locomotor ataxia, Dr. Erb had established the modern standards for diagnosing and treating the symptoms of the disease with electricity.

The Hersheys turned to Dr. Erb at a time when the Continent still dominated world science, and research there was producing major discoveries in bacteriology, radiology, psychology, and other disciplines. Medicine was leaving the era of bleeding and emetics and entering the age of antitoxins, vitamins, X rays, and antiseptic surgery. These advances offered hope to the sick who could afford to travel.

Rest and fresh air, massage, low-power electric jolts, and a variety of medications from phosphoric acid to mercury and camphor were among the standard treatments of the day for locomotor ataxia. Few details of Catherine's care in Europe survive, but the regimens she used at home included massage and doses of Buffalo Lithia Water ("Enables a Miserable Dyspeptic to Eat Bacon, Cabbage and Turnips," noted its bottler). The water, priced at five dollars for three gallons, would have had no curative powers, but the lithium it contained was later found to be a powerful mood stabilizer, and today is widely prescribed by psychiatrists treating bipolar disorder.

In the early part of the twentieth century, syphilis patients had trouble telling whether any treatment helped them because the disease has a tendency to flare into an acute crisis and then recede into apparent remission. But most understood that there was no true cure. Dr. Erb warned the Hersheys that eventually the disease would weaken Kitty so completely that she would die of pneumonia. Perhaps the only good news in her diagnosis was that at its later stages, syphilis is not usually contagious.[4]

Trips abroad gave Milton Hershey a chance to recover from the hard work he did whenever he was in Lancaster. Those who traveled with him would recall he slept through a good part of the outgoing voyage, and did the same on the way home.

When he got back from Europe in 1900, a well-rested M.S. Hershey was ready to attack the challenge of developing a big new business around a better chocolate that could be made in huge quantities and priced for the masses. He saw magic at the point where cost and quality converged with the general public's idea of an affordable indulgence. There he would offer a five-cent chocolate bar for which there would be constant and growing demand. He called it "a continuous market."

With the help of J.M. Lehmann's company, Hershey had visited chocolate manufacturers in England, Germany, France, and Switzerland. Rumor had it that he made several attempts to get a job inside one or more of these factories, but failed. Once a group of touring businessmen from Lancaster came home to say they had seen a man who looked just like M.S. Hershey at work in a cheese factory in Switzerland, but he had scurried away before they could make certain it was him.

Milton Hershey would never confirm his effort to infiltrate Europe milk chocolate makers, but he couldn't deny other evidence of his competitive zeal. There were the workers he lured from other firms. And then there was the industrial espionage he sponsored when he got back to the States in 1900. Walter Baker was again the target, as Hershey sent one of his trusted workers, William Klein, to Massachusetts where he found work in the country's biggest chocolate factory and spent months there learning what he could. Hershey termed this mission a paid vacation for a most loyal employee. (In fact, Bill Klein had regarded M.S. as a role model ever since he was a boy who shoveled snow at the Hershey home in Lancaster.) Klein returned to Lancaster confident that he knew everything that was going on in Baker's business and he reported it all to his hero.

The trouble was, Walter Baker still made ordinary hard chocolate, the type that was already coming off the line in Lancaster. Klein may have picked up a few bits of valuable information. But it's not likely that anyone in Massachusetts, or the rest of the United States, could have told him how to find the holy grail pursued by everyone in the industry—a workable recipe for smooth, creamier-tasting milk chocolate. Somehow, the Swiss had managed to keep their secret for more than twenty years.

Why was it so hard to make milk chocolate? The main problem is that milk is almost entirely water and chocolate contains a lot of oil, in the form of cacao butter. They do not mix well. The solution to this problem required removing water from the milk through evaporation. But this was very tricky business. Variations in the rate of heating, in the highest temperature used, and even in the way the milk was cooled affected its quality.

Once the first milk chocolate appeared on the market, companies across Europe tried to replicate it. But they had trouble re-creating the Swiss method for condensing milk. And when they got close, they were tripped up as they tried to add the rest of the ingredients. The originators added cocoa powder and sugar and then squeezed out excess liquid. Kneading produced what was called a "crumb," a base to which more cocoa butter, sugar flavorings, and salt were added. More steps, and a full week's worth of work, would be required before a batch of milk and cocoa was turned into milk chocolate.

Difficult as the process might seem, large-scale production was made even more complicated by factors that the Swiss discovered through trial and error. One was that they needed enormous amounts of milk, far more than they could obtain nearby. They also discovered that the imperceptible differences in the taste of milk produced by various breeds of cows, and the quality of their feed, were magnified many times when the water was removed. The variation was so significant that condensed milk from the wrong cows could actually ruin a batch of chocolate

With no background in chemistry or engineering, Hershey would need years of experimentation—much of it an attempt to copy the Europeans outright—to arrive at his own method for making milk chocolate. In the beginning the work was done in open kettles. Ingredients were added to cream as it was heated and reduced. The result was a thick blob that tasted stale and spoiled quickly.

Things got a little better when M.S. switched from cream to whole milk. Some of what Hershey made this way was good enough to sell, and he did offer customers the first Hershey's Milk Chocolate bars in 1900. Although smooth and sweet, this early type of milk chocolate turned rancid in a matter of days, which meant it couldn't be distributed beyond Lancaster.

Whether M.S. was the first to make and sell real milk chocolate in America is a matter of debate. Others advertised the stuff for sale at about the same time. What is known is that the new bars were part of a line of Hershey's chocolate that produced more than $620,000 in annual receipts for the company by 1901. The company continued to grow the next year, posting higher sales every quarter.

As they continued to experiment, Hershey and his small crew began using vacuum pans, a closed kettle that allowed them to more gently boil milk and draw off the water vapor produced by the heat. (Some of these

vacuum pans were so large that a man could crawl inside to clean them.)
This process was delicate, and as often as not it ended with a scorched pan
and ruined milk. But Hershey pressed on.

As a boss, M.S. had his quirks. He discouraged on-the-job socializing,
and he couldn't stand to hear a worker whistling on the job. He also insisted that even his most outlandish ideas be tried, even if his employees
knew they wouldn't work. The trick to satisfying him was to be brave
enough to fail. To his credit, M.S. never complained about the time and
money lost when workers who followed his orders wound up with curdled,
soured, or sickly sweet results. He only wanted them to try, and keep on
trying, until he was sure an idea wouldn't work. Of course, big failures produced big messes and even more work to clean them up. And Hershey had
so many ideas that he often drove his helpers to exhaustion.

"We used to look at one another," recalled Bert Black, who was one of
Hershey's young helpers. "We'd both be afraid to say we were tired and
wanted to go home. Night after night, and Sundays. We even spent the
whole night there till we were done out. You can't think anymore. You
can't do anything."

With all the failures, M.S. came to realize that he needed better control
over the various elements of his experiments, and a place where he could
experiment in secrecy and maximize the amount of time he could be on
the job. For these reasons, he decided to move out to the homestead.
There he would keep his own cows, controlling their food and water, and
build a small dairy to process the milk. Near the dairy he put up a small
milk-condensing plant and a chocolate production line.

The experimental factory that Milton built at the homestead delighted
his father and intrigued the neighbors. The sleepy household was suddenly
alive with activity, but those who did the work were secretive about it. A
group of about eighteen men, led by M.S., would rise at 4:30 A.M. to milk
the herd of seventy-eight cows, eat breakfast, and then go to work behind a
door where a sign warned, "No Admittance." Sometimes they didn't come
out until the next morning. At night Hershey had a watchman patrol the
grounds to keep spies away.

About all anyone knew about the mysterious goings-on at the homestead was that M.S. Hershey was up to something important. If you wanted
to be part of something new and big, you tried to get involved. In February
1900, a teenager named Harry Tinney went to the homestead looking for a
job. He told M.S. the only thing he wouldn't do was work with mules—

they scared him. Tinney was hired to help in the creamery and was soon working long days and nights and sleeping in one of the new rooms Hershey had built in a barn. Tinney would recall that most of the work done there went into chocolate, but the boss might have them experiment with almost anything.

"He came round one time, sat down on a peach basket, and said, 'Do you have any cream?' He told me to take pure cream, powdered sugar, and the yellow gratings of eleven lemons. When it got thick, Mrs. M.S. Hershey came out to watch. After it was finished it was so rich, like butter, you could not eat it. He told me to take it down and dump it in the garden. 'Well,' he said, 'that didn't work.'"

With everyone working and living together like a family, the mood at the homestead was good. Kitty Hershey often came to visit, so she could at least catch a glimpse of her husband, and she would spend long hours in playful conversation on the homestead's porch. She and Henry Hershey were the main sources of entertainment for the workers in their rare off-hours.

Harry Tinney enjoyed listening to Henry's ideas for inventions and felt a little sorry that "Dad," as many people called him, didn't have the money to develop any of them. But he and the other young men at the homestead were also amused by Henry's stories and his drinking. "M.S. paid him every two weeks, but just enough for his Rock and Rye, and honey for his bread. He was very fond of honey," recalled Tinney.

Henry wasn't always a teller of tales warmed by sips of whiskey. He could be disagreeable. This trait emerged after Milton had decreed that everyone at the homestead, including Kitty when she visited, ate together. One day his father took his plate to a little private table in another room. "Mr. Hershey went at once and brought him out and sat him with us," said Tinney, years later. "Dad never tried that again."[5]

If Dad Hershey was upset by his son's rule at the homestead, he didn't show it. Instead he liked to brag about Milton and would make bold predictions about a future Hershey empire that people in the Lebanon Valley found hard to accept. A big new community was going to rise in the valley, he would say. It was going to be organized around his son's new factory. There will even be skyscrapers, he said. One of Henry's friends, Howard Bomburger, was so excited by what he heard that he tried to persuade the editor of a local newspaper that the story was true. As one contemporary recalled, Bomburger and Henry Hershey were both renowned "screwballs" and the editor "didn't put it in the paper."

Since he was a source for continuous speculation about wonders to be, Henry Hershey's talk about his son's plan for the future of Derry Church could have been dismissed as one more wild-eyed vision. But Henry knew that his son had abandoned his original plan to build a factory back in Lancaster, on a farm near Franklin and Marshall College. Milton had been discouraged by the price of land there, and by city politics—some local party bosses had come to him for a big contribution. After M.S. turned them down, he learned he could expect a big increase in his property taxes.

In the early twentieth century, political corruption was hardly unique to Lancaster. At the time when party hacks tried to shake down Milton Hershey, Lincoln Steffens was traveling the country to research his landmark book *The Shame of the Cities*, which revealed much of American politics to be a cesspool of graft and influence peddling controlled for the most part by dishonest businessmen. To the dismay of homegrown progressives, who feared the effect this civic disease might have on their state's future, Pennsylvania was particularly corrupt. The situation was so bad that historians would eventually count political corruption as a major element in the state's eventual decline as a center for finance and manufacturing.

Hershey responded to Lancaster's political climate by announcing his intention to build his new business somewhere else. He considered locations in four different states, and at one time or another he was rumored to be focused on Baltimore, Yonkers, or Kingston, New York. But in March 1902 he went by himself to the town of Palmyra, which was a few miles east of the Hershey homestead.

It was a cold, wet day and Milton wore a heavy winter coat and rubber boots. After getting off the train he walked to the Washington Hotel. He stood in the bar and announced that he needed to hire a horse and wagon and a driver. A young man named G.H. Moyer put down his newspaper and volunteered.

The two men took Moyer's buckboard and team west toward Hummelstown, along a rutted turnpike that flanked the tracks of the Pennsylvania and Reading Railroad. Here the Lebanon Valley, which runs roughly southwest from Palmyra, is about two miles across, with the Blue Mountains to the north and the Cornwall Hills on the south. The highest elevations on both sides are about three hundred feet from the valley floor.

A mile outside of town, Hershey and Moyer found themselves in a patchwork of small family farms, most under one hundred acres. The people were mainly of German, Swiss, and Scotch-Irish stock, descendants of eighteenth-century immigrants who had battled local Indian tribes to get control of the land.

Unfortunately for those who settled there, the soil in the region wasn't quite as fertile as the earth in the hills of Lancaster County, and the farms were not as productive. The families of Lebanon Valley struggled against the long, steady decline in prices paid for their crops. They were not alone. In the period around 1900, advances in transportation and in packaging and preserving food had changed agriculture. Buyers could play producers in one region against those in another to drive prices down. As a result, farmers on less productive land could be overwhelmed by efficient producers from far away.

The downturn in the national farm economy affected everyone who lived in agricultural regions, whether or not they actually worked the land. Lebanon Valley's grist mills, for example, were losing their struggle against Midwest competitors who were using new rail lines to invade East Coast markets. But the valley had certain local economic problems, too. Its iron foundries were struggling to compete against the behemoths of the industry in Bethlehem and Pittsburgh, and the quarries that produced brownstone for buildings were under pressure from competitors that were closer to major cities.

All of the struggle and decline would have been obvious to Hershey and Moyer as they inspected the mostly empty countryside. At Derry Church, where a spring bubbled up from the earth to feed a stream that flows westnorthwest, Hershey told Moyer to stop. He got down from the buckboard and climbed over a split rail fence. Crossing through soggy hayfields, he turned east and reached the edge of a large deposit of limestone.

According to Moyer, Hershey spent several hours inspecting the area without ever revealing his name, or why he was making such a careful survey, except to say he had been raised in the area. When they got back to Palmyra, Moyer received $1.50 for the use of his horse and wagon and $1 for his service as a driver.

As spring turned to summer, M.S. Hershey returned to the valley many times, often bringing his lawyer, John Snyder. Having chosen Derry

Church for his factory, he hired a local real estate agent, Christian Maulfair, to obtain options to buy property along the spring-fed creek. Farmers named Zimmerman, Curry, and Gingrich, whose families had held land in the region for generations, were among those who quickly agreed to sell.

Word that Maulfair was trying to buy land for a wealthy third party spread through the valley. Prices did rise, and sellers were soon able to tell which parcels were of prime interest. For example, the one-acre plot that would one day hold Hershey's new home would cost him $1,750. This was ten times the price he paid for land elsewhere in the valley. But the seller probably sensed that the buyer just had to have it. In general the process went quickly, though, and the agent was able to bring 1,200 acres under option for less than $200,000.

The trips to Derry Church and the options on all that acreage were part of a plan that had been developing in M.S. Hershey's mind and was finally crystallizing into a commitment. One afternoon at the factory in Lancaster, he went to the side of the building where William Blair ran the caramel-making plant for LaFean. He told his cousin that he was going to build a huge factory to make chocolate in rural Lebanon Valley.

According to the official version, recorded by a historian authorized to write a Hershey biography in the 1950s, M.S. paused when he finished outlining his plan and waited for Blair's response. When it didn't come right away, he added, "Don't you have an opinion?

"If you want my opinion," replied Blair.

"Of course, yes."

"My opinion would be that your friends should go to court and have a guardian appointed for you."[6]

M.S. Hershey didn't have a competency hearing. He went instead to an office on East King Street to meet with a civil engineer named Henry Herr. It was mid-January 1903, and Hershey wanted Herr and his men to survey the property he intended to purchase and lay out his dream upon the land. Herr's first question was one that many people in Lancaster would have asked: Where exactly is this place?

Although it was just thirty miles away, Derry Church was so small and insignificant that Herr, who had surveyed much of the region for railroad companies, wasn't able to point to it on a map. The idea that someone would choose such an isolated spot for a major industrial complex—instead of the major cities favored by everyone else—was puzzling for many reasons. First, it was so far from population centers that it was hard to imagine how Hershey would find and keep workers. Second, the site lacked most of the vital resources—gas, electricity, and supply houses—that factories needed to operate. Finally, Derry Church was wholly without the basic social amenities that workers and executives would need in their off-hours. There were no theaters, libraries, shops, clubs, or parks. Simply put, there was nothing there.

But where others saw an empty landscape, Hershey imagined an efficient factory that would help him create and dominate a national chocolate industry worth many millions of dollars in annual profit. It would be flanked by an idyllic small town that would be home to workers and executives alike. And it would be surrounded by modern dairy farms that would provide an uninterrupted supply of wholesome milk.

It didn't matter that Derry Church lacked a basic infrastructure to provide energy or transportation. And Hershey didn't care that there was no commerce and no society, except for the Grange, a lodge hall for farmers, and the Presbyterian church that gave the place its name. He believed that by the time he was finished, he would preside over an industrial and agricultural utopia, a company town devoted to the production of a wholesome food that everyone loved, where farmers and factory workers and their bosses and their families could live in happy comfort with all that modern technology could provide. A beacon of humane and moral capitalism, it would be the perfect American place.

Surprising as it may have seemed, especially given the site he had selected and his choice of a local firm for the planning, M.S. Hershey's ambition wasn't entirely unique. Utopian experiments are as old as western civilization. And American industrialists had played with the idea of creating the perfect company town as early as the 1790s, when Alexander Hamilton proposed building one in New Jersey. More recently, businessmen had considered industrial utopias to be an antidote to labor unrest. A nice place to live, coupled with a decent job, should be enough to keep workers happy, they reasoned.

The capitalists were joined in this dream by architects and intellectuals who had begun to consider ways to improve cities and towns. The center of this discussion was located in the city beautiful movement, which was led by progressives like Frederick Law Olmsted's stepson John and by Daniel Burnham, who had presided over the design of the Columbian Exposition. (The campus of the White City was perhaps the greatest manifestation of city beautiful ideals ever built.) Burnham, Olmsted, and their allies believed that clean, well-run cities with artfully landscaped parks, broad avenues, neoclassical buildings, statues, and other public decorations would inspire people to live virtuous, peaceful lives. In short, they believed that good architecture could cure much of what ailed society.

Few attempts were made to actually create a city beautiful, but one place that tried was Harrisburg, Pennsylvania, which lay just twelve miles from Derry Church. In 1900 civic leaders there were the first to use the words "city beautiful" in a concerted campaign to remake a major community. This crusade was sparked by a dynamic, wealthy woman named Mira Lloyd Dock, who rose at public forums to denounce the "hideous conditions" in corners of her city and call for sweeping improvements. By the time Hershey began acquiring the land for his new town, the voters in the state capital had approved a $1 million bond issue to develop parks, pave streets, build sewers, and turn the banks of the Susquehanna River from a dump site into a promenade.

Although cities like Harrisburg received more attention from progressives, who wanted a more perfect life for the average American, small towns and farm regions also had their advocates. In the early 1900s the country life movement led by Liberty Hyde Bailey of Cornell University tried to improve the quality of life of farmers and rural communities. By 1908 President Theodore Roosevelt, the progressive champion, would appoint a commission on country life that would lead to the creation of many federal programs to support rural regions. Beyond these practical steps, the country life movement reinforced the image of rural America as the source of native virtue. Among the signs of the movement's success in the early 1900s were the many books published to teach middle-class children the Latin names for plants and vegetables.

As he went to work for Milton Hershey, Henry Herr began to translate the ideals of both the city beautiful and country life movements into a farm-town idiom. On January 28, 1903, he brought a team of surveyors to Derry Church. In the weeks that followed, they surveyed four thousand acres of pasture, woods, and farm fields to create contour maps so detailed that every five-foot change in elevation was noted. The hills and other features of the landscape would play an important role in the ultimate design for the factory, neighborhoods, and even the trolley lines Hershey would build to neighboring towns.

The problem with too many communities, thought Herr, was that they overwhelm nature. He said that a person deprived of mountains, water, forest, and sky "loses his identity, and in a big way, the power of self expression. . . . Isn't it worth something to an industry on its own account, and to its employees," he asked, "to have its own hills, valleys, sky?"[7]

With Henry Herr and his men tramping through the countryside with surveying equipment, Milton Hershey's land agent and lawyer began exercising the options taken on property for the factory and the village. On February 19, 1903, a newspaper in Harrisburg announced that Hershey had bought "all the land bordering Spring Creek, from its source until it empties into Swatara Creek." The article said that "the chocolate man" was planning to spend $1 million to create a town that would resemble industrial communities in England. At about the time this article appeared, Kitty Hershey took a break from a visit to the homestead to see where Herr's crew had placed stakes to show the outline of the factory. "Milton," she said, "you ought to go and have your head examined."

By spring, fifty workers—all "Italians," according to the Harrisburg paper—were using hand tools, horses, and dynamite to reach the stone substrate that would be the base for construction of a factory that would cover six acres. While this site work was being done, quarrymen were mining Hershey's own land for the limestone that would be used for outer walls and stone-crushing equipment was turning out gravel for roads.

Henry Herr laid out the routes for the trolleys, the grid of streets for the town, sewer lines, and water pipes. Names from streets in Lancaster—Plum, King, Queen, etc.—were used as place holders on the map until Hershey decided to call the main roads through town Cocoa and Chocolate Avenues and relied on places related to cacao production—Java, Caracas, Granada, Ceylon—for others.

A Lancaster architect named Emlen Urban was hired to design the factory and the grand public buildings that would soon spring from the rocky earth. The highest hill in the town was reserved for M.S. Hershey's own home. Although High Point would be large enough and fancy enough to be called a mansion, this house would be modest compared with the homes of the era's most prominent men.

The scale of High Point reflected some basic truths about M.S. Hershey. Although he indulged in luxury when he traveled, he would always present himself to the folks in Pennsylvania as a sensible sort. When it came to houses, yachts, or any other affectation of wealth, he would never compete with other millionaires. However, in business Hershey was more than willing to think and act in a big way. With the construction of his factory and his town, M.S. took an audacious gamble, especially when one considers that the product he planned to produce and sell in order to recover his investment was not yet perfected.

Fortunately, business conditions favored risk taking. America's population was growing and corporate profits had risen steadily for decades. Entrepreneurs were finding ways to create new valuable products or ways to make existing staples—food, clothing, even plumbing—better and cheaper. Anyone who wanted to see how far ambition might take you only had to look at John D. Rockefeller, who was about to become history's first billionaire, and Andrew Carnegie, who earned a staggering $23 million per year.

The phrase "irrational exuberance," coined to describe conditions in the 1990s, fit America circa 1903 perfectly. With the Wright brothers taking to the air, and Marconi sending telegraph messages without wires, it was easy to believe that anything was possible. Everywhere people like Frederick Winslow Taylor, social worker Jane Addams, and philanthropist Carnegie were trying to promote the perfect society with ideas, words, and money. As described by the national press, Milton Hershey fit this mold. In Pennsylvania, one magazine announced, he would put "a thousand employees into improved conditions which work for the good—socially, physically, and morally—of all concerned."

But Hershey's ambition reflected more than just a progressive's desire to do well and do good. In choosing a rural site for his factory, and making it the economic engine to power a new town and a collection of farms, he was expressing certain Mennonite ideals—taught by his mother and her family—about rural life and service. He was also indulging the egotism and eccentricity he inherited from his father. After all, everything he was going to build would bear the Hershey name.[8]

"HERE THERE WILL BE
NO UNHAPPINESS"

7   There remained one problem. Milton Hershey did not know how to mass-produce milk chocolate.

At the homestead he had tinkered with the recipe hundreds of times. He had changed the heat, the cooking time, and the order of ingredients. Sometimes he poured sugar into cold milk and then raised the temperature of the kettle. Sometimes he added the sugar after the milk was already condensed. He had not made the breakthrough he needed, but he had made plenty of work for the crew who cleaned up after him.

"If you put too much sugar in and the vacuum goes back, it would just settle and there is nothing to do but just dig it out," explained Bert Black. "When it settles, someone had to get in through the manhole. First turn on the hose to cool the kettle down. Whoever could get in the kettle, got in" and scrubbed with a wire brush or a rough-faced brick to remove the sticky blob. Although it consumed time and money, this kind of failure didn't bother the boss, and his attitude made his men more willing to try whatever he suggested.

Trial and error gradually persuaded M.S. that skim milk from Holstein cows—their milk was lower in fat to start with—offered the best protection from spoiling. He replaced his herd of Jerseys with Holsteins, installed cream separators at the homestead, and soon had all the skim milk he needed. He would turn the leftover cream into a Hershey brand of premium, higher-priced butter, which was sold at an exclusive shop in Philadelphia.

The men who helped Hershey experiment would recall this time with sentimental pride. Sixteen-hour shifts were typical, and sometimes they worked for days at a stretch, grabbing bits of rest when they could. When they did get a break, they enjoyed sitting on the homestead porch with the boss's beautiful wife or listening to the stories his father told. Henry Hershey could supply dinner table conversation when everyone else was too tired to speak. He also brought a little excitement when he set the fire on his coal stove so high it caused a small fire in his room, which was quickly extinguished.

Henry's little conflagration, his mealtime speeches, and visits from Kitty couldn't relieve all the pressure felt by the team of experimenters. They were working against a deadline. By the fall of 1903 the factory walls were rising on the site along Spring Creek and the first brick smokestack—six feet in diameter and one hundred fifty feet tall—was almost completed. It appeared that the men building the plant would finish before the recipe was found.

Despite his aversion to experts, a desperate M.S. hired a chemist to provide him with advice. When this led to a burned batch of milk and sugar, he dismissed the chemist and summoned a trusted hand from the Lancaster plant. On the day he was called John Schmalbach got to the homestead in time for supper and then went alone with Milton to work at one of the huge copper vacuum kettles in the creamery. First they took turns getting inside the kettle to scrape at the burned remains of the last experiment. When they were done cleaning, they poured in skim milk and added a large amount of sugar. Schmalbach then took control, gradually raising the temperature of the kettle and gently cooking the contents.

After a few hours of low-heat evaporation, Schmalbach let the mixture cool a bit. When the kettle was finally opened, he discovered a batch of warm, smooth, sweetened condensed milk that accepted cocoa powder, cocoa butter, and other ingredients without getting lumpy. Later Schmalbach would recall the boss's excited reaction, word for word.

"'Look at that beautiful batch of milk,' said Mr. Hershey. 'How come you didn't burn it? You didn't go to college.'"

It would take time to confirm Schmalbach's breakthrough. But when this was done, Hershey had a mild-tasting milk chocolate that had the perfect bite—like al dente pasta—that melted smoothly in the mouth. In time they would learn that this product could be stored for several months without spoiling. They would also discover that the method and recipe devised at the homestead could be adapted for mass production. In fact, because it used liquid condensed milk instead of the powdered milk that the Swiss favored, Schmalbach's mixture was easier to move through various processes—it could be pumped, channeled, and poured—and it required less time for smoothing and grinding. Hershey would be able to make milk chocolate faster, and therefore cheaper, than the Europeans.

The only difference was the taste.

From the very beginning, Hershey's milk chocolate has had a distinctive flavor. It is sweet, like the others, but it also carries a single, faintly sour note. This slight difference is caused by the fermentation of milk fat, an unexpected side effect of Schmalbach's process.

Anyone who knew Swiss milk chocolate would have detected the unusual taste and may have found Hershey's candy unpleasant. But in the mouths of people who had never tried the stuff made in Europe, Hershey's milk chocolate would be a revelation. It would also come to define the taste of chocolate for Americans, who would find harmony in the sweet but slightly sour flavor.

John Schmalbach got a $100 bonus from the pocket of M.S. Hershey, but no royalty or big promotion for breaking the milk chocolate code. He accomplished this on the one and only day he ever worked at the homestead.[1]

Once the experiments ended and M.S. Hershey had his formula, work at the homestead focused on refining the process and adapting it for large-scale production. By the winter, the new factory building alongside Spring Creek was covered by a roof and workers were quickly outfitting the interior. Two railroad spurs were being built to connect the plant to the Philadelphia and Reading Railroad.

As 1904 arrived, the outline of the village proper could be seen in the unpaved streets that had been carved out of former pastures and the lots being cleared for construction. There were places for a business district and a school. But the houses would come first, and masons, carpenters, and other tradesmen were busy putting up the first few. Some of the work went on into the night, with men hammering, sawing, and plastering by lamplight. When certain projects were finished, work was stopped to celebrate the milestone. For example, on the day the first towering smokestack was completed, a small crowd gathered to watch a mule pull on a line-and-pulley system that was rigged to hoist a man all the way to the top, where he attached a lightning rod.

Everyone could see that, at long last, one of Dad Hershey's grand predictions was coming to pass. There weren't actually skyscrapers rising from the valley floor, but the smokestack for the boilers was the tallest thing around. (According to one report, the bricklayers who worked on the highest portion of the stack had to fortify themselves with alcohol before climbing up to its top.) Considering all this activity, no one could doubt that soon hundreds of workers would come to take jobs in the great new factory and, with their families, occupy homes in town, where everything was new and up-to-date.[2]

Henry Hershey did much of his bragging in Erb's General Store. It was his habit to make a morning trip to the store, arriving at about ten o'clock and then settling in for hours of conversation and drink, which he charged to his son.

The Erb family was more than tolerant when it came to misfits and wanderers. They kept a room just for tramps, and never turned away a man who needed a warm place for the night. They enjoyed Henry's big personality and his elaborate monologues. He won over the Erb children by giving them some of his paints and brushes and encouraging them to make pictures. (He suggested they try painting what they saw around them — farm fences, silos, even a giant cabbage he brought from his experimental garden.) Once he had even taken a horse and wagon to a nearby school to fetch little Edna Erb, who had fallen ill. She would remember this kindness for the rest of her life.

Late on the afternoon of February 18, 1904, Henry left the store to see his doctor, Martin Hershey, a distant relative who maintained a practice in Derry Church. At the doctor's Henry mentioned that he was glad that Milton had gotten married, to "a working girl" no less. By the time the visit was over snow had begun to fall. Henry left on foot, even though the storm was getting worse.

Somewhere on the road, a neighbor on an errand came along in his spring wagon, and invited Henry to climb aboard. Henry got off at a bend in the road near the homestead and said he would walk the rest of the way. The neighbor drove on.

It was almost five o'clock. The snow was falling harder and the temperature was dropping. Harry Tinney, who was working in a shed that housed a big boiler that served all the buildings at the farm, looked out to see Henry stumble in the yard. He thought the old man had enjoyed a little too much Rock and Rye.

In fact Henry, who always said he would live to see one hundred, had suffered a heart attack. He got to the boiler room door and stopped to rest, leaning against the building. Albert Snavely and Hoffer Bowman, who worked in the creamery, rushed out to help.

"I remember him standing at the corner of the building. His lips were getting blue," recalled Bowman decades later. "As we led him in he said, 'I'm perfectly paralyzed.' Those were the last words I heard from him."

Henry was brought into the homestead and laid on a settee in the big room on the north side of the house, where a stove threw off plenty of heat. In old age, Henry was always trying to get warm. Bowman went to telephone the doctor, but Henry died before help could arrive.

Harry Tinney fetched the undertaker while others sent word through the lawyer John Snyder to Milton and Kitty, who had just traveled to Florida to escape the winter cold. Fanny Hershey was also contacted. After years of calling herself a widow, she was one.

Three days would pass before the family could gather at the nearby meetinghouse for the funeral and burial. At the family cemetery, where Henry's spot was marked by the biggest monument, Milton was heard to wonder, aloud, whether his father had ever "made up his mind" about the afterlife. No one recalled what Fanny Hershey said about her husband that day, but what she did after the funeral would never be forgotten.

Back at the homestead, Fanny went to Henry's room, which happened to be the same room where she had given birth to Milton forty-six years before. She enlisted a relative named Monroe Hershey to help her take all of her husband's beloved books, the library he had carried across America, load them in a wheelbarrow, and cart them outside to the furnace in the boiler house.

The furnace was Harry Tinney's responsibility, and on that winter Sunday he followed Fanny Hershey's orders and fed the entire library to the flames. There were so many books that the chore took some time. Monroe Hershey would have to make several trips with his barrow.

"She stood back a little and watched," said Tinney when he was himself an old man, "but she didn't say anything."

Years later, a member of the family would suggest that despite the book burning, Fanny felt as much grief as anger after Henry died. "I think they were always in love," said Mary Hershey Pfautz, "only they didn't know it."[3]

• • •

Some parts of Henry Hershey's spirit—his love of travel, beauty, and finer things—lived on in his son. And with Catherine, Milton let this part of himself bloom. She was, in his words, the most beautiful woman he had ever met, but his love was based on something more than simple attraction. People who knew them said that Milton and Kitty held similar philosophies of life. Both were open-minded about religion and almost naïvely optimistic about their promise of Progress in their time.

Although Milton was deeply involved with the demands of building his factory and town, Kitty was clearly the most important person in his life. He gave her gifts—Tiffany jewelry was a favorite—and he always seemed to be taking her to New York. While there, he would sometimes trade in commodities, betting on the future price of cocoa beans, for example. She looked for clothes, especially fine hats with feathers and bows. Her taste was hardly extreme by the standards of sophisticated society, but this didn't keep people in Lancaster from clucking.[4]

There was little Milton could do about the gossip, but he made it clear that he didn't like it. He wouldn't do business with anyone who talked about Kitty, and as time passed he became even more openly devoted to her. While anti-Catholic sentiment was strong among the Pennsylvania Dutch—his own mother shared this feeling—Milton gave generously to his wife's church. When the Catholic hospital in Lancaster was raising money for operating room equipment, he didn't simply send a contribution; he paid for everything they needed.

Given Catherine's illness, the Hersheys were deeply interested in health and medicine. Despite periods of remission, when she'd tell him "you are not going to get rid of me in a hurry," Kitty's locomotor ataxia was a constant worry. Each time the pain, weakness, and loss of coordination returned, they were worse than the time before. Once she took a hard fall at the Broad Street train station in Philadelphia. Trying to make light of it, she wondered aloud if she should wear a card around her neck that might tell people who she was in case she fell again and was knocked unconscious.[5]

When she felt well, Kitty went to Derry Church to watch her husband's dream rising out of the earth. She got around in a surrey pulled by a favorite horse, a lively chestnut with white socks. She would have needed a good horse and rig to keep up with her husband. In the heady days of construction, he was everywhere, checking on the houses being built for workers, inspecting the tracks being laid for the trolley, and watching the crews excavate sites for commercial buildings in the downtown area, where Chocolate and Cocoa Avenues met.

The few accounts left by men who built the Hershey complex describe a boss who needed to be personally involved, the way he was in the experimental factory at the homestead. He had the plasterers teach him bits and pieces of their trade. He ate lunch at the cafeteria set up for laborers. He bought the beer for a big party the masons held when they finished the stone work on the factory.

As a boss, Hershey could be both generous and short-fused. After the first few houses had been constructed, he noticed that they weren't based on individual designs, the way homes in a fine neighborhood might be built, but were instead little places that all looked the same. "That's the way slave dealers used to do [it]," he said, referring to plantation settlements in the South. "We don't want that here." Angered to discover that his own vision had been ignored, Hershey took the job away from the man who had supervised the builders. It didn't matter that he was Harry Lebkicher, his longest-serving employee.

In contrast with the way he handled Lebkicher and the houses, M.S. took a very deliberate approach to the matter of an itinerant worker named Jimmy the Hobo and the flying hatchet. Jimmy had hurled a hatchet at his foreman, John Shaeffer, after he was told the job he had just finished wasn't satisfactory and would have to be repaired. The whirling blade missed the foreman, lodging deeply in a wooden door.

M.S. Hershey had been nearby when the argument began and he had seen the tool-turned-weapon stuck in the door. But instead of firing the man who threw it, M.S. did a little investigating and decided that the supervisor had no good reason to criticize Jimmy's work. In the end it was the foreman who was let go. The decision was popular among the workers because "John Shaeffer was a slick article who stole another man's wife and three children," recalled a plasterer named William Miller.

Stories like the one about the hatchet and Hershey's response to the design of the first homes were repeated over and over again. They were told to make certain points about the man's character. He was tough-minded but fair. He wanted his workers and their families to live in dignity. This image

of M.S. made it easier for rank-and-file workers to feel loyal and even grateful for their jobs. This positive tone was also valuable to Hershey and his
company because resentful employees were more likely to demand higher
pay or turn out inferior products.

Labor peace and a positive public image were essential if Hershey was
to succeed, as they were to any company that intended to sell a consumer
product in the national marketplace. But a good reputation was not easy to
acquire, or maintain. In the early 1900s large companies and their owners
were the subject of much political criticism, muckraking journalism, and
public concern. The most impressive example of this trend was the pro-
tracted war against the Standard Oil monopoly waged by the writer Ida
Tarbell and her political allies, including the trustbuster Teddy Roosevelt.

Critics of the big corporations charged that the most powerful used their
wealth unfairly, selling below cost to undercut smaller competitors and
then starving them out of business. This was how, in just one six-year period (1898–1904), 1,800 companies in various industries were consolidated
into fewer than 160. The effects of consolidation were obvious. On one
hand, massive new companies produced high-quality goods at reasonable
prices. On the other hand, dominant industries could control so many jobs
that workers had no choice but to accept low wages and dangerous conditions.

In this time, organized labor stepped up the use of boycotts and strikes
to pressure companies for better pay and safer work environments. The
most militant union, the Industrial Workers of the World, or "Wobblies,"
sought a socialist society through aggressive organizing. The Wobblies and
others made terms such as "robber baron" and "monopoly trust" part of the
vernacular. They also led many Americans to suspect there was something
fundamentally unfair in the way some great fortunes had been amassed.
Millions of people supported populist critiques of the super-rich and their
political allies. The same people got behind such "radical" remedies as the
eight-hour workday, a progressive income tax, and more government regulation of corporations.

In Derry Church, the great majority of workers and townspeople put
M.S. in a different category from the robber barons and monopolists. As
scores of oral history accounts and interviews attest, Milton was widely
considered to be a good rich man. He would buy an employee a suit, if he
needed it, or pay for his child's education. Gifts he gave as wedding or
housewarming presents were handed down through the generations, along

with the stories of their provenance. He rewarded loyalty and never punished an honest mistake, even when it cost him money. In his office he hung a sign that read "Business Is a Matter of Human Service." The slogan reflected his best impulses.

But there was, from the very beginning, a minority of workers who didn't recognize in Hershey a benevolent creator. Instead, they saw an egotistical captain of industry, a hypocrite who enjoyed a drink himself while he chastised workers who did the same. He was so serious about work that he once fired an employee when he saw the man playfully tap another on the backside. He was so conscious of his status that when a junior office worker made the mistake of asking him for some water, he ceremoniously filled every glass in the room and then fired the man who had said that he was thirsty.

The man who dismissed people abruptly and the man who was impetuously charitable were, of course, one and the same. And a clear picture of Milton Hershey at the time when his industrial utopia began to take shape must include all the qualities on display in the stories that survived the generations. It's worth noting that after years passed, M.S. rehired the worker he had caught poking another man's rear end. "Go back and get a job," he said paternalistically, "and cut out your God damn goosing."

In retrospect, Hershey may have deliberately overreacted so that his workers would feel just a little insecure. If this was his strategy, it worked. Hershey employees generally understood that they served at the pleasure of a mercurial leader and that they better stay sharp. Of course, the unlucky few whom he made into examples with sudden dismissal paid a high price.

Those who knew Milton S. Hershey would debate his true nature to his death and beyond. But the larger American public, who wouldn't know or care about the men Hershey fired, embraced him as a kindly type of industrialist and an oddly selfless capitalist. This reputation depended, in part, on the playful sweetness of the product he made. People naturally expect a candy maker who turned a luxury item like milk chocolate into a five-cent treat for the masses to be a kind of Santa Claus, distributing happiness in a wrapper. The press played on this ideal by calling M.S. Hershey the Chocolate Man, and rarely failing to describe him as a good-hearted soul.

Hershey's audacious plan for a new type of company town only added to his aura. From the very beginning, the development he proposed for the Lebanon Valley was described as a utopia in every sense of the word and as a product of his morally superior vision. Because the eventual profits made at the factory were to be shared with his community, Hershey and his company were also associated with progressive idealism. This meant that people who purchased Hershey Chocolate weren't just buying a treat, they were contributing to a grand experiment that was going to prove that big business, often feared and resented, could do remarkable good.

The Hershey idea, a business that would create something nobler than profit, arrived at the very height of the progressive movement's power. Theodore Roosevelt, one of the few politicians whom M.S. Hershey admired, elevated the movement's agenda when he became president after William McKinley's assassination in September 1901. Long a critic of corrupt politics and the industrial monopolies owned by a group he called "the criminal rich," Roosevelt immediately directed his justice department to file scores of antitrust lawsuits. One of his first successes was against Northern Securities and banking giant J.P. Morgan. He also moved to protect organized labor and promote child welfare. And since progressivism was, at its core, religiously inspired, TR also advanced optimistic Christian morality, clean living, and responsible stewardship over the environment.[6]

Roosevelt became a folk hero by attacking ruthless corporations and using his bully pulpit to rail against "the malefactors of great wealth." Thirty years after Mark Twain had coined the term "Gilded Age," a large number of Americans had finally concluded that there was something wrong with a system that allowed corporations to own U.S. senators, manipulate markets, and bully competitors into bankruptcy. Although the public once accepted the pseudoscientific idea that greedy businessmen were merely practicing the sort of natural selection that Darwin identified in the animal world, by 1902 this view was under broad attack. In this moment, a wise entrepreneur would try to distance himself from corruption and immorality that "Roosevelt the Progressive" had rallied the country against, and attempt to do business in a new, more humane way.

All of the ideals expressed by the progressives and their standard-bearing president could be seen in miniature in the Hershey plan, which called for a perfect American town in a bucolic natural setting, where healthy, right-living, and well-paid workers lived in safe, happy homes. Similarly, M.S. Hershey presented himself as a thoroughly modern, progressive man. He was refined, but hardworking, enthusiastic, industrious, and devoted to a cause beyond profit. If he sometimes went a little overboard, slipping into the role of social engineer, this made him a genuine progressive, too. These were, after all, the do-gooders who brought America the eugenics crusade, which sought to improve the national gene pool by preventing so-called undesirables from having children.

M.S. and his men had little trouble convincing visitors that they were going to make a dream come true in the Lebanon Valley. In 1903 a business writer from New York had only to see the plans in order to declare the place, which he called Chocolate Town, a civic perfection that would return mankind to "Nature" and promote the social, physical, and moral well-being of its people. "It will have its individual form of local government, but there is no provision for a police department, nor for a jail," wrote Joseph Solomon. "These are not expected to be necessary under the conditions. Incarceration and punishment are for criminals—unhappy mortals. Here there will be no unhappiness, then why any crime?" Taking a cue from this journalist, Hershey's own publicity machine would soon add to the hype, painting Milton as that rare, noble, and altruistic industrialist and promoting his town as a genuine utopia.[7]

By the autumn of 1904, houses had been built on Trinidad Avenue north of the factory and in a neighborhood along the south side of Chocolate Avenue. The homes were completely modern, with electricity, indoor plumbing, and central heating. These were genuine luxuries to the families who moved in, many of whom had always relied on water pumps, gaslights, and outhouses. Indeed, as of 1905 fewer than 8 percent of the homes in America were wired for electricity. A few settlers had trouble adapting to the new technologies, choosing, for example, to use kerosene lamps until they warmed up to the idea of electric lights. But once they made the change, the luxury became a necessity. "What an improvement for a family who had never turned a switch before," recalled Monroe Stover, whose parents were among the first to settle in the community.

Along with the ready-built homes, Hershey had laid out more than a hundred lots that would be sold to people who would be permitted to build their own homes, just as long as they adhered to certain restrictions. The houses would have to be two stories tall, with pitched roofs. Owners couldn't use their property for any "offensive purpose or occupation"—piggeries, saloons, and blacksmiths were expressly forbidden—and they could not build a fence without M.S. Hershey's approval.

These covenants were intended to foster the development of a quiet, orderly, well-built town where real estate would grow in value. "A neighborhood where there are restrictions means that it is a high-grade neighborhood," declared one advertisement for the lots.

Buyers readily accepted the restrictions because the strategy worked. The new town was neat and inviting. Hershey did his part by planting trees, flowers, and shrubs that lent a parklike quality to the town's streets and wide main boulevards. The new residents also understood that plans were in place for the kinds of public facilities—parks, a swimming pool, a gymnasium, and a public library—that were rare in much bigger communities. Even the five-cent trolley line, which began running in the fall of 1904, signaled that the good life could be found in this place. It also gave M.S. Hershey, who loved railroads so much he often went to the station to watch trains come and go, a certain delight to own one.

On its first run, the trolley carried dignitaries in black coats to the new factory, where M.S. Hershey took them on a tour of his nearly completed plant. Really eighteen different buildings connected by hallways, the plant was seven hundred feet long and half as wide, yielding six acres of floor space. Limestone walls and slate roofs made the factory almost fireproof, and its one-story design meant that in the event of an emergency, workers wouldn't have to deal with dangerous flights of stairs.

The men who toured with M.S. Hershey would have been especially impressed by the power plant, which housed enormous industrial boilers and dynamos that would make electricity for both the factory and the community. The tour ended with a banquet in the Hershey Chocolate Company's new office building.[8]

Although not as big as Machinery Hall at Philadelphia's Centennial Exposition, which a young M.S. Hershey had put on his first business card, the new chocolate factory was one of the largest and most modern confectioneries in the world. Add to it all the houses, commercial buildings, and infrastructure that was being built in the surrounding community and you quickly realize that M.S. Hershey had been steadily increasing the $1 million bet he first made when he announced his plan for the Lebanon Valley.

All the development at Derry Church was being leveraged by the continued earnings of the Hershey Chocolate Company, which was still operating in Lancaster. Sales had grown by 20 percent in 1902 and by another

20 percent in 1903, reaching $862,000 (about $18 million in 2005 dollars). But as time, energy, and focus were devoted to the future in Lebanon Valley, the business that was still working out of Lancaster faltered. During every quarter of 1904, sales were lower than they had been in the same period the prior year. When the twelve months were added up, the total was $780,000.

The trend suggested that the sooner Hershey shut down the Lancaster plant and gear up his efficient new factory, the better his chance of long-term success. In late fall 1904, workers began to install equipment—most of it imported from Europe—in Derry Church. Production was gradually shifted from Lancaster until June 1905, when the last of the machines were removed from the old plant and set up in the new one.

Although it seems unremarkable today, the design of the new Hershey plant reflected an attempt to match architecture with function. Boxcar loads of cocoa beans, sugar, and other dry ingredients arrived on a railroad siding at the east end of the plant and would march their way through the plant to completion and a shipping department.

Much of the manufacturing effort was focused on the beans, which were first cleaned and then sent westward for roasting in revolving drums. From there they traveled on to hullers, where the cocoa "nib" was separated from the shell. Grinding and milling turned the nibs into cocoa liquor. Some of this liquid was used to make candy. The rest became either cocoa butter or cocoa powder.

The other key ingredient, fresh milk, was produced daily at local farms and arrived at a creamery on the north side of the plant, either by wagon or aboard special trolley cars. After it was processed into skim, the milk was combined with sugar, condensed, and then sent for mixing with cocoa, liquor, and cocoa butter. Drying, rolling, and four days' worth of mixing in conching machines finally produced chocolate that could be transferred to molding machines. The molds were big metal trays that had to be overturned and hammered to free the chocolate bars. Once they left the big, noisy "knock out" department, the bars were wrapped, boxed, and delivered to the shipping department, which occupied the western side of the factory and was served by another railroad spur.

Because they were organized along Frederick Winslow Taylor's principles, the jobs at the new plant were reduced to efficient routines. And like workers on similar production lines, the Hershey employees were expected to keep up a fast pace. The combination of routine and the demands for production made some jobs such as wrapping, or knock out, fairly monotonous. But there were other assignments, like condensing milk, or roasting beans, that required more expertise and attention and were therefore more satisfying.

"The Java bean was a golden yellow bean, very yellow, and then the Granada and the Trinidad and Areba were coal black," recalled George Bowman, a roaster in the early days at the plant. "We didn't roast too many low quality cocoa beans. . . . We would make one roast every hour, four hundred pounds to a ball, and ten heaps a day."

Bowman's workday started at 6:20 A.M. and ended at 6:00 P.M. In that time he would operate oil-heated roasting drums, which he could monitor by looking through a hole the size of a half dollar, to produce two tons of roasted beans. It was a tricky operation in a room that often reached 120 degrees Fahrenheit. As the shells of the beans opened, they dried and became highly flammable. If Bowman let them burn, an entire batch would be lost and the oven could be damaged. If he removed the beans too soon, they would taste raw. With the factory unable to produce without the roasted beans, the pressure on Bowman and other roasters, who worked mainly by feel, was intense.[9]

In the first full year of manufacturing at Derry Church, from June 1905 to June 1906, net sales for Hershey chocolate topped $1 million. This was 25 percent higher than the previous twelve months and roughly equal to the sales of another big new national brand, Jell-O.

With workers performing simple but carefully choreographed routines and using new machinery in a building designed for efficiency, Hershey was able to make high-quality chocolate at very low cost. The only real problem he encountered early on came from the outside, in the form of a lawsuit filed in September 1905 in federal court by the Société Générale Suisse de Chocolats. At issue was the design for the original Hershey bar wrapper. Like some of Hershey's other ideas, the color scheme—gold letters on maroon paper—had apparently been borrowed from, or inspired by Daniel Peter's products. Negotiations led to changes in the Hershey wrapper. The lawsuit was dropped, and Hershey could go right on making chocolate, and money.

The cash flow produced by the Hershey bar would be used in part for the acquisition of land and the further development of the town. As revenues grew over the next few years, a cluster of graceful public buildings would be built, including a commercial center called Cocoa House, and a school named for President McKinley. A large department store would rise on the corner of Cocoa and Chocolate Avenues. A park established on the north side of the village would grow to include a zoo, a carousel, a miniature railroad, and a band shell. The parks and other recreation facilities were free. And while the town's businesses and utilities were sometimes self-sustaining, they served a purpose beyond profit. Hershey would subsidize them in order to keep prices low and service consistent. This was because he saw the town and the factory as a single project. The trolley system, for example, ran regular deficits. But it got his employees to work on time and improved the quality of life in town.

It all worked because Hershey had created a remarkably strong local economy. The basis for this strength, and the key difference between this place and other company towns, was home ownership. Instead of renting to his workers, Hershey arranged for them to purchase houses and become in essence investors in their community. Homeowners were more certain to maintain their properties, and they were far more likely to stay put in the town, and in their jobs.

Other factors worked in the town's favor. For one thing, the Hershey Chocolate Company was built to exploit a brand-new product. It also had no real competitors. The factory was the equivalent of an oil field, sending a rich dark product into a market with an ever growing appetite. It received, in return, a flood tide of cash. Once costs and profit were taken care of, the money was distributed to workers, who, given the relative isolation of their community, had a tendency to spend it right in town. As the dollars circulated, they produced more profit for various Hershey entities. This cycle was repeated every payday, as the outside money collected by the company was poured into a pipeline that looped right back to the corporation.

To illustrate how this worked, M.S. Hershey sometimes told a story about a man he met on the street who didn't have the fare to ride the trolley. He gave the man the nickel, knowing that the fare box was, essentially, his own pocket. Once the man got on board the car, Hershey had his money back. The tale, which Milton told with pride, revealed the genius in the system he had built. It was a businessman's version of a perpetual motion machine.

It wasn't just M.S. Hershey, or his townspeople, who profited from the interlocking local economy. After his first round of acquisitions in 1903, Milton had continued buying farms, which he converted into dairies that supplied milk to the chocolate works. (Often the sellers of these properties stayed on to manage them for the corporation.) But even though he would eventually acquire almost 10,000 acres, Hershey couldn't produce all of the milk he needed. The rest he bought from independent farmers, who suddenly had a large and growing new market. Many farmers served only Hershey and would see orders for their milk increase every year for decades.

With all the revenue he was generating, M.S. was able to develop new products, buy equipment, and continually increase production to satisfy the sales orders being written by the scores of salesmen he sent into the countryside. Following the model established when William Murrie sold caramels, the Hershey sales force depended on face-to-face contact with retailers to secure orders. They continuously searched for new outlets—bowling alleys, stationers, tobacco shops, ice cream parlors—and took pains to make sure Hershey's items were displayed prominently.

The salesmen got a boost whenever new candies became available. In this time, the most successful were a Hershey bar with almonds and a little conical-shaped drop of chocolate called the Sweetheart. First made in 1907, this bite-sized candy wrapped in foil was soon renamed the Hershey's Kiss and would help propel sales over the $2 million mark by 1910.

The enormous success of Kisses and almond bars would lead Hershey toward a business strategy that was new to confectioners. Instead of making hundreds of items of varying prices, Milton would produce huge quantities of a few varieties and price none higher than a nickel. This low cost meant that every grocer, druggist, and candy store owner in America could stock Hershey products—and most of them did. The demand created as salesmen found new outlets would drive sales to $3.6 million in 1911 and $5 million in 1912.

The growth of the Hershey company financed construction of the town, but it also created occasional labor shortages. If help was needed in the chocolate works, Milton would take men who had just completed a building project and give them jobs in the plant. This would force his construction managers to travel to New York to recruit newly arrived immigrants for building jobs. These men were nearly all Italians, and they would settle in a shantytown just west of the plant. Soon they too would find long-term employment in the factory and buy homes. The recruiters would have to go back to New York. In this way, a large Italian community grew in a crowded, low-lying neighborhood called Swatara Station.[10]

Despite language problems, the newcomers fit well into the factory. But they did meet with prejudice. This took the form of social sleights and slanders. Typical was a suggestion note submitted to managers by a company janitor:

> Since many of your employees complain to me that next to their locker is that of an Italian, and because I know very well the conditions of an Italian home having repaired many for the Hummelstown B.S. Co., they contain any thing in the insect line from a bedbug down and all smell like limberger [sic] cheese factory. Therefore I would advice [sic] respectfully that indiscriminate distribution of lockers be abandoned, that foreigners be given their lockers in a continuous [sic] section by themselves. . . . The above frank straightforward statement is exclusively between you the management and me.[11]

Fortunately, anti-immigrant feeling rarely led to anything more than talk. When violence *was* threatened, M.S. Hershey took personal responsibility for keeping the peace. For example, when he heard that a group of farm boys were planning to attack some immigrant workers at quitting time, he turned to a contractor named John Wickersham for help. Wickersham was one of the men who had gone to New York to hire the Italian workers and he enjoyed their trust.

"I took with me two of my foremen," recalled Wickersham many years later. "There were about twice as many farmer boys as there were Italians. I stepped in front and said, 'Now we're here in our working clothes and we don't give a damn what happens to us. And there are three of us and we're supposed to beat the merry hell out of the first man who starts something. If you want to see what happens, begin while I'm looking at you.'"

In the tense moment that followed, Wickersham stared down the would-be attackers. They had no leader, and "each one was scared that the three of us would beat the hell out of him," he explained. In the end, the boys just walked away and the factory workers went home safely.

Wickersham offered the tale as an example of the level of control and responsibility M.S. Hershey assumed in his town. But there was one area where he met some trouble: naming the place he had built.

In 1904 the company had held a contest—with a prize of $100—to find a name for the new town. (Although sweepstakes were barred by law, these kinds of contests were popular at the time.) The entries that were submitted show that the fawning press reports about the Chocolate Man and his town had convinced the public that something special was happening in the Lebanon Valley. Among the suggestions were Ideal, Majestic, Oasis, and Zenith. Milton Hershey's very positive public image inspired one entrant to suggest the place be called St. Milton's. The contest winner was Hersheykoko, submitted by Mrs. T.K. Doyle of Wilkes-Barre.

Many people, including Catherine Hershey, didn't like the winning entry. She asked her husband to reconsider. "How will it be when you go to the Waldorf-Astoria and sign your name, Milton Hershey, Hershey-koko?" she asked.

M.S. was spared having to reject Mrs. Doyle's invention when the post office declared that it was just too commercial. M.S. went back to the pile of contest entries to discover that the most popular submission of all—one sent by two thousand different correspondents—was simply Hershey. M.S. submitted this choice to the federal government. It was accepted, and the first bag of mail addressed to Hershey, Pennsylvania, arrived on February 7, 1906, on the train from Harrisburg.[12]

Milton and Catherine were not there to see the mail arrive. They had left for New York, where they would spend a week at the ultrafashionable Gotham Hotel, which had opened the year before on Fifth Avenue. The twenty-three-story Gotham was then the tallest building in the city and had become a landmark the instant it opened.

In their eight years of marriage, Kitty and M.S. Hershey had developed a routine that called for frequent travel, which gave M.S. a chance to let down his guard. As one of his drivers remarked, "He was a different person" when he left Hershey. "He was a wonderful fellow when you were out in strange country." Catherine and Milton enjoyed long stays at resorts in the mountains of New Hampshire and at Hot Springs, Arkansas. Regular trips to New York allowed Milton to do business with commodities traders and gave Catherine relief from the gossip and boredom of small town Pennsylvania.

(One of the rare bits of negative publicity ever printed about Hershey dwelled on the provincial quality of its townspeople, and it may explain why Kitty enjoyed travel. Appearing at a Hershey theater where admission was free, actor/humorist Leo Donnelley couldn't wrench a single laugh out of the audience. In an essay he published about this experience, he wondered if the townspeople "had promised their parents when they were children that they would never laugh at anything.")

In New York, Milton and Catherine shopped for furniture, artwork, rugs, and other items to fill their new home, the mansion called High Point, which was slowly taking shape from atop its hill overlooking the factory. At a time when the giants of the Gilded Age competed to build the greatest home—George Vanderbilt's château, Biltmore, in North Carolina took the prize—High Point in Hershey was not the kind of place that would make headlines in the national press. But for a small town, it was an impressive house.

Built with local stone, the Hersheys' mansion represented a modest attempt at the popular Beaux-Arts style, which borrowed from the ancient Greeks and Romans. High Point's exterior was defined by four large, scroll-topped Ionic columns and was decorated with balustrades and pilasters. One of the main features inside was a grand staircase that rose from the front hallway. Upstairs bedrooms were decorated in different colors. The blue and green rooms were reserved for guests. Milton and Catherine kept separate bedrooms: his was gold, hers rose pink.

While High Point gracefully dominated the view from many parts of town, the mansion gardens, which were open to the public, made an equal impression on those who visited. When it was finally mature, the landscaping at High Point included thousands of tulips and hyacinths, more than one hundred rosebushes, three hundred chrysanthemums, more than a thousand boxwoods, and a Japanese pond. Spring flower beds were planted in bright patterns. One was said to resemble an oriental carpet. In summer, the specimen plants, flowers, trees, and shrubs grew so densely that in some sections the grounds were almost tropical.

Many photos from their time at High Point show Catherine and Milton in the gardens and on the veranda. By this time Milton was a rounder, softer, prosperous-looking middle-aged man with a high forehead, hair that was more white than brown, and creases around his eyes. Kitty, almost fifteen years younger, was still slight, still fair, and her face was unlined. In one photo the Hersheys and half a dozen friends line up behind a huge flower bed and pose with their hands on one another's shoulders. In another, Milt and Kitty lounge with three other couples on the grass beneath shade trees. The men in the photo wear suits, high collars, and neckties. The ladies are in long white dresses. A close look reveals two little white bunnies hopping among them.

When Catherine wanted to be outdoors alone she could escape to a platform her husband had built high in a spreading oak that overlooked Spring Creek. Accessible by a gently sloped, winding ramp, it was called the "bird's nest," and she would spend hours there when the weather permitted. In the summer she also enjoyed the shade from large trees on the east side of the property.

Hershey's attention to trees, shrubs, and gardens at his home and in the town he built marked him as a man of his time and status. In the early twentieth century, landscaping was considered a true art form and elaborate gardens—with rare specimen plants and statuary—were a sign of sophistication, refinement, and the kind of wealth that allowed a man to spend lavishly on mere beauty. Although he would never be regarded as a man of great taste, M.S. understood the value of beauty and sought out the best. In addition to the elaborate plantings he made at his estate, he commissioned a prominent sculptor, Giuseppe Donato, to produce a fountain of granite and bronze.

In another sign of his status, Hershey hired people to tend the grounds, prepare meals, clean the house, and take care of his horses, carriage, and, later, his cars. The staff was also in charge of a parrot that had a habit of cursing people who passed by and then played dead when disciplined with a swat. The bird also noticed when a horse was brought from the stable and cried out, "Wait for the wagon!"

But while Milton could afford to make the mansion beautiful and paid to keep it running, the house never won Kitty Hershey's heart. She felt uncomfortable there because it was such a visible landmark, and a place where Hershey company executives, tourists, and even rank-and-file workers expected to find the boss at any hour. With her physical condition worsening, she sometimes had trouble getting around the place and she craved privacy more and more. To find it, she often escaped to the homestead. There she would put on a sunbonnet and lie on the grass and absorb the warmth of the day.

Friends she invited to visit at the homestead noticed how her illness had progressed. The spells when she felt pain and had trouble controlling her body were getting worse. Although only thirty-seven years old, she often needed a cane, and sometimes two, to get around. Both Hersheys tried to deal with her illness without becoming discouraged. Milton doted on his wife, bringing her meals and supporting her gently when they took walks together. Kitty, believing her husband had been neglected as a child, tried to make up for it by mothering him.

But with all the wealth and good cheer they enjoyed, the Hersheys were being forced to accept some sad realities. With Kitty approaching forty and M.S. now in his fifties, they were not going to have children. Indeed, her health was so bad at times that their main concern would be keeping her alive.

When she was feeling her worst, Catherine would sometimes hint at the desperation she felt by telling a story about a farmer in upstate New York who struggled to get his trusted horse through a harsh winter. The farmer would whisper, "Just live on horse, and you'll get spring grass," she would recall. Her voice betrayed the fact that she was talking about herself.[13]

BENEFICENT JOVE

 8 Six-year-old Nelson Wagner had no idea that he was making history. Nelson's father had recently died. Now he and his mother and his little brother, Irvin, were walking up to an old farmhouse that Nelson had never seen before. They stepped up onto a big front porch that was decorated with fancy scrollwork.

Inside the Hershey homestead, Nelson met M.S. Hershey, now a grayer and rounder man of fifty-three, and a couple named George and Prudence Copenhaver. While his mother talked with these adults, a doctor whom Nelson had never seen before examined him as closely as a farmer checking out a new horse.

Forty-six years later, when he was a middle-aged man himself, Nelson Wagner would still hold a vivid memory of the moment when he realized that the big farmhouse was going to be his new home, and that he and Irvin would live there without their mother. "I can remember," he said, "that when my mother walked out . . . that walk, I cried terrifically." That night he and Irvin shared a bedroom high in the southwest corner of the house.

Nelson's mother would recall things a bit differently. A widow with two rambunctious little boys and a third still nursing, she had been relieved to receive a letter admitting Irvin and Nelson as the first two residents of a new home for orphan boys. As she recalled it, "The boys never complained."

In September 1910, as Nelson and Irvin slowly adjusted to their new lives, they started attending school and doing chores. Eight more boys soon arrived, and they found creeks to play in and farm fields to explore, and eventually accepted the place as home. Nelson and Irvin's mother visited once each month, and became so convinced that Milton S. Hershey, the pleasant man whom she had met when she dropped them off, was raising her boys well, that in 1912 she would give him her third son, William, who had reached age four.

When William arrived, the orphanage that Milton Hershey had started at his family's homestead had grown to include classrooms in an old cow barn, all overseen by the Copenhavers. The program for the younger children was styled after the teachings of Friedrich Froebel, inventor of the kindergarten, who emphasized play and physical activity as keys to child development. Older boys received standard academic courses, but were also trained for farming or a trade.

Mr. Hershey, who wasn't much for advanced academics, believed that agriculture was the noblest profession of all, and he expressed this bias as he set up his school. But with the boys, he wasn't as resistant to outside experts as he was in business. Before the school opened he had sought advice from several sources, including the Russell Sage Foundation. (Established two years earlier by the widow of a hugely successful New York financier, the foundation was devoted to finding ways to improve education and social welfare.)

People who knew Kitty and M.S. understood that the boys at the Hershey Industrial School, as the facility was known, were, in part, replacements for the children the couple could not have on their own. This was especially true for Milton, who reviewed every application and helped to choose the youngsters who got rooms at the homestead. Unlike Kitty, he visited them regularly. He also brought groups of boys, who were dressed in their Sunday best, to the mansion for special breakfasts. Tables and chairs were set up outside—sometimes on the lawn, sometimes on the veranda—and the awestruck boys would show their best manners. Obviously they were his sons, and he was giving them the stability, safety, and community he had missed as he followed his father and mother from place to place.[1]

The charity in Milton Hershey's heart was sincere. Echoing Carnegie, he said, "It's a sin for a man to die rich." And the idea of the school had been in his mind for years. His grandfather and his lawyer, John Snyder, had both served on the board of the Emaus Trust, which funded an orphanage in nearby Middletown, Pennsylvania. According to some sources, Milton had begun to imagine funding a place like the Emaus home as early as 1886.

In this time, wayward, needy, and orphaned children, whose ranks increased with every epidemic, war, and natural or man-made disaster, were a great social concern. It was fashionable to worry about these children. They were at the top of the progressive agenda and the subject of intense political debates.

Hundreds of public and private orphanages and larger institutions were founded between 1880 and 1910 to both serve children and protect communities from those deemed delinquent and dangerous. Orphan trains took thousands to foster homes in the rural West. In early 1909, President Roosevelt hosted a White House Conference on the Care of Dependent Children, which produced a report that emphasized the need to prevent needy children from becoming a danger to society. The experts at this meeting stressed the value of family life, noted the problems in large institutional settings, and urged that new orphanages house children in cottages. By 1914, the soon to be famous Boys Town, based on the cottage system, would open in Nebraska.[2]

When the Hersheys decided that they too would help deserving children, they focused on needy boys, who had become a special worry for progressives. The new social sciences warned that without intervention, these boys would become shiftless and criminal men who would spawn another generation of undesirables. "If we do not pull him up," one activist said about this type of boy, "he will pull us down."[3]

The Hersheys also came down on the side of those who valued institutions as an efficient alternative to foster care. Like Boys Town, they followed the most modern model, choosing to house boys in homes headed by couples rather than in large dormitories. They also thought well into the future as they funded their school. Besides endowing their trust with more than ten thousand acres of property and the majority of Hershey stock, they fashioned the deed that governed the use of the money in a way that forbade changes.[4]

The deed of trust written in 1909 was modeled after the one created by Stephen Girard in 1831. The wealthiest man of his time—he had financed America through the War of 1812—Girard had endowed a school for orphans in Philadelphia to be overseen by the city. His relatives hired lawyer Daniel Webster and challenged the will on a variety of grounds, including the fact that Girard allowed for boys to be raised without the Christian religion. Webster lost when the U.S. Supreme Court found the document to be crafted in a way that forbade changes.[4]

In Hershey's case, the Girard-style deed not only established funding but set the rules of the industrial school's operation. It would give preference to boys from three counties near the town of Hershey—Lebanon, Dauphin, and Lancaster—and then admit orphans from Pennsylvania and the rest of the United States. Instruction would focus mainly on preparing them for jobs in industry or agriculture. (Although academics would be taught, Milton did not set up the school to prepare boys for college.) The school would stress religious tolerance, clean living, and modesty. The boys were to be fed with "plain wholesome food" and clothed "without distinctive dress." The deed of trust declared, "Each scholar shall be taught to speak the truth at all times" and will learn the "habits of economy and industry."

For their part, the boys in the school would be required to meet strict standards for behavior, academic performance, and character. The industrial school was not established to deal with the most challenging cases, and admitted only those boys deemed "healthy" in every way and capable of adapting to its program. In the beginning, the school had some trouble applying these standards. Four of the first ten boys admitted—including student #1, Nelson Wagner—would be expelled because they disobeyed so often that they were deemed "incorrigible" or "undesirable." But in the decades to come, the officials at the school would find ways to limit such bad outcomes and reduce the rate of expulsions to fewer than 5 percent annually.[5]

Besides providing opportunities for needy boys, the endowment and the values established by the trust allowed M.S. Hershey to shape his own legacy. And like all good deeds, the creation of the trust benefited the giver, too. It resolved Milton's long-standing worry, shared by Catherine, over the future of their fortune. It also allowed him to make a dramatic and principled statement—one steeped in his Mennonite background and progressive idealism—about the purpose of money and the meaning of life. Carnegie's strategy for solving the moral problem of wealth was more ostentatious, but it had to be considered against his mistreatment of workers. Hershey had responded to the challenge of wealth more fully and more consistently.

"I never could see what happiness a rich man gets from contemplating a life of acquisition only, with a cold and legal distribution of his wealth after he passes away," he would explain. "After all, what good is one's money unless one uses it for the good of the community and humanity in general?"[6]

• • •

Milton Hershey could comfortably—and secretly—endow the trust without worrying about his own financial needs. He understood how much cash was flowing into the firm's accounts and that the current was getting faster every month. In the candy trade, Hershey's success was clear to retailers who stocked his bars and competitors who lost shelf space. It inspired imitation. In January 1911 Milton authorized his lawyer to sue a competitor named Jacob Kreisler for copying the Hershey bar. "He is a bad actor," said M.S., "and will encourage others."

Hershey's plan for creating a national market for a new product made at the lowest possible price had succeeded beyond expectations. The factory, which was designed with excess capacity and supposedly completed in 1905, had actually continued to grow, season by season. By 1911 it had tripled in size, to eighteen acres of floor space, and employment reached seventeen hundred.

With all the expansion, much of the efficiency that was built into the original layout was lost. The plant grew up, as well as out, which meant that raw ingredients had to be transported via freight elevators. Instead of conveyor belts, workers used carts and even bathtubs on wheels to move materials around. The lack of automation meant more jobs in the factory. This suited area families just fine, as sons and daughters went to join their parents at jobs inside the chocolate works. The plant ran night and day, six days per week, filling boxcars with Hershey bars and Kisses and blanketing the valley with the acrid yet sweet scent of roasting cocoa beans.

The Hershey Chocolate Company's success rippled into the countryside to benefit the railroad, local tradesmen, and businesses that supplied everything from paper to wrenches. Dairy farmers across the region expanded their herds and still sold all the milk they could produce.

As the factory had grown, the town that Henry Herr had drawn up in 1903 had become real, with a graceful downtown shopping district, electric lights, telephone service, and municipal water and sewer. Although he was not a widely known urban planner, Herr's design was quite sophisticated. He refused to lay out the streets in a monotonous grid, as the famous landscape architect George Miller did in Fairfield, Alabama, a town built by U.S. Steel. Instead Herr favored curving roads. He also allowed for wide variation in home architecture and building materials.

The town of Hershey had free schools, a public library, countless clubs, and athletic teams outfitted by the company. All of these services and amenities were subsidized by the company, which meant that property taxes were about half what they were in other places.

Although most of the civic improvements were for locals only, the 150-acre Hershey Park was becoming a major tourist attraction. Company executives persuaded the railroads that served the region to hand out color postcards of the park to spread the word about its attractions. They sent the same cards to churches, suggesting Hershey as the destination for Sunday school outings.[7]

The publicity blitz worked and tourism became the community's second big business. On the busiest summer days ten thousand visitors would come to ride the carousel, swim in the pool, gaze at animals in the zoo, and listen to concerts at the band shell. Those who wanted to walk off the meals they ate in the park could take a stroll in the gardens at High Point and hope to catch a glimpse of M.S. Hershey himself.

The park was an amusement for M.S., and he went there often. On one visit he conducted a playful experiment intended to show that he could get people to buy anything. Taking over a booth to sell a "new and exciting delicacy," Hershey added chopped onion to vanilla ice cream. The first customer fought the disgusting taste and, eager to trick someone else, said it was just fine. As one person lied to another, Hershey quickly sold all the onion ice cream he had made.

The development of the park, and everything else in Hershey, was paid for by the sale of building lots, the profits from various businesses established to serve the town, and the revenues of the chocolate company. The Hershey company had more than enough cash to handle the load, and was poised for almost endless growth. In the decade since M.S. Hershey had announced his plan for an industrial utopia, annual sales had increased sevenfold, to more than $7.7 million. The income from this business was so great that neither the town, nor the constant expansion of the factory, nor the growing school for orphan boys, could soak it all up.

Inevitably all of the success—the growing company, the beautiful little town, the factory, the park, the school—led to the kind of local pride that any Babbitt would have recognized. The company-produced newspapers—*Hershey's Weekly* and later the *Hershey Press*—were filled with good news and outright bragging. Readers would be reminded that they lived in "America's most remarkable town" and worked for "one of America's best employers." Praise would be heaped on "boy farmers" and the nutritional benefits of sugar ("a real food of very high value") would get ample attention.

Even the animals acquired by Hershey's farms got good press. The arrival of a prize bull named Chocolate Segis Pontiac Alcarta (the Finest Young Bull in America) merited a front-page portrait and hundreds, including M.S. Hershey and lawyer John Snyder, turned out at the train station to greet him. His subsequent death by sledgehammer, an accident that occurred when a slaughterhouse worker failed to recognize the great beast, would be recalled as a moment of tragedy for decades to follow.[8]

With such rare exceptions as the slaughter of Chocolate Segis Pontiac Alcarta, the news in Hershey was all good news. Thanks to the company, jobs were plentiful, housing was affordable, and playful diversions were easy to find. In this happy place, populated mainly by young families, death itself was almost a stranger. Hershey didn't have a mortician, a funeral home, or a cemetery.

In any time, M.S. Hershey's accomplishments—building a dominant brand, a national company, and a beautiful town—would have been exceptional. But the fact that he did so in the first decade of the twentieth century made his success even more remarkable. In this time, big business was the subject of widespread scorn and suspicion. Aggressive journalists, President Roosevelt, the U.S. Justice Department, and a gaggle of state attorneys general were all pursuing the crimes and manipulations of a host of well-known companies and their leaders. At the top of the list were Standard Oil and John D. Rockefeller.

While Milton S. Hershey had been creating his do-good, forward-looking company and contented little town, Standard Oil had come to symbolize the dirty business practices of the past and its founder had become an object of ridicule and caricature. The oil baron didn't help his image when he took to flitting about the countryside like a fugitive from justice to escape process servers bearing subpoenas that demanded he appear in various courtrooms. In hiding, Rockefeller couldn't even see his newborn grandson and namesake, and he was humiliated for this in the press. In 1907, Rockefeller and others at Standard Oil were indicted for nearly 1,000 alleged crimes. In 1908, William Randolph Hearst made public documents leaked from Standard Oil offices that proved that Rockefeller executives had paid off members of Congress. By 1911, the company had been taken apart by the courts and Standard Oil was no more.

Every bit a Roosevelt booster, M.S. was open in his admiration for a man whom his *Weekly* called a "rugged, ferociously bold and courageous" leader "firing the hearts of millions." Milton himself got fired up enough to jump into the national debate over politics and economics. In 1912 he briefly overcame his reticence about political speechmaking to oppose Woodrow Wilson's bid for the presidency. Wilson and the Democrats were in favor of revising tariffs in a way that might affect sugar prices. M.S. rose against them at a meeting of state Republicans. Contemplating a Wilson victory he predicted, "Some of us will have to go back to the farm. Hershey will be hard hit and all of us will suffer."[9]

Though Wilson won the election, Hershey somehow avoided catastrophe. But being wrong on both counts didn't end Milton's interest in public affairs. Obviously convinced that he had accomplished something remarkable in his little utopia, he planned to publish a magazine that would bring his philosophy, an amalgam of populism and capitalism called the "Hershey Idea," to a national audience. (Here again Milton followed the Cadbury way. After he started his chocolate town, Bournville, George Cadbury began publishing a widely distributed newspaper called the *Daily News*, which promoted his ideas for social reform.)

Work on the magazine had begun before M.S. stood up against Woodrow Wilson, when two of his most trusted men had traveled to upstate New York seeking guidance and inspiration.

Harry Lebkicher and Milton's distant relative Joseph Snavely, who was editor of *Hershey's Weekly*, visited a long-haired, pop philosopher named Elbert Hubbard. Based at Roycroft, a craftsman's commune in East Aurora, New York, Hubbard was a widely read author and publisher of political tracts and social commentary. He promoted "right thinking" and "right living" through American-style business, cheerfulness, and a hybrid spirituality that counted Tolstoy, Thoreau, and Whitman as prophets. Women's rights, nutrition, and spirituality were favorite topics. He was also a big fan of agricultural education, sunshine, fresh air, and spinach.

Besides representing the progressive philosophy that lay beneath all things Hershey, Elbert Hubbard was also a successful community builder. Five hundred workers lived and labored at Roycroft, turning out publications, furniture, and homey goods made from metal and leather.

When they arrived at the settlement, Snavely and Lebkicher joined Hubbard for lunch at the Roycroft hotel, where the rooms were not numbered but rather named for the founder's heroes: Burroughs, Ruskin, Emerson, etc. The dining room where they ate was decorated with slogans and catchwords reflecting Hubbard's teachings. Some, like the word "fletcherize," were written on boards that were then hung from the rafters on chains.

In the early 1900s to "fletcherize" meant to chew food thoroughly, to the point where it became liquid, in order to improve digestion and prevent overeating. The word came from Horace Fletcher, a self-anointed nutrition expert who costumed himself in a white coat and inspired large numbers of people, including John D. Rockefeller, Upton Sinclair, and John Kellogg, to excessive mastication. Fletcher and others would turn Americans toward a dieting craze that would destroy the generations-old Fat Man's Club of Connecticut and continue to this day.

Snavely and Lebkicher were not converted to fletcherism, but Hubbard made them think. That night they attended a play in Buffalo and talked about one of Hubbard's aphorisms, which held that anyone can have a great idea but the successful man perseveres and "brings the ship into port." In a moment of sentimentality, Lebkicher noted that M.S. Hershey wouldn't have had a ship to pilot if not for those who helped him early on, especially Mattie Snavely. Dead for years, Mattie still held the old man's heart.

Elbert Hubbard was able to offer the men from Hershey more than a few good sayings. Through his many publications he had access to large numbers of readers who were receptive to new ideas and progressive politics. In the summer of 1913 Milton would place a full-page ad in one of these magazines to announce the creation of a new journal called *The Hershey Idea*. Besides soliciting subscribers, the advertisement described an editorial agenda that might have been lifted, in part, from one of Henry Hershey's old dinner table sermons. According to the ad:

> "The Hershey idea" will fearlessly attack the oppression of dishonest Capitalism, and the unjust assaults of Labor upon Capital, and will also emphasize the great need everywhere of conducting public business in the nation, state, county and municipalities in the same honest and economical way that private business is conducted.

As he offered a special rate to the first ten thousand subscribers, M.S. Hershey also promised his new journal would stand for "all the *live* and *pro-*

gressive issues of the day." It would "enter the whole world of political, economic and social journalism, and in an absolutely unbiased and judicial manner discuss all such questions."

With its promise to be a fearless voice on the national political stage, *The Hershey Idea* represented a radical departure from M.S.'s cautious approach to publicity. He even pledged to support "civil rights for women" and, for some reason, to promote the health benefits of ginger. But then, after all this buildup, the magazine idea was dropped without any public explanation. M.S. Hershey would satisfy his interest in publishing close to home, with journals like *Hershey's Weekly*. Years later he would consider the idea of buying and publishing *Life* magazine but quickly dropped this idea, too.[10]

Small as it was, Milton's hometown magazine could still serve as an outlet for his progressive impulses. (In fact for a while it was called *Hershey's Progressive Weekly*.) For as long as it was published, it promoted the movement's recipe for good living in all its forms, including the delights of nature, the value of social clubs, and the importance of temperance. It also allowed M.S. Hershey to position himself as a wise counselor and friend to the working class. In one edition his weekly would describe a Rockefeller heir as "a millionaire above the law." In another issue it would oppose aggressive labor organization like the Wobblies as "sheer anarchists."

In many cases, the voice of the *Weekly* was shrill. A snippet on the $50 million estate left by brewer Adolphus Busch noted the "thousands of humble homes" made into "hells" by the intoxicating product that had generated all the wealth. The article was titled "Blood Money."[11]

When it came to policing alcohol consumption, Hershey and his key executives went beyond propaganda. At Christmastime in 1911 they hired Kraver's Bureau of Secret Service to spy on the beer drinkers at the Haefner House Hotel, one of the few businesses they did not control. Over the course of three weeks "Operative MT-1" reported such vital observations as "Hungarians" drinking "a large quantity of beer" and roaches in his coffee cup. He discovered that a local doctor and his hired helper seemed to take turns getting drunk on certain days, and the hotel proprietor was cautious about selling drink on credit. In the end, MT-1 had to admit that the Haefner House was operating within the law. Nothing came of the investigation.

Although the Hershey company's managers attacked the problem of drink and the workingman in secret, they were more open about other items on their social reform agenda, including those that would later be deemed excessive and even racist. In the December 26, 1912, issue of *Hershey's Weekly*, an article warned that intermarriage or "race suicide" was a grave danger and another lent credence to an Ohio preacher who declared that Jews would soon rule the "entire world." As if to balance this latter item, the paper also published, around the same time, a note praising Jews for a wholesome lifestyle that allowed them to live longer than their Christian neighbors.

Jews were not the only people singled out for special attention. The local paper made sure to point out that foreigners were more likely than native-born Americans to act as assassins and that Pennsylvania needed to work harder to control the so-called feebleminded. Similar bits of prejudice would have been published in many small papers of the day. They don't mark the Hershey publications as special. But few, if any, would have tried to turn a mortal man into a sainted figure in the way that the *Press* and the *Weekly* tried to canonize Milton S. Hershey. Whenever a chance arose, M.S. was credited with the good things that were reported. And when major articles described the community's growth, the founder was portrayed in such florid terms that only a direct quote can capture the tone:

> It is, in a word, the story of how one man, inspired with acute foresight and shrewd business acumen, combined with a sense of justice—rare combination!—and recognizing the tremendous value of cooperation, raised a monument to himself by elevating the conditions of others.[12]

A great many factors had helped to build the image of M.S. Hershey. Fawning publicity, which certainly aided his company's sales, was one of the forces that slowly turned Milton from man to icon. The fact that he had actually done what he said he would do—create a town, a booming business, and a national brand all bearing his name—was also important. The final element was Milton Hershey's schizophrenic style of leadership.

M.S. had a temper and might fire someone for a ridiculous reason— goosing, for example. And while he spent freely on luxuries for Kitty, he habitually tried to catch his employees wasting the tiny amount of electricity needed to burn an extra light. But just when someone might decide, once and for all, that M.S. Hershey was a cheapskate, he did something generous. In 1912 he paid every one of his workers a 20 percent bonus, matching the dividends he paid to investors. The bonus, which he would continue to pay for many years, honored labor alongside capital and reflected a basic tenet of Taylorism—that industrialists could purchase both loyalty and efficiency with cash. Much of the money came back to Hershey anyway, as his workers used it to make down payments on homes in the company town.

In setting up this cycle of wealth, M.S. was well ahead of Henry Ford, who would gain fame in 1914 by sharing his profits—raising pay to $5 per day—in order to retain workers and in the process turn them into customers for his cars. Although M.S. was rarely credited for pioneering this strategy, his generosity was both a wise business policy, because it kept good workers on the job, and a vivid illustration of his values. Ford tied heavy strings to his wage, requiring that recipients be of good character, which meant sober, churchgoing, and thrifty, and he created a force of investigators to make sure they were. Although he too valued these qualities, M.S. Hershey never sent men into his employees' homes, as Ford did, to make sure they shared them.[13]

Given his complex personality and inconsistent actions, Milton Hershey was like an unreliable parent to his dependents, who included the workers in his factory, the farmers who supplied him milk, and the citizens of his town. Since they couldn't be certain about his kindness and, thus, their own security, they put a lot of time and energy into praising and pleasing him. By focusing on the positive traits they hoped would prevail, they constructed an almost mythical M.S., a character who was brilliant, congenial, generous, and just. He accepted the role, as creator and ruler of all things Hershey, and played it well.

The defining performance of this *tableau vivant* took place on Friday, May 30, and Saturday, May 31, 1913, when the chocolate company and chocolate town celebrated the tenth anniversary of Hershey's move to Derry Church. The factory, the park, and all the buildings along Chocolate Avenue had been decorated with American flags, red, white, and blue bunting, and shields of stars and stripes. As Friday morning dawned, the High Point mansion was so elaborately decked out that it resembled a political party's headquarters on election day.

"Twenty-six kinds of ever-changing spectacles" were on the two-day anniversary program, although Teddy Roosevelt, who declined an invitation "with very keen regret," was not. The band from the Bethlehem Steel Company, where owner Charles Schwab and the state police had recently broken a major strike, played eight different concerts. The comedy team of Carter and Bluford entertained folks at the outdoor theater. More than twenty thousand people turned out to see James B. "Birdman" McCalley and his eighty-horsepower Curtiss biplane attempt to break the world's altitude record.

Much like auto racing today, early air shows promised an audience a display of speed and daring, and the real possibility of a fatal crash. Birdman had won the $2,000 contract for the Hershey show with a promise to attempt the altitude record and perform his famous "ocean roll" and the perilous "dip of death." Advertisements for his flights noted that eight of McCalley's "personal friends" had been killed in crashes and that Birdman had broken his wrist during a recent landing when he had steered into a fence to avoid hitting a crowd that had "surged upon the field."[14]

As luck would have it, the crankshaft on McCalley's plane broke days before he was scheduled to appear in Hershey. Fortunately another aviator, R.V. Morris, brought his plane to the celebration to put on four shows with Birdman on the ground. Men in straw boaters, women and girls in dresses, and boys in knickers lined a makeshift airfield to watch as Morris climbed in the plane and McCalley directed things on the field.

Although Morris wouldn't attempt to set an altitude record, as McCalley had promised he would, the crowd got a good look at what a flying machine could do in the air. Then came the landing. As he buzzed down and rolled along the field, Morris somehow misjudged the distance to a rocky gulch that would have destroyed his aircraft. With the huge crowd looking on, McCalley risked his body as he tried to slow the plane, but was knocked over and reinjured his wrist. Morris managed to steer into a crate that had been left near the runway, damaging his plane but stopping before the little crevasse.

The plane was repaired, and in the next day and a half Morris would make three more flights that were "tame enough" according to the local paper. There were no ocean rolls and no dips of death, but the sight of an aircraft in flight high above the town was exciting. A week afterward, poor McCalley was still missing a gold watch, which he had lost when Morris plowed into him.

The air show may have provided the great drama for the weekend, but it wasn't the only big draw. A large crowd turned out to watch a parade with forty-five floats, two bands, and more marchers than Hershey had citizens. Women with parasols rode in open cars decorated with flowers. Men in white suits marched in orderly formation.

At two o'clock on Saturday afternoon, people stood shoulder to shoulder to hear Omar Hershey, a Baltimore lawyer and renowned public speaker who was known for promoting the idea that business must eventually work to create world peace. No relation to M.S., Omar opened his address, "The Hershey Idea," with a little anecdote about sharing his last name with the Chocolate Man:

> Wherever I go, be it in Maine or California the first thing they ask me is "Are you the Hershey who makes the chocolate?"
> I tell them, "No, I'm the Hershey who eats it. And it costs me five cents a bite too, even if I am a Hershey."
> Hershey makes the chocolate. I eat it. You see the effects. He has all the money, and I all the size.

Pictures from the moment show a crowd of well-dressed men and women surrounding the great orator and flags and bunting all around. The only person not standing is Milton S. Hershey, who sits in a big chair, looking like a rather bored king at court. What he heard that day, as Omar praised him and all he had made, would have made royalty blush.

Milton Hershey was "not only making chocolate, but history, here," said Omar. Noting national labor unrest and public concern about industry, he added, "If Big Business adopted *the Hershey idea* there would be less danger in some of these ominous murmurings. You have demonstrated that where simple justice and plain, ordinary common sense prevails, some of the problems quickly adjust themselves." M.S. Hershey is, he added, "a doer of things, a builder . . . an inspiration to the youth of the land."

By the time an hourlong fireworks display marked the end of the two-day celebration, M.S. Hershey would have soaked in more praise from other speakers and heard both an eight-stanza poem and an anthem called "The Hershey Song," which was set to the tune of "America."

> May our wise founder be
> Spared in his time, to see
>   Success replete.
> May his great task begun,

To full fruition run.
And ere the waning sun,
His works complete.

Not satisfied with poetry, song, speeches, and a parade, M.S. Hershey's employees also marched up to High Point, accompanied by the drums and
horns of the factory band, to give him a sterling silver loving cup, lined
with gold, and decorated with silver oak leaves and laurel. As *Hershey's
Weekly* explained, the heavy cup, made by the famous jewelers Bailey
Banks and Biddle, was meant to honor him as the town's "beneficent
Jove."

M.S. had reached that level of celebrity where his reputation and his
name were every bit as powerful as his physical presence. The persona of
Milton S. Hershey had become so important that it governed the mood
and activities of his company and his town even when he was absent. This
powerful dynamic would come in handy as he spent more and more of his
time far away from Hershey.[15]

Years before this tenth-anniversary hoopla, M.S. had begun to let his un-
derlings manage his company's day-to-day affairs as he traveled abroad with
Kitty, whose health was worse than most townspeople could have imagined. Catherine nevertheless tried to enjoy the places and activities she always loved and even enlisted a young servant boy to pull her wheelchair
up the ramp to the "bird's nest" in the oak tree outside High Point.

More and more the Hersheys were focused on Kitty's illness. They frequently traveled to Europe to seek treatment and seem to have been willing to try anything. The syphilis/locomotor ataxia expert Dr. Wilhelm Erb
had retired to an emeritus position at Heidelberg University, but Catherine
was seen by doctors he had trained. Once, in Wiesbaden she tried something called the "grape cure," which involved grinding fresh grapes to
make juice.

When they weren't seeking cures, the Hersheys enjoyed in Europe the
privacy and time together that they could never have in Pennsylvania.
Considered years later, it seems as if Milton knew that his opportunities
were running out. With every passing year he lavished more time and
more money on Kitty. Only on occasion did M.S. conduct business
abroad. Once, William Murrie asked him to investigate a new French

method for condensing milk. He also looked into selling chocolate in England. But in the main, M.S. traveled to escape Hershey, find treatment for his wife, and feed his own curiosity about the world beyond.

This man, who championed the village and the farm and criticized urban living, thoroughly enjoyed first-class travel to the big cities of Europe. In 1912 he even made sure to book passage on the super-ship *Titanic's* first voyage. When business required him to sail three days early, aboard the steamer *America*, he escaped the disaster that claimed many other millionaires, including an Astor, a Guggenheim, and a Straus.

Although he was hardly a fixture on the society pages, M.S. delighted in meeting other rich and famous men who traveled by ocean liner. He once spoke of taking the barber's chair next to the one occupied by J.P. Morgan. He also gambled with the chewing gum magnate William Wrigley Jr., but left the game suspecting he had been cheated and vowing revenge. On dry land, M.S. favored expensive hotels and dining rooms, and invariably found his way to local casinos. During one visit to Monte Carlo, young women in the casino started calling him "Mr. Maximum" because he often placed the highest bets allowed.

On their European tours, the Hersheys could enjoy their wealth and share the company of sophisticated people, without being held to the harsh social standards of the Pennsylvania Dutch. Kitty could wear the diamond tiara Milton had bought her as well as the $8,000 diamond dog collar necklace, which he had given her as a Christmas present years earlier. And she could get away with the childish behavior that made Milton think of her as a sometime teenager.

The trips turned M.S. Hershey into a worldly man who could discuss Europe's art and ancient ruins because he had visited them. They also supplied more adventure than Kitty and Milton could ever have at home. For a 1912 journey through France they hired an aging race car driver as a chauffeur. Somewhere near Cherbourg he lost control of the car and smashed into a tree. The car was wrecked, but the tree survived, and it became a landmark they enjoyed seeing on later excursions. The same driver later served Milton in Cairo, where M.S. found a racetrack and won a wager on a horse that offered forty-to-one odds. According to one source, the track had to use all its available cash to make good on Milton's bet. When Milton was ready to leave for home and had trouble selling the Packard he had brought for touring, he gave it to his driver.

In Hamburg, where Kitty sometimes sought treatment, the Hersheys socialized with the medical elite. During one elaborate meal a prominent English doctor received an urgent letter while at the Hersheys' table. He rose, and went around the table discreetly informing people individually that the Queen was sick and he had been called to attend her. When he told this to Kitty, she blurted out, "God save the Queen!" The dining room went silent for an uncomfortable moment, until the doctor threw his head back and laughed out loud.

"She was a very charming woman," recalled Ruth Hershey Beddoe, the daughter of Henry Hershey's doctor, Martin Hershey; she became Kitty's frequent companion. "When my father called [on her], all he talked about afterward was her beautiful eyes. She was very popular with the men." Catherine liked to laugh, to tease, and to show her affection. She could always get a rise out of her husband by recalling how she had hired an investigator to check his financial status before agreeing to be his bride.

For his part, Milton managed to make Catherine laugh over his struggles with foreign languages. At a restaurant in Marseilles he ordered pork and heard the waiter call out "*jambon.*" Believing he heard the waiter say "Jumbo"—the name of P.T. Barnum's famous elephant—Milton desperately called out, "I don't want an elephant!"

The Jumbo story was repeated by Milton himself for years, to show how much fun he had with Kitty abroad. But even with all the laughter, sights, tastes, and sounds they enjoyed while traveling, the Hersheys did not escape their sorrows completely. Ruth Hershey Beddoe would forever remember watching Milton study a little boy aboard a ship that was taking them to Alexandria. As the ship was docking, a man came up to the boy and took him in his arms. The child hugged him around the neck and kissed him. "M.S. looked on, fascinated," she recalled.

Just as they couldn't escape the fact that they would never have children, Milton and Catherine could never quite ignore the reality of her illness. But they carried on as best they could. Milton would lift her out of cars or into bed. Catherine had boutiques send their finest things to her hotel room, so she could still shop for the latest fashions.

In whatever city they found themselves in, Milton was always able to find a flower shop when he took his regular walk, and took great care selecting roses for her. He even climbed into display windows to grab just the right ones. Once, when they were in Nice on Washington's Birthday, he brought a little cherry tree into their hotel's dining room and set it on the table as a centerpiece. He then counted all the cherries—there were twenty-three—and calculated what each one had cost him.[16]

By the time the Hersheys departed on their most ambitious trip, in the fall of 1912, Kitty often needed a wheelchair, but still tried to hide the extent of her paralysis. She managed to fool her husband for a while. But then, during dinner, he watched to see whether she could cut her own meat. She couldn't.

The stories that Ruth Hershey Beddoe would tell about that trip through Germany, Switzerland, Italy, France, and Egypt are filled with poignant examples of how Kitty and Milton struggled to be happy. Kitty often spent days in bed and received therapeutic massage in their hotel rooms. She needed so much rest that Milton—a fast-walking, fast-talking ball of energy—had to find a way to fill his days. When they reached Nice in January 1913, and settled into the Hotel Majestic, he found the perfect outlet.

An annual festival called Bataille des Fleurs, or Battle of the Flowers, was days away. The highlight of the celebration came when contestants decorated coaches with flowers and competed for judges' approval in a parade. Milton threw himself into the competition, renting a coach, and emptying his wallet to decorate it so thoroughly that even the spokes of its wheels were covered in mimosa flowers.

Since the rules required each coach be decorated with a young woman, as well as flowers, Ruth joined Milton and Catherine for the 4 1/2-mile parade. They were armed with bunches of violets, which they threw to people in other coaches, and on the street.

Upset by the amount of money her husband had spent on the carriage—she often tried to curb his impulse toward extravagance—Kitty refused to enjoy the Battle of the Flowers. She and Milton argued along the entire parade route, while young Ruth handled the violet-throwing duties. As Ruth would recall, it didn't help when Milton's carriage actually won the fifth-place prize, a silk banner decorated with fake jewels. "She was mad at him," explained Ruth. "He could not take any pleasure in it."

Milton had his chance to be angry with Catherine when, during the same vacation, they were in Egypt for a tour of Cairo and the Pyramids. (Fascinated by ancient civilizations, Milton had started on this leg of their trip alone, when Kitty was too tired to travel. She and Ruth Hershey eventually caught up with him.) It was there that he discovered that Catherine was spending a small fortune on international telephone calls to a practitioner of Christian Science healing. Although Christian Science was criticized by mainstream religious leaders and respected physicians, Milton didn't take issue with his wife's interest in healing prayers. Religious tolerance was something he valued, and she was desperate for a cure that mainstream medicine couldn't provide. But he was briefly incensed over the payments she made to hear such prayers said over the phone.

The arguments about flowers and telephone calls were just two moments out of many recalled in the 1950s by Ruth Hershey Beddoe, who during those months got as close to the couple as any person could. She saw in Milton an eccentric, inscrutable man of real intelligence, who was alternately loving, frustrated, generous, demanding, and kind. He had trouble resisting horse races and casinos, but managed to limit his losses. He thought of Kitty as someone who was charming and childish, beautiful and exasperating.

Kitty could be immature, selfish, and self-centered. Many of her friends seemed, to Ruth, to be frivolous "children of the vapor." But Kitty mothered Milton and also pitied him for the love and kindness he had missed in childhood. And on that long jaunt through Europe and Egypt, both of the Hersheys had an excuse for their excesses and mood swings.

"That was a longer trip than most because her health was failing," recalled Ruth. "She felt that the end was near. She was studying the Bible, not for its own sake, but in connection with the Christian Science lessons."[17]

In August 1913, two months after the tenth anniversary festivities, Dr. Martin Hershey, Ruth's father, was so alarmed by Catherine's labored breathing that he ordered her to leave Pennsylvania for a cooler, drier climate. Milton leased a Pullman sleeping car—it cost almost $500—and dispatched her to Bretton Woods in the White Mountains of New Hampshire. To keep her warm in the winter he bought her a fur coat valued at $40,000.

Catherine's dependence on Milton was almost complete. During her worst spells, when she thought of the horse in winter longing for "spring grass," she couldn't walk or even hold a book. She was reluctant to let her friends see her when she was sick, and she was not especially close to her own extended family. Once she startled a friend when she said she had a brother somewhere. She had never mentioned him before. He was disabled, she said, and she wondered aloud if he might be dead.

Kitty had lost her main ally on Milton's side of the family when Henry died. Fanny, who had moved into a house on Chocolate Avenue, may have warmed to her a bit. They did correspond when Milton and Catherine were abroad, and they were photographed together. But they were not especially close. And it couldn't have soothed Catherine to know that whenever he was in Hershey, Milton began almost every day with a stop at Fanny's house.

Elderly and old-fashioned, Fanny was a more visible figure in Hershey than Catherine and many people regarded her as the beloved if somewhat eccentric Queen Mum of the kingdom. "She was a good soul, a good Christian soul," reported Milton's chauffeur, who often drove Fanny around town.

Fanny Hershey was known to rise before dawn most mornings for a walk followed by chores. She regularly occupied a rocking chair on her front porch, in sight of one of the factory doors. In her kitchen hung a picture of a woman wielding a broom. Below was a caption reading, "If you want to know who's boss around here just start something."

Although she lived in the second biggest house in town and her son provided her with everything she could need, Fanny never stopped worrying. She recalled the poverty of Milton's childhood, when he would hungrily lick his plate to clean every bit of the yolk from an egg. Fanny insisted on being useful and would often sit and put fresh Kisses in their tin foil wrappers, which were brought to her from the factory almost every day. (Milton was humoring her, and did not sell these candies because they were not handled in sanitary conditions.) On Sundays she'd walk around the quiet factory building, testing the doors to make sure they were locked.[18]

People catered to the old lady. Unwilling to trust local delivery boys with such an important task, the aging Harry Lebkicher met an early morning train to get the newspapers that Fanny read every day. And whether her son was present or not, executives escorted her on a tour of the chocolate works at least once a year. They understood her place in the Hershey hierarchy. Her hold on Milton's heart was obvious. "Milt was more afraid of her than of anything else," explained John McLain. It was "not that she was sharp tongued, but she was an idol to him. Nothing was too good for his mother."

For those who came to work and live in Hershey, Fanny was to some degree an extension of M.S. Hershey himself. George Bowman, the cocoa bean roaster, would make sure his department was cleaned up and operating smoothly when she came through the factory. But he wasn't especially afraid of her. In his mind, "she was a wonderful person."

George Bowman found much about living and working the Hershey way to be rather wonderful. He had applied for work on October 1, 1911, and started the very next day, earning fifteen cents an hour. He was lucky enough to find a place to rent, in town, and moved his young wife right in. Soon he was a head roaster, and his boss, plant superintendent George Epply, was telling him he was the best man in his department.

The Bowmans watched the little town grow, and were there for the parade, the air show, and the fireworks that ended the tenth-anniversary celebration. They loved living in a modern community with every convenience and entertainment. But they also grew to recognize that Hershey was not an escape from reality. George Bowman recalled the strains that could develop among workers and managers in a plant that ran full bore all the time. This was especially noticeable after his beloved boss, George Epply, was replaced by Frank McGee, "the meanest son of a gun I ever met in my life."

In time, others would reach the same conclusion about McGee. One was a short-tempered foreman who worked in the cocoa department, where a soft brown dust covered everything and everyone. He came to work one night to find the superintendent waiting with a list of minor complaints. The conversation began poorly and grew worse. The foreman, a big redheaded man, grabbed McGee and threw him down on the floor. The two fought, getting themselves covered with cocoa dust, until the foreman grabbed McGee and put his fist in his face.

"He said, 'I'm not going to give you a chance to fire me,'" recalled George Bowman. "He said, 'I'm going to quit myself.' And he did. He walked right out . . . those were the things that were going on there."[19]

A THIRD LIFE

 In early 1915 the Reverend Billy Sunday named the three things "which will ruin any town and give it a bad name." They were licensed saloons, stores open on the Sabbath day, and "a dirty, cussing, swearing gang of blacklegs on the street." No community that allows these sins can grow and attract new citizens, he said. "You could never start a boom half big enough to get one man there."

At the time, people listened to Billy Sunday. A former major league ballplayer, the square-jawed evangelist was America's favorite campaigner for Jesus and against alcohol. He was an exciting saver of souls who rallied thousands to his sermons in major cities and small towns. And he sparked religious revivals in the places he visited, as even local preachers who may have resented having to compete with an out of towner caught the spirit.

The famous evangelist's remarks about the "things that ruin a town" struck a nerve in Hershey. On January 12 the editor of the *Weekly* published his points at the top of the paper's front page, and then fretted over the town's fate. The Founder had spared the community two of Sunday's three evils. Saloons were outlawed and stores observed the Sabbath. But the *Weekly* had to admit that Chocolate Avenue was afflicted with cussing men. "They and their kind do not belong in Hershey," said the paper, "and they should be made to move on."[1]

The outrage over profanity shows how much Hershey's overseers wanted to manage every aspect of life in the town. But as the bad habits of certain denizens of Chocolate Avenue suggest, M.S. and his men couldn't control everything. In retrospect they generally succeeded when a project involved spending money, or time, to build, organize, or operate a new enterprise.

The Lancaster Caramel
Company began in 1886
in a small space in a large
building on Church Street,
which also housed an
organ manufacturer, a
brewery, and a carriage
works. In six years Milton
Hershey's firm would oc-
cupy the entire four-story
building. Inside caramel
cooked in rows of big kettles. Teamsters lined up
their rigs to deliver fresh
milk and sugar and cart
away finished caramels.

After failing as a printer's
devil, Milton S. Hershey
found success as an ap-
prentice for Lancaster
candy maker Joseph
Royer. Hershey is shown
here, on the right, in a
photo from 1873 when he
was sixteen years old.

By 1889, thirty-two-year-old Milton S. Hershey had made himself a financial success. This portrait was taken by a photographer in New York, where Hershey had an active wholesale trade.

Milton's mother, Veronica "Fanny" Hershey, is shown here in 1918 outside High Point at age seventy-three. She would live two more years before dying of pneumonia.

Henry Hershey considered himself a self-taught expert in everything from art to horticulture. He is pictured here in 1898, at age sixty-nine, long after he had ceased living with Milton's mother and after she had begun to refer to herself as a widow.

This photo of Catherine Hershey was taken at about the time she and Milton were married in 1898. By some accounts she had begun experiencing bouts of weakness associated with the illness that would eventually kill her, but she was generally energetic and high-spirited.

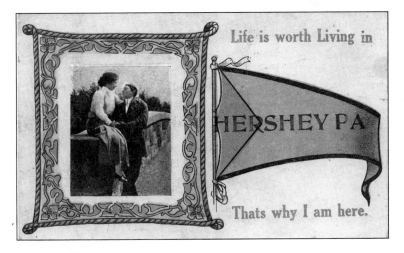

Postcards, like the one pictured here, promoted Hershey as a tourist destination and utopian community. (Neil Fasnacht Collection, Hershey Community Archives)

Milton S. Hershey liked to say that he let the quality of his products serve as his advertising. In fact, in the founder's lifetime, the company regularly advertised in candy trade publications and occasionally bought ads to appeal to the public, like this one noting the flight of Douglas "Wrong Way" Corrigan who mistakenly flew to Dublin when he intended to go to California.

Until the 1960s, women who worked in manufacturing jobs at Hershey were generally restricted to jobs that were not physically demanding. Here, in a photo taken in the 1930s, a woman employee dressed in a sanitary white uniform works at a wrapping machine.

The high temperatures of the ovens and the heavy labor required to shovel and shift the beans made the roasting department, shown here sometime between 1900 and 1915, a demanding assignment. The skill required to process the beans properly, without burning them, also made the roasters some of the most valued employees.

In this photo, from approximately 1915, downtown Hershey bustles with traffic. The trolley system was designed to take workers from their homes to work and then back at night for a five-cent fare.

Hershey's Tenth Aniversary Celebration, 1913.

In 1913 a parade that featured social clubs, zoo animals, and hundreds of marchers marked the tenth anniversary of the founding of the town of Hershey. "Twenty-six kinds of ever-changing spectacles" were on the two-day anniversary program, including concerts, a comedy show, and a demonstration of daring by a flying ace.

Orphan boys as young as four were eligible for enrollment at the Hershey Industrial School, which began at the Hershey family homestead in 1910. By 1923 there were enough Hershey school boys to surround Milton as they sat together on the steps at the homestead.

After the sale of the caramel business in 1900, Mr. and Mrs. Hershey took a trip to France, Austria, Germany, and Egypt. While they took in many tourist sights, they also traveled to find medical treatment for Catherine.

The 1937 sit-down strike at the Hershey factory ended when farmers and other "loyalists" entered the plant and forcibly removed union organizers. The strike and community response brought into view long-standing social conflicts between immigrant workers and locals. Animosities begun in that time lingered into the 1950s.

The Hershey strike was part of a larger organizing effort by unions nationwide, which had led to conflict in other communities. Opponents of the strikers marched to show their loyalty to Milton S. Hershey and to protest the activities of the small local Communist party chapter, which distributed pamphlets critical of the company.

In 1941 the Hershey Country Club hired superstar-to-be Ben Hogan as its pro. The move was considered a publicity coup for Hershey and a sweet deal for Hogan (pictured here with Milton Hershey), who performed minimal duties in exchange for one of the best club pro salaries in the country.

By 1937, at age eighty, Milton Hershey had given his mansion, High Point, to the community for use as a golf course clubhouse. He lived in a two-room apartment on the second floor surrounded by photos of his deceased wife, Catherine. Three of these pictures sit atop the console radio in the upper right corner of this photo.

But when a new thing required the assent or active participation of the average citizen—when people could actually decide whether to go along—the outcome was far less certain.

Consider, for example, the Hershey Department Store. Opened in 1910 at the corner of Chocolate and Cocoa, the big store had twenty-eight sections, selling everything from coal to cars. The store could furnish your house, fill your stomach, and put shoes on both your child and your horse. It also kept home, in Hershey, all the dollars that would have otherwise been spent in nearby Harrisburg or Lebanon.

Sensitive to grumbling about the monopoly the store enjoyed, M.S. eventually proposed to turn it over to the community. Like so many others, this idea was inspired by a European example. In the mid-nineteenth century a group of English weavers had created the Rochdale Society of Equitable Pioneers, a cooperative that ran a factory that produced textiles for the world market and income for its members. They also started a store, which allowed members to buy food and other goods at wholesale prices. Their success bred hundreds of imitators. And it led M.S. Hershey to suggest it might work for the inhabitants of his new town.

The Founder said the department store was profitable and poised to expand its business. Even if prices were cut to benefit the co-op's members, it would still be a going concern. Nevertheless, he was ready to give it away.

"From out of the fertile brain of Mr. Hershey have already evolved many useful and pleasant things," explained the *Weekly*. This one "will be worth thousands of dollars per year to the people of Hershey and vicinity, provided they are willing to stretch out their hands and take the benefits he offers."

Having had almost every other Hershey idea simply deposited in their community, the townspeople were less impressed by the offer of a department store than they were by the fact that they had the power to decide the matter for themselves. In the public debate that ensued, M.S. pointed out that hundreds of co-ops had been started in America. According to a pamphlet the company printed and distributed to townspeople, the co-op serving federal employees in Washington returned 90 percent of its profits to its members in the form of rebates on purchases.

These facts couldn't compete with the suspicions that hid in the minds of some Hershey residents. No one, no matter how bighearted, would simply give away a profitable department store, they said. Obviously Milton Hershey was hiding something. And what if they did accept the offer?

Wouldn't it oblige them to do all of their business at the corner of Chocolate and Cocoa?

Although he believed that "co-operation is the basis of the ideal state of the future," in the end M.S. was forced to abandon his idea for making the department store a co-operative. There just weren't enough eager townspeople to form a workable co-op. He would always believe that the men of Hershey, whom he considered a levelheaded group, had been willing to give it a try. It was the women who wouldn't go along, and the failed co-op proposal marked one of those rare moments in Hershey when the Founder needed help to get something done and he didn't receive it.

M.S. Hershey felt undermined when he couldn't control his community's response to the co-op idea, but he was absolutely helpless in the face of his wife Catherine's progressive illness. By the winter of 1915, Kitty was so debilitated that she rarely left home. She was no longer able to attend when her husband invited the boys from the industrial school to breakfast at High Point. She couldn't write or hold a book. But she held enough hope in the future that she ordered a spring wardrobe, including party dresses, to be shipped to Hershey.

Although she was no longer able to travel great distances, Catherine was nevertheless restless. In March she went to stay in Atlantic City. Late in the month she decided to go home, by way of Philadelphia. She rode in a convertible, with its top down. (According to one source, her paralysis left her impervious to the cold.) Near Philadelphia Kitty became quite sick. She went with her nurse to the Bellevue-Stratford Hotel. A local doctor saw her in her room, and diagnosed her with mild pneumonia. She didn't seem terribly ill when Milton joined her.

In nearly seventeen years of marriage, Catherine's illness had lurked like a monster in the darkness. Doctors had told the Hersheys that this incurable disease, locomotor ataxia, eventually claimed its victims with organ failure or pneumonia. This was why every cough had sent her to Hot Springs or New Hampshire, and it was why Milton rushed to be with her at the Bellevue-Stratford in Philadelphia.

Only secondhand accounts of what happened in that hotel room survive. According to the *Hershey Press*, the doctor expected Kitty to recover. Ruth Hershey Beddoe would say that Kitty had hidden the full extent of her suffering from Milton. She even wondered if Catherine had intentionally exposed herself to the elements to make her end come more quickly, for her husband's sake. Milton didn't appear to grasp the gravity of the situation as he tended his wife, who lay on a sofa in the hotel room.

"Well Kitty, what would you like to have?" he asked.

She suggested champagne. As he went to get it, a nurse called to him saying, "Mrs. Hershey has changed her appearance. I think she's gone."

When Milton returned to her side, Kitty was dead.

"Mr. Hershey just went to pieces," reported a housekeeper who had been in the room.

After he composed himself, he sat down to write out a list on hotel stationery of those who should be notified of his wife's death.

Just forty-two years old, Catherine Sweeney Hershey had risen from poor Irish immigrant's daughter to become wife, companion, and partner in philanthropy to one of the more prominent men in America. With a level of wealth that few people ever knew, Kitty had indulged freely in travel, shopping, music, and the theater. She had seen much of the world, met the kinds of people whom others only read about in newspapers and magazines, and felt the devotion of a man who truly loved her. These facts of her life made the mystery of her introduction to Milton—was she a small town innocent in Jamestown or someone else entirely in Buffalo?—irrelevant.

But life had denied Kitty as much as it had given. For most of her marriage she was unable to be the bright, engaging woman whom M.S. first met. Her illness robbed her of vitality and, most likely, denied her children. These losses were doubtless harder to bear in the community that was supposed to be her home. In Lancaster, and later Hershey, too many people made her the object of common gossip. Too few offered her friendship.

This was evident, even in her death. Among the condolence letters saved for posterity by M.S. Hershey are many from out-of-town friends and business associates. He heard from people in the candy trade, cocoa importing, and finance. George Boggs of the Rock Island Railroad wrote, "I never in all my life saw anyone with a brighter, happier disposition and although it has been a long time since I saw her, I am sure she maintained that until her last."

In contrast, few locals, including members of the family in Hershey and Lancaster, sent cards or letters. One of those who did, Milton's uncle Elias Hershey, a preacher, revealed complex feelings about both Milton and his wife.

I have learned of your bereavement with a feeling of sympathy for you in your loss of a companion who, as I knew her, was cheerful and cordial.

Relations and conditions here are uncertain and by our varied experience we learn the lessons of human frailty. Your life is not free from what is common everywhere. You have made great worldly development. May you be ready for the end of this scene, but may God be pleased to continue your usefulness to others.

Your uncle,
Elias Hershey

As he had while she lived, M.S. Hershey spent lavishly on his wife in death. Workers in Hershey got a day off and he paid the fare for those who wanted to travel to the service. Mourners who arrived in Philadelphia aboard the train called *The Queen of the Valley* were met by a fleet of twenty-seven limousines. At the funeral home they found a large room, overflowing with flowers, where Catherine lay on imported satin inside a solid bronze casket. The hired cars also brought the crowd to the Cathedral of Saints Peter and Paul for a funeral mass. Since Hershey had no burial ground, Catherine's remains were then placed in a vault at a local cemetery.

Kitty Hershey's death was noted by the *Hershey Weekly*, but it was not front-page news because, as the paper reported, Mr. and Mrs. Hershey generally avoided publicity about personal matters. For the next four years, when a Hershey town cemetery was finally ready for the transfer of her casket, Milton would make sure that fresh flowers decorated the vault in Philadelphia where Kitty's body lay.[2]

Over time, Milton Hershey had come to live two separate lives. One, which Kitty had preferred, existed away from his little town, in places like New York, London, and Paris. While he ordered the editor of the *Weekly* to publish warnings on the evils of urban life, M.S. clearly enjoyed everything great cities had to offer, indulging his taste for fine food, luxury hotels, and the excitement of casinos and racetracks.[3]

When he returned to Pennsylvania, Hershey became a very different person. He dressed conservatively and made sure everyone knew he preferred the kind of food found at a farmer's table. In this life he was so hard-driving that it sometimes seemed like he never slept at all. Those who worked with him described a leader who walked fast, produced countless proposals and orders, and held others to a very strict code of conduct. He was, in short, the kind of man his mother admired.[4]

In the months after Kitty died, M.S. stayed in Hershey and focused on his business. People in town and at the factory generally knew when the boss was home, the way royal subjects always know when the monarch is around. But those who did the essential work in the factory, turning milk, sugar, and cocoa into money, wouldn't have thought much about M.S. They were too busy.

Typical was George Bowman, who worked in the roasting department ten hours a day. On an otherwise normal summer day he was tending several different batches of beans when a fire broke out in one of his ovens.

The fire started when one of the bricks that lined the oven came lose. It broke open the container that held the roasting beans and spilled them. The dried shells of the beans instantly caught fire in the high heat.

As Bowman struggled to stop the fire, a large flame burst toward him through the oven door. Just as this happened, M.S. Hershey entered the room with an older man and two little girls who were following him on a tour.

"When Mr. Hershey seen that," recalled Bowman years later, "he turned around and they rushed out of there."

With the fire demanding his full attention, Bowman didn't follow to explain that similar fires had happened before, and that due to the design of the ovens they were in fact bound to happen from time to time. He simply turned back to his work and soon had control of the oven. After he got things back to normal, the big boss returned with Bowman's two immediate supervisors, a foreman and the plant superintendent. They called him away from the ovens.

"He wanted to know what had happened that we had this fire. And I told him. . . . And he said, 'Don't you know losing four hundred pounds of cocoa beans in the fire is a big loss to me?'

"I said, 'Yes.' I said, 'I know that.' But I said, 'I couldn't help that.' I said, 'It happened.'"

The supervisors and Hershey left without resolving the issue. But soon one of the managers returned. He told Bowman, the company's best roaster, to go to the payroll office and collect his last check. He no longer worked for M.S. Hershey. Bowman, in a state of shock, found a cloth bag to carry the personal tools he had brought to the job, collected them, went to the office for his pay, and then walked home to his wife. Their life in the seemingly secure, almost perfect place that was Hershey, was suddenly over. On that summer day, which had started like any other, they sat down in their tidy Hershey home and cried.[5]

In casting out George Bowman for an accident that was out of his control, M.S. Hershey showed more temper than usual. But in the months after Catherine's death he was generally more aggressive and impatient. For example, in the fall of 1915 he went to court with Giuseppe Donato to fight over the bill the artist had delivered along with the sculpture that Milton and Catherine had commissioned five years earlier.

Donato's vision for the piece—a bronze entitled *Dance of Eternal Spring*—had changed as he worked. With each revision he had consulted with either Milton, Catherine, or their landscaper designer. According to Donato, who wore a goatee and presented himself as a mercurial *artiste*, he had received permission to complete a much grander statue than the one first imagined. He bought materials, engaged a model, and with years of effort finally produced a fountain that featured three female nudes dancing in a circle and holding a cherubic baby aloft.

The bill that Donato submitted for this work, the equivalent of $500,000 in 2005, was roughly eight times the price quoted when the commission was first made. M.S. decided to dispute the price when the bill arrived, and he left the crated statue in storage at the Hershey train station. Donato sued for payment, and the two faced off in a Harrisburg courtroom before an audience of curious citizens and eager reporters.

The facts of the case would have delighted the crowd in the court. Donato's model for the nudes had been the beautiful dancer Maud Sansbury, who was considered one of America's most glamorous women. Sansbury's star power, the titillation associated with nude modeling, and Milton Hershey's wealth and fame meant that the Philadelphia papers covered every twist and turn of the trial. They dubbed M.S. "the Chocolate King" and granted Donato "the eccentricity of genius."

At the start of the trial Milton tried to deny he had possession of the statue, because it had been held in an unopened crate at the train station, but the judge brushed this argument aside. Then Milton argued that he had never agreed to all the changes and increases in cost that Donato had sought while the work progressed. In his testimony he said he only wanted a fountain, and the dispute was over a contract, not the artistic merit of the work.

When Donato got the chance to tell his side of the story, he described Milton Hershey as an eager patron of the arts who had asked for the sculptor's best work, regardless of the cost. It was Hershey, he said, who insisted the work be made bigger and he had approved both the final design and the expense. To emphasize how his sensibilities had been wounded, Donato bemoaned the fact that M.S. had placed a bronze female figure holding what looked like a coal scuttle on her shoulder on the granite base that had been reserved for his three nymphs.

"Why it's just plain hardware," said the artist. "It's iron plated with bronze and it looks as if he got it from the studios of the Bethlehem steel works."

An independent art expert hired to review the case said that Hershey's replacement statue was worth "just about as much as it would cost to pull her down and haul her to a river somewhere and dump her in." On the other hand, Donato's sculpture was, according to this critic, a masterpiece.

Before the trial was over, reporters would accompany the jury to Hershey on a field trip to see the statue. According to his own newspaper, Hershey got his first look at the piece on that field trip, when it was finally uncrated so the assembled jurors, court officials, reporters, and others could take in its sensual beauty.

In the end, the jury sided with Donato and his unwilling patron was forced to pay roughly 80 percent of the price the sculptor charged. On the afternoon when the trial ended, M.S. Hershey visited Mayor John K. Royal of Harrisburg and donated the statue to the city.

"If that thing was on my place I'd get mad every time I looked at it," M.S. told reporters. "If it is set up in Harrisburg, perhaps I can admire it."

Days later Hershey sounded a more magnanimous note in a letter he wrote to the mayor making the gift official. He wrote that the *Dance of Eternal Spring* was "highly praised by persons who are reputed to be competent to determine artistic value." For his part Donato called Hershey a man "who loves all that is beautiful and poetic." And "naturally," he added, that included *Dance of Eternal Spring*.

The statue eventually found its way to the garden at a local hospital, where nursing students developed a tradition of clothing the figures in lingerie every year on the night before graduation. But this did not quite end the story of M.S. Hershey and Giuseppe Donato. Over time the sculptor would become so convinced that he and his patron had parted on good terms that he would write requesting a new commission. In 1934 he suggested he place a copy of the original statue in a pool at Hershey Park. A bust of Milton "would be appropriate also," wrote the sculptor. M.S. thought otherwise.[6]

The contest over the *Dance of Eternal Spring* might have occurred no matter how M.S. Hershey felt in the months following Kitty's death. But there's little doubt that he was in a fighting mood. This showed as he went after an opponent much bigger than Giuseppe Donato. That year M.S. also attacked William Wrigley Jr., his fellow entrepreneur, on two different fronts. The battles would be both a matter of business and a certain personal animosity.

Something had happened between the men. According to longtime associate John Myers, Hershey believed that Wrigley had cheated him in some gambling game during a transatlantic crossing. He reported that M.S. vowed, "I am going to put Wrigley out of business." Hershey had also heard that Wrigley was planning to make chocolate. This was enough to turn the two men who had made parallel fortunes building national brands in the same era into a couple of overly competitive bulls.

Declaring that he would "fight fire with fire," M.S. sent his nephew Clayton Snavely to New York to buy the equipment and supplies to start making chewing gum. At the same time Milton also dispatched John Myers to Philadelphia to investigate the possibility of buying the Phillies baseball team to go up against Wrigley's Chicago Cubs. (Milton was enough of a baseball fan that he had gone to Philadelphia the year before to watch the Athletics get swept by the Boston Braves in the World Series.)

Ultimately, M.S. Hershey didn't even get up to bat in the baseball business. Myers, who was not impressed by the team's players, concluded they were not worth the price the owner wanted for the team—$350,000; on his advice the idea was scrapped. The truth of the matter was not what Myers suggested. The Phillies were a very good team. In 1915, they won the National League pennant but lost the series to the Boston Red Sox. The Phillies then featured the best pitcher the franchise has ever had, Grover Cleveland Alexander.

Although he never would challenge Wrigley in baseball, Hershey got much further with gum. In New York, Clayton Snavely met with an entrepreneur who had put together the equipment to make a new brand of gum but lacked the financing to follow through. Without ever mentioning the Hershey name, Snavely spent three or four days learning how to operate the machines. The seller took him to meet wholesalers, where Snavely placed an order for Mexican chicle, and they settled on a price of $500 for the whole lot of equipment.

The chewing gum equipment was delivered to the second floor of one of the factory buildings in Hershey. While it was being set up, Clayton Snavely went back on the road to take tours of three plants in New York where Beech Nut Gum was supposedly made. (One turned out to be a ketchup factory.) A week later he was back in Hershey, gearing up to produce what would be called Easy Chew gum.

Unlike the start of the chocolate works, Hershey had no trouble with getting the gum recipe right. The stuff that came off the small production line was so good that more equipment was bought to permit large-scale production. The only delay was caused by a marketing twist devised by William Murrie. He suggested that Easy Chew packs be loaded with six sticks, instead of the usual five. M.S. liked this idea well enough to order a time-consuming overhaul of the two dozen wrapping machines.

Once the business got rolling, it was good enough to occupy a hundred workers for fifty-four hours per week. Easy Chew (later called Hershey's Chewing Gum) would never overtake the other big brands, but Wrigley executives felt enough pressure that when the country entered World War I they turned to the government for some anticompetitive help. They demanded that Hershey pay a 20 percent surcharge on the special war tax applied to gum, because Hershey packs contained that one extra stick. The federal authorities agreed. Suddenly Hershey had to bear the cost of the additional tax, and the extra stick. This was the beginning of the end for Easy Chew. Though Hershey would continue to pester Wrigley for another six years, poor sales and problems with getting raw ingredients would eventually kill the brand.[8]

While baseball and chewing gum may have been the focus of M.S. Hershey's competitive passions, the main Hershey enterprises—the town, the chocolate company, and the industrial school—were continuing to grow as he had planned. A 4,000-seat convention hall, conceived when the Church of the Brethren inquired about holding a convention in Hershey, was opened in May 1915 and would become the site of hundreds of big events. At about the same time a new water supply, with a modern filtration plant, was put into operation for the town. Not yet completed, but under construction along Chocolate Avenue was the four-story Hershey Press Building, which would become the largest structure in the village, outside the factory.

With sales increasing by roughly 30 percent, to more than $10 million, the chocolate factory added five new stone and cement buildings, bringing the total to thirty-one, with another ten acres of floor space. The Hershey farms were expanded to 8,500 acres. The roughly seventy-five separate herds owned by M.S. were housed in spotless barns and tended by expert dairymen. They produced most of the milk the plant needed. Meanwhile, the industrial school had grown to sixty students and fourteen staff.

M.S. Hershey's success in all three realms—business, charity, and community building—made him stand out among the rich and ambitious men of his time. Andrew Carnegie certainly built a bigger industrial empire and gave vastly more money away, but he was at times a brutal employer and he made no attempt at community building. In fact, the areas where Carnegie's workers lived were notoriously dangerous, desolate, and dirty places befouled by his steel mills. Ford and Rockefeller had not tried to build utopian communities either, and George Pullman's railroad town, run like a feudal state, never recovered from the animosities of the 1894 strike.

Only Hershey was able to fulfill the progressive utopian ideal of using the fruits of capitalism to raise the spirits, and the standard of living, of all involved in his company. This exempted him from the populist attacks suffered by Rockefeller and Morgan, who were widely considered to be heartless and greedy, and guaranteed that muckrakers like Ida Tarbell would leave him alone. He also escaped the guilt that plagued Carnegie before he died in the summer of 1916. As biographer Peter Krass would note, in 1914 Carnegie would say during a visit to Braddock, Pennsylvania, site of his Edgar Thomson mill, that he expected to be found "not guilty" when God finally judged him. "Clearly," wrote Krass, "being guilty was on his mind" in Braddock, where the men who risked their lives as mill workers lived with their families in dismal conditions. It may also explain why Carnegie was so public in his philanthropy: history's inevitable verdict was on his mind.[9]

To be fair, any analysis of Hershey's success as a philanthropist, utopian schemer, and businessman must note that he enjoyed certain advantages.

For one thing, he got rich as the public and press began to turn on the super-wealthy, and he was able to latch on to progressivism to avoid the same fate. He also benefited from favorable economic trends. Chocolate sales increased steadily because the national population was growing, and all consumer brands—Heinz, Campbell, Ivory, Kodak, etc.—were getting stronger on the power of advertising and promotion. People were looking for consistent quality at a low price.

However, one thing that did make Hershey exceptional among the big brands was that M.S. hardly needed to advertise at all to build business. The most extensive promotion the company devised involved picture cards that were wrapped inside five-cent bars. Many showed farm scenes—barns, herds of cattle, a forlorn cow hooked up to a milking machine—but some promoted the town and park as tourist destinations.

One of the major draws at the park was the largest free private zoo in America. Begun in 1910 when Harry Lebkicher acquired three native deer, the collection had steadily grown to include native possums, squirrels, and birds. Trained bears became a big attraction in 1911 and were minor celebrities in town. Bob the bear appeared on a float during the tenth-anniversary parade and was sorely missed when he died a year later from liver disease. (His death was not as ironic as that of his mate, Mag, who passed away after eating a large quantity of Hershey Kisses, foil wrappers and all, that had been left by zoo visitors.)

By 1916 the zoo would acquire new bears and grow big enough to rival the collections found in major cities. It displayed hundreds of animals including a leopard and a two-year-old lion named Minnie. A lucky visitor might even see escaped monkeys scampering around the property. One, a rascal named Jake, managed to get out of his cage and steal a man's watch, but the head keeper got him to return it.

For locals, the monkeys of the Hershey zoo would become community pets of a sort. Children and adults would delight in the occasional escapes, when they might find a little primate in a front-yard tree or scampering across a lawn. In 1924 workers inside the sugar warehouse at the chocolate factory would follow tiny footprints in order to capture a monkey who had brought a little excitement to a workplace where efficient routine was the norm.[10]

Since his various creations in Hershey could be maintained and even grow larger without his daily involvement, M.S. was free to explore new territory. In early 1916, as cold winter bore down on Pennsylvania, he turned his attention to the south, to Cuba, and the possibility of a second empire in the land that his hero Teddy Roosevelt had turned into an emblem of American superiority.

In the years after the United States had intervened in Cuba's war of independence and prevailed against Spain, the island was first ruled directly from Washington and then became a protectorate subject to periodic interventions by the United States. The use of American troops on behalf of pro-Washington politicians was justified by the so-called Platt Amendment to the Cuban constitution, which was written by U.S. officials and adopted during the time when America ruled the island.

Under the Platt Amendment, Cuba had become a land of opportunity for American businessmen, especially those who cared about sugar. They bought up war-ravaged plantations and mills and quickly set about restoring them. It was, depending on your perspective, the rebirth of Cuba's essential industry or a hostile takeover conducted at bargain prices.

By 1906, investors from the United States had poured roughly $200 million into the Cuban sugar industry and the railroads that served it. Sixty percent of the island's rural property was owned by Americans, many of whom believed that God required them to bring civilization to a country that was both backward and immoral.

The idea that Cuba was a beautiful but tainted place had been planted in the American mind by a long line of writers, including Richard Henry Dana Jr. and Anthony Trollope. Artist Frederic Remington described Cubans as "in aggregate, the most ignorant people on earth." Much of what these observers described could have logically been blamed on the slave economy created in Cuba by the Spanish, who were of course white Europeans. But this fact was largely ignored in favor of colorful descriptions of apathetic blacks and "mulattos."[11]

The prevailing American attitude allowed politicians in Washington to describe the nation's adventure in Cuba in terms that were more religious than commercial. Albert Beveridge, a United States senator who was a fervent advocate of American empire, explained:

God has not been preparing the English-speaking, Teutonic people for a thousand years for nothing but vain and idle self-contemplation and self admiration. No! He has made us the master organizers of the world to establish system where chaos reigns. . . . This is the divine mission of

America, and it holds for us all the profit, all the glory, all the happiness
possible to man. We are the trustees of the world's progress, guardians of
the righteous peace.[12]

Senator Beveridge was seconded by businessmen who came back to America from Cuba exclaiming that it was the best place in the world for the
ambitious to seek their fortunes and diplomats who described vast tracts of
land available at prices that were far below values before the 1898 conflict.
These prices reflected the effects of war, but were also tied to a thirty-year
decline of the Cuban sugar business, which had failed in its competition
with beet sugar producers in Europe and the United States.

The investments made by Americans who snapped up Cuban plantations and mills paid off when World War I disrupted Europe's sugar industry, reducing its output from nearly 9 million tons per year to less than 4
million. As supplies dwindled, the small group of refiners and financiers
who dominated the world sugar trade began to raise prices.

In the United States, the flow of sugar was controlled by the heads of
two firms, American Sugar Refining and National Sugar Refining, who enjoyed what was, for all intents and purposes, a monopoly. These companies
processed sugarcane and sugar beets into granular sugar for industry and
households. In times of shortage, they held real power over buyers like soft
drink and candy manufacturers. The crisis that occurred during World
War I highlighted this problem and led many to wonder whether it might
be possible to break free of the sugar giants. It was at this moment that Milton Hershey left Pennsylvania for a vacation in the Caribbean.[13]

Formerly a mansion belonging to one of Havana's wealthiest families, the
Hotel Plaza, where M.S. Hershey began his Cuban adventure, was the best
tourist address in the old city. The Gran Teatro, top-flight restaurants,
nightclubs, and the casino were all nearby. Outside the streets teemed with
traffic as automobiles, newcomers to the city, turned narrow streets into
what one writer called "a savage beehive."[14]

Soon after he arrived, Milton summoned a Cuban he had met in the
States, Juan Batista Salo, who would become one of his guides. Salo then
recruited Angel Ortiz, who knew the sugar business. Together the three
men went to explore the countryside.

They set out in a 1914 Ford driven by a chauffeur called simply "the

Mexican," whom M.S. had hired at the Plaza. Traveling east along the coast, they passed through vast fields of sugarcane, where men with machetes cut the tall canes—some grew as high as fifteen feet—and then piled them on two-wheeled carts. Most of these cutters worked for landowners called "*colonos*," who in turn sold their cane to *centrales*, the local mills. There the juice was squeezed and ground out of the woody stalks to create syrup that was then evaporated and purified to produce raw, unrefined sugar.

After a stop for lunch, M.S. and his advisers inspected a small mill where cane was being pressed and ground. The place, called Central Puerto, was in bad shape, so they pressed on, toward the city of Matanzas. They planned to stop along the way to look at a ten-thousand-acre plantation and mill called Central San Juan Bautista.

Before they reached the second mill, the Ford ran into a stretch of road so thick with mud that it got stuck. The team of oxen that came to M.S. Hershey's rescue was supplied by F.F. Aguirre, who happened to own the San Juan facility. After they met along the muddy road, Aguirre took M.S. and the others to see his mill. It was larger than Central Puerto and a bit more modern, and it was available for less than half a million dollars.

Once M.S. Hershey decided to purchase the acreage and mill at San Juan, he searched for a site where he could build the tropical version of his perfect town in Pennsylvania. He found it near Santa Cruz del Norte, a town on the seacoast roughly midway between Havana and Matanzas. There in the Yumiri Valley, a picturesque region of small farms nestled between low-rising mountains, lay thousands of acres for sale at a good price.

The Yumiri Valley was considered one of the most beautiful places in Cuba, and it offered several spots that would suit a factory. But what caught Hershey's attention was a large spring-fed river with a steady flow. Just like Spring Creek in the Lebanon Valley, this water supply would nourish both the industry and the community that were to rise under the Hershey name.[15]

Although it was partly the product of one man's ego, the plan for Central Hershey Cuba also made business sense. Sugar prices were continuing to climb, and would double again, reaching more than nine cents per pound by 1918. With the war in Europe stalemated, the fighting could go on for years and make sugar all the more scarce. But with his own cane, his own workers, and his own mills, M.S. Hershey would not be held hostage to the swings in the international market. Just as he had secured a supply of milk in Pennsylvania, he could establish a reliable source of sugar—produced at a lower cost with Cuban labor—that would keep his chocolate works humming along in peacetime and in war.

As he tramped around the island, M.S. Hershey gradually recovered from the sadness that affected him after Kitty's death. He became, once again, the ambitious and energetic builder. Dressed in a white linen suit and a panama hat, he was much more vigorous than a typical man of fifty-nine. He took his coat off, slung it over his shoulder, and set a pace that younger men struggled to match. "We went tapping, with canes, to locate the underground spring," recalled Angel Ortiz. "He was the strongest old fellow I have ever seen."

Hershey told his companions stories about his past and discussed his plans for the future. The Cubans who worked for him generally liked him. Unlike many other rich men, he enjoyed the company of workingmen and he shared coffee and cigars with them. They were amused by his bits of homespun advice. "When you go out in the field," he once told Ortiz, "get a couple of soft-boiled eggs and some rice as the best thing for the stomach."[16]

Although the properties Hershey acquired on Cuba's northern shore were picturesque and productive there was one problem—transportation. The nearest railroad line passed far to the south, leaving the region dependent on roads that were often impassable. But in a country where costs were dramatically lower than they were in the United States, M.S. Hershey could afford to think big as he considered a solution. He decided he would build his own railroad—not just a trolley line but a full-scale rail line with 120 miles of track—to link his properties to the ports of Havana and Matanzas. Engineers, including Henry Herr of Lancaster, came from the United States to map the route and a plan was submitted to the national railroad commission.

Opposition to the planned Hershey railway came from a British-owned company that controlled all the tracks in Havana and much of the surrounding countryside. The commission brushed aside United Railway's claim that Hershey was violating its franchise to provide service in the region out of an "evil desire for competition contrary to law." But while the British couldn't stop the new line, they were able to deny Hershey a link to the city of Havana itself. His railroad would have to terminate in Casa

Blanca, on the eastern side of Havana Bay. There the shallow water would make it impossible to dock oceangoing freighters. Hershey would have to use smaller vessels to deliver his sugar to ships in the harbor. In his dreams, M.S. imagined solving this problem by building a bridge or tunnel across the bay, but this idea never got much past the talking stage.

Construction of the Hershey Cuban Railway, the first electric line in the country, was to start in Santa Cruz. With Ortiz managing the work, and M.S. pushing him to complete the project as quickly as possible, rails were ordered from America. They would be transported by ship to Santa Cruz. These supplies could be off-loaded with the labor and equipment available locally, but Hershey worried about how Ortiz would handle something as massive as a locomotive. "We will pull it with our teeth," explained Ortiz, and his boss was satisfied.

After a few sections were built, Ortiz rented a team of bulls to help wrestle the first cars onto the new track. Then he used the same animals to pull the cars down the new tracks after they were loaded with supplies. Until a steam locomotive was in place to take over the job, the bulls kept pace with the men who built the bed, laid the ties and rails, and drove the spikes.

The matériel demands of World War I, which America would enter in April 1917, made it harder to acquire steel and other commodities, but not impossible. M.S. was able to push forward the construction of the railroad, the new plant, and the town at Central Hershey, all at once. Once again, Milton Hershey built the best houses around—about 180 in all—with modern utilities. He set them on paved streets that were carefully landscaped with flowers and trees. He built sports fields, a golf course, and a store where workers and their families could get food and household goods. Eventually he would also establish a free school, a hotel, and a medical clinic. All of it was intended to benefit his workers and other locals.

"Forget the profits," he said to those who managed the store he created to serve Central Hershey Cuba. "I don't want to lose much either, but I want the store to help my people."

Eager to take advantage of efficient technologies, Hershey decided that the entire development would be served by a new electric system with its own generators, substations, and a grid of power lines. Electricity would also be supplied at a low cost to Central Hershey residents and to villages that were close enough to the railway to tap into the lines.

In promising electricity to his neighbors, and building a railroad available to all passenger and freight traffic, Hershey created enormous goodwill among the people in the region, where the liberal political party dominated. This became important in 1917, when American force was used to suppress an armed insurrection that followed the fraudulent re-election of conservative president Mario García Menocal. Although liberal rebels destroyed the property of other American companies, Hershey's holdings were untouched. By then people in Cuba had come to regard him as "a benevolent old gentleman who liked to give money away." [17]

The projects that M.S. Hershey set in motion in Cuba in 1916 marked the start of a third kind of life, after the ones he had created in Pennsylvania and then as a sophisticated traveler in the United States and Europe. In Cuba he would be free from the gossips of Lancaster and Hershey and yet at home. He would have his businesses, his town, and his pleasures all in one place. The island became perhaps his favorite place in all the world. And whenever he went there, people back in Pennsylvania were left to wonder when, if ever, he might return. Once, in 1917, while the Founder was in Cuba, the *Hershey Press* reported on its front page: The chief question in Hershey for the past three weeks has been: "When will Mr. Hershey be back?" Of course no one knows. No one ever knows, for it is the habit of Mr. Hershey to drop in from anywhere whenever he wants to.

Although Cuba agreed with M.S. Hershey, his Caribbean adventure caused some concern at company headquarters. William Murrie, for one, would never be very supportive of the whole sugar enterprise because he worried about the financial burden it might create. But the marketplace seemed to confirm that M.S. was on the right track. In early 1917 Germany announced that all ships in the Atlantic, including vessels loaded with sugar, would be subject to submarine attacks. That spring America entered the war. With shipping in question, and the U.S. Army gearing up to feed a million soldiers, sugar prices continued to rise.

The Hershey Chocolate Company could benefit from the mobilization as long as it had the supplies to keep operating. The firm was assured access to sugar when the army ordered huge quantities of Hershey's cocoa and more than 2 million chocolate bars. In order to meet the contract, the company called for volunteers to help wrap and box the bars. Three hundred women turned out to do the job.

War was good for the company's books. Annual sales increased from $11.7 million in 1916 to $20 million in 1918, the last year of the conflict. Townspeople got into the spirit of the war effort, raising money for the Red Cross. Milton did his part by giving three of his own Packard automobiles to relief agencies.[18]

Although the war made travel difficult—German submarines were also active in the Caribbean—M.S. continued to go to Cuba, usually by way of Key West. In March 1917 he met there with Henry Ford, who had arrived aboard his yacht, a five-hundred-ton steamer called the *Sialia*. Long interested in ethanol, because it was clean burning and beyond the control of the oil industry, Ford was exploring the idea of buying sugarcane plantations and a mill as the first step toward producing the fuel himself.

It was not uncommon at the time for American millionaires to meet and play together in Havana. Those who did business on the island, where the weather was eternally springlike, enjoyed making personal surveys of their investments. Those who did not own property in Cuba came for the sunshine, luxury hotels, casinos, and other diversions. In some seasons a tycoon was as likely to bump into one of his peers at the Plaza in Havana as he would have at the Plaza in New York.

After they met in Havana, Milton and Henry Ford sailed the coast aboard the *Sialia*, and then went ashore so that M.S. could take Ford on a tour of his growing island empire. They found that the new railroad was far enough along that a steam engine had replaced the snorting bulls acquired by Angel Ortiz and that many miles of track had been finished. The small mill at Central San Juan Bautista was busily grinding sugarcane. And construction of the big new mill at Central Hershey was well under way.

The two men, each of whom had turned an idea into an icon, became friends but they had their disagreements. They both liked to give advice, but neither enjoyed receiving it. On one of their drives, they were met by men who warned them there might be robbers ahead. Ford wanted to turn back. M.S. suggested they press on. "We both need the publicity," he joked. "What a headline it would make: Ford and Hershey Captured by Bandits!"

Ford was not amused by his companion's sense of humor, but as a master of efficiency he must have appreciated Hershey's design for his new industry. Instead of shipping unfinished sugar to the United States for refining, Hershey would do everything on the island, becoming the first in Cuba to handle every step, from planting canes to bagging granular sugar.

With a modern facility, and a refinery workforce that earned a fraction of their counterparts in America, he could make his own sugar at a cost far below what he might pay to American refiners. Not only would he free himself from their monopoly, he would beat them at their own business.

Hershey planned for other innovations that would save him even more money. For example, instead of moving the sugar in heavy jute bags, which were expensive to purchase and required costly manual labor, M.S. would use special rail cars, designed as hoppers, to transport his product by rail the way that mines moved coal, sand, and salt. (This idea may have been borrowed from Europe, where all sugar was handled this way.) New freight services that ferried rail cars from Cuba to the Florida Coast Railroad terminal in Key West made it possible to load a car once in Cuba and send it directly to any destination in North America.

The potential savings Hershey could achieve by producing his own sugar, refining it more fully, and shipping it in special cars grew month by month as the world price for this commodity continued to increase. Other American companies saw the value in the Cuban sugar business and rushed to buy mills and plantations and consolidate them into more efficient operations. Output per mill grew exponentially, as did the size of the Cuban sugar crop. Investors from the United States also poured money into local railroads and American banks, including Hershey's preferred lender, the National City Bank, set up dozens of branches on the island.[19]

Between the bankers, the railroad men, and the sugar kings, the expatriates made up a very wealthy little society that included a great many men who traveled on their own with plenty of money to spend. To them Havana was the place that writer Basil Woon would soon describe in a guidebook titled When It's Cocktail Time in Cuba. Casinos to rival Monte Carlo beckoned with baccarat tables and roulette, while restaurants, burlesque houses, and bordellos offered every variation imaginable to satisfy a man's appetite. Although the city had just 250,000 people, Havana had more than 200 brothels, and prostitution was so openly practiced that the government operated a small hospital devoted entirely to the care of those who worked in the trade.

As he oversaw the construction and then operation of his tropical enterprises, M.S. allowed himself many of the sensual luxuries Cuba had to offer. He had a taste for Cuban cigars, tropical fruits, and champagne. But his real vice was gambling. As time passed, he would spend hundreds of thousands of dollars in casinos and at racetracks. He would also become so comfortable with who he was in Cuba that he made no effort to hide his habits.

When John Myers and his wife came to visit from Pennsylvania, M.S. brought them to one of Havana's casinos. (If it was his favorite, the Nacional, all he had to do was flash a hand signal to make a bet.) After the Myerses had seen the casino, Hershey sent them off with his chauffeur to a nightclub known for an exotic floor show featuring dozens of dancing woman. With each dance, the ladies appeared wearing fewer clothes, until the master of ceremonies announced that they would be nude in the next number.

"Of course my wife did not approve of that," recalled Myers, "and she made me leave."

The Myerses made their way back to the casino, where John's wife gave Hershey several pieces of her mind. M.S. waited patiently until she was quiet, and then asked, "Are you through?"

"Yes," she said.

"What's your lucky number?"

"I don't approve of gambling," she said.

Hershey persisted, and she finally relented, telling him she thought the number 25 might be lucky. He went to the roulette wheel and put $100 down for her on 25. The wheel went round and finally slowed enough to let the ball drop just one space from Mrs. Myers's pick, on number 24.

"Now, Mrs. Myers," said Hershey, "if you wouldn't have been so ugly to me, you would have won thirty-five hundred dollars." [20]

Like the Myerses, a long line of Hershey's most prominent citizens would make the pilgrimage to Cuba to experience the pleasures of the Caribbean and glimpse, if only for a moment, M.S. in full tropical flower. It would become his routine to spend most of each winter and spring on the island, returning to Pennsylvania for summer and autumn.

This pattern meant that M.S. missed certain key events back home. In February 1918, for example, a fire broke out in the cocoa storage department in Building 25. As men rushed to seal off the room where the fire started, a violent explosion sent them running. Eventually the blaze destroyed much of the building and 2 million pounds of cocoa. Hours after it was put out, chocolate-colored water continued to drain out of the building. Milton could have done little to change events that day, but he would have been amused to see the street turn brown with cocoa. Later in the year, M.S. would miss out on another big event, the Hershey premiere of D.W. Griffith's *The Birth of a Nation*, which played in a theater in the park. Regarded by many as a landmark in racist propaganda, Griffith's three-hour film was also the first American epic movie and a showing meant that Hershey was a cultured and sophisticated place.

When he was home in Pennsylvania, M.S. left day-to-day management of his enterprises to trusted executives and focused his attention on major projects. The most important of these he researched and carried out in secret. On November 13, 1918, he secretly placed every bit of his Hershey Chocolate Company stock into a trust benefiting the industrial school. Under the rules of the trust, the money generated by these shares, which were worth more than $60 million, could be spent only on the school for orphans in the town of Hershey.

To get a sense of how big this gift was, it helps to compare the Hershey company's value with other big consumer product manufacturers. A year after Milton made his gift, the Coca-Cola Company was sold by its founder for a total of $25 million.

This one act would create something unique in both philanthropy and capitalism. It made the industrial school, under its trustees, the majority owners of a national company that was poised to double in size, many times over, in the decades to come. The cash generated by this arrangement would make the orphan boys some of the most financially secure children in the world and guarantee the school the funds necessary to grow within the boundaries set by the terms of the trust.

At the same time, the gift set up an unusual relationship between the industrial school and the townspeople of Hershey. The school would be the majority shareholder in all Hershey enterprises, from the factory to the park and the department store. Taxes were low, and life was good in Hershey in part because the company—actually, the school that owned it— subsidized services. For as long as M.S. lived and controlled the board of the trust, this was not likely to change. But anyone who looked further into the future could imagine a time when the school's power might trouble the people who made their lives in Hershey.[21]

A BETTING MAN

10 Most of us will never know what it feels like to place a multimillion-dollar bet based on a personal view of the unknowable future. Milton S. Hershey knew that feeling in January 1919 as the giant mill at Central Hershey Cuba began grinding its first crop of sugarcane. Trains had begun to run on his new electric railway the previous September, and the price of a pound of sugar was heading past twenty cents. It appeared that there was no better business in the world than making sugar in Cuba.

Producers weren't the only ones benefiting from the price run-up. Their profits rippled through the island economy creating what was termed the *"vacas gordas"* or "fat cows" years. During this period bank deposits rose an astounding 1,000 percent. Annual imports of goods from the United States reached the $1 billion mark and tax payments made to the Cuban government increased dramatically. One product of this windfall would be a new presidential palace, built at a cost of $3.75 million and outfitted with $100,000 worth of bed linen and a $60,000 painting done by one of President Menocal's cousins.

The burst of wealth had its greatest effect in Havana, where the shops on Calle Obispo began stocking luxuries never before seen in Cuba. The newly rich crowded the casinos and theaters and scrambled to join new social clubs. Real estate values rose so high that building lots in so-so neighborhoods fetched $100,000.

Nothing illustrated the change wrought by the sugar wealth better than the evolution of the traditional evening *paseo*, the promenade enjoyed by Havana's elite. A few years earlier, people still came out in elegant two-wheeled carriages called *volantes*. Now, every day at six o'clock, the seaside avenue called the Malecon was filled with bug-eyed Rolls-Royce convertibles and Hispano-Suizas. Wives and daughters rode in the backseats, dressed in gowns from Paris. Husbands and fathers sat in front, beside their chauffeurs as they headed toward the Prado, a wide boulevard with a park-like median that was lined with nineteenth-century mansions.[1]

The bubbling society that emerged in Cuba's sugar boom was called the Dance of the Millions, and almost everyone caught the rhythm. Besides the flood tide of money, the optimism that washed over the island in 1919 was inspired by the end of the war in Europe and the world's gradual return to normal life. After disrupting shipping for fours years, German U-boats no longer prowled the Atlantic and ocean liners could again safely cross the sea. Taking advantage of the peace, M.S. Hershey returned to Europe for the first time since Kitty's death.

From September through December 1919, Milton traveled to places where he and Kitty had enjoyed some of the best moments of their life together. He was in Paris in October, Marseilles in November, and Monte Carlo in December. He didn't leave much of a record of these visits, but he enjoyed himself in the casinos on the Riviera. His financial files from this period note frequent letters of credit posted for $1,000 or $2,000 over the course of the month he was there.

Milton returned to the United States when he heard that his mother had been stricken with pneumonia. He found that she was tended by a pair of nurses. One was a long trusted friend of the family named Katherine Baker. She had often cared for Fanny, accompanying her to High Point for Sunday dinners and on drives in the country. Sometimes they read the Bible together. The other nurse, the one who actually directed Fanny's care, was a newcomer from Baltimore. Later Katherine Baker would recall her with a tone of suspicion.

"Mrs. Hershey didn't talk much in the end because her nurse doped her" with an opiate called morphia, which the nurse hid in a drawer, said Baker. "This nurse told me she wanted a six-week patient and when that was up she was not interested in Mother Hershey. I could not do anything because I was not in charge, but I knew what was going on."

Five weeks into her illness, in a time before antibiotic cures, Fanny died. The funeral was held at her home across from the chocolate factory and her body was buried in the new Hershey cemetery in a grave next to Catherine's. Milton would soon order that his father's remains be exhumed from the old family cemetery and placed in the same plot. It may not have been something that Fanny wanted, but her son would make sure the family that was often divided in life was together in death.

Of the four people who had known Milton and helped him from his start in the candy business, only Harry Lebkicher, who had been at Hershey's side through failures and success, remained. Old Lebbie, as he was now called, would live another nine years.

Always difficult, in old age Lebkicher became an even more peculiar and crotchety man. He had trouble keeping his clothes clean and his attempts to spit tobacco juice generally left his shirtfronts stained brown. He wandered the town and factory, taking notes on what he saw and warning others, "By God, I am going to tell Mr. Hershey." Eventually Milton would hire a man to shadow Lebkicher around town to make sure he didn't get into any trouble. Lebbie once got so annoyed and confused by this guardian that he threatened to shoot him.[2]

In the months after his mother died, Milton would divide his time between New York, where contracts for future sugar supplies were traded, and Cuba, where he produced the stuff. Hershey was trying "to do the same with sugar that he had done before with milk," noted Tomas Cabrera, his accountant in Cuba. "He wanted to be independent."

The plants at Central San Juan and Central Hershey would produce more than 30 million pounds of sugar in 1920, but this figure fell far short of the chocolate factory's needs. Looking forward to the coming years, M.S. searched for more property and another "central." He found and bought a steam-powered mill at a place called Rosario. It came with a beautiful old hacienda with tropical gardens and a driveway lined with towering royal palms. The cost was reported to be $8 million.

Though the Rosario mill promised a big jump in future production, the harvest was almost finished when Hershey made the purchase, so it wouldn't meet his immediate needs. To guarantee that the chocolate works would be fed through the months ahead, M.S. turned to the New York traders. He bought millions of dollars' worth of future contracts to purchase substantial amounts of sugar. Although he might have tried to cope with the high price of sugar by switching to other sweeteners, as other manufacturers did, Hershey refused to risk the quality of his product. "He never flirted with that question," recalled W.S. Lambie, one of Hershey's bankers. "He made the best he could."

The prices on Hershey's sugar futures contracts were high—some were over twenty-six cents per pound—but M.S. had studied the market intently. He believed that when the time came for him to take delivery of the sugar, others would be paying even more on the open market. This confidence in the face of risk was consistent with a man who loved to gamble with his own money and his business. Who else would build a chocolate factory before he even knew how to make the stuff?

This time, however, M.S. Hershey failed to understand the game he was playing. Unlike other futures players, he bought contracts with the idea of actually taking delivery of the sugar. Most traders never want the commodity they agree to buy. Instead, they use purchase contracts as a bet that the price will rise. If it goes up beyond their contract limit, they sell it to someone else at a premium. Their profit is made buying and selling contracts, not actual sugar.

As the deadline for Milton's contracts approached, a trader did make an offer for them. He could have accepted the deal and suffered just a small loss. But he was convinced that he had figured out the market trend. He knew that prices would continue to climb and make his contracts all the more valuable. He refused to let go of them.

Anyone who saw Havana in the spring of 1920, where money from the sugar boom filled cash registers and bank vaults, would have likely made the same choice. Few places on earth ever offered more grand displays of confidence, wealth, and extravagance. New luxury liners operated by the Ward Line and the United Fruit Company arrived in the harbor bearing hordes of wealthy Americans who were seeking relief from the restrictions of Prohibition, which had just taken effect back home. They spent enormous amounts of money on hotels, food and drink, gambling, and other vices. Racetracks, boxing promoters, and even the local opera brought the greatest talents in the world to perform.

Havana was so exciting, so filled with pleasures and distractions, that spring that it was hard to recognize that the boom was just about to end. In fact, the developments that would cause the market to crash were taking place in the eastern Cuban province of Camagüey and Oriente territory. In this region, where sugar had never been grown, speculators were carving out vast new plantations—leveling priceless forests of mahogany, rosewood, and ebony as they went—and building enormous new processing plants. Like M.S. Hershey, the investors behind these projects had seen that huge profits could be made in sugar and they intended to cash in.

They were encouraged by the construction of new railways that ended the isolation that had previously limited development in the region. Their efforts raised the value of U.S. investments in Cuban sugar to a dizzying $1.2 billion, as Americans controlled just over half of the island's sugar mills.

For a brief time, the new *centrales* and plantations thrived, and even the tenant farmers who became cane cutters when their plots were sold off earned some of the spoils. Then, in the summer of 1920, the world suddenly realized that the sugar shortage was over. Indeed, there was such an oversupply that, in the words of one observer, "the market, satiated with sugar, turned sick with nausea and fright."[3]

Beginning in June, from a height of almost twenty-three cents a pound, the price of Cuban sugar rapidly declined. By the start of 1921 it had sunk to less than four pennies per pound. It would go even lower in April as the U.S. government, concerned about the domestic sugar industry, put an extra tariff on imports from the island. As the Dance of the Millions ended, Cubans began the years of "*vacas flacas*" or "skinny cows." Local banks that had lent money to plantations and mill owners based on the record-high price of sugar collapsed. Farm workers saw their wages slashed. A few of the once rich men who found themselves suddenly bankrupt killed themselves.

The Cuban people, who had become dependent on the single-crop economy, would suffer the most from the sugar debacle. But foreign speculators were also affected. Having agreed to pay as much as twenty-six cents for a pound of sugar, Milton S. Hershey found himself holding some very expensive contracts. In 1920, these contracts pushed the Hershey Chocolate Company, which had a $6 million profit the year before, into the red for the first time in its history. M.S. knew that he alone was to blame for the crisis and, while he seemed unfazed to most who saw him in this time, he took the losses to heart.

With the brokers who had handled his futures trades demanding to be paid immediately, Hershey was forced to turn to National City Bank to help him avoid losing his company. (Because National City owned mills in Cuba, its officers were familiar with the industry.) The bank handled a $20 million bond issue and took a $10 million mortgage on his factory. Hard as it was for Hershey to accept this debt, it was not the worst consequence of his sugar escapade. The worst blow was the arrival of a National City overseer named R.J. DeCamp.[4]

• • •

In the annals of Hershey history, R.J. DeCamp of the National City Bank would become the most reviled enemy of all time. He was, in the words of a company executive named Samuel Hinkle, a "smug and conceited Wall Street snob." Of course Hershey loyalists had reason to resent DeCamp. Nevertheless, the man's colleagues at the bank agreed with this assessment.

"He was the kind of man who would walk in with spats, and he sat on his tail and directed everybody and do [sic] little himself," recalled Stanley Russell, who worked with DeCamp at National City. "That man had the opportunity of a lifetime," added Russell, suggesting that DeCamp could have turned his assignment into a high-level appointment at the Hershey company. "He ruined it by the way he conducted himself."

Even if he had been the most effective bank-imposed overseer in the history of American finance, DeCamp would have found little he could do to improve the operation of the chocolate factory. Over the years the company had designed new machinery that brought efficiency and automation to many stages of the process. (A machine that wrapped Hershey Kisses, installed in 1921, was a big step.) At the same time the company's workers were devoted to the Founder and had stepped up their efforts when they learned of the company's financial troubles.

The crisis had been announced by M.S., John Snyder, and William Murrie on a Monday in November, when they met with nearly fifty of the company's most prominent employees and a few town leaders at a luncheon in the Hershey café. Milton predicted a period of "readjustment" as together they "put our house in order." Murrie called for loyalty in a time of emergency and Snyder tied the company's trouble to postwar economic conditions.

The three men wanted to inspire their midlevel managers to lead workers and townspeople to make every effort possible to pull the company out of its financial trouble. But it was Milton who put things in emotional terms. He said that his goal was not personal wealth but the preservation of his school for orphans. Toward that end, he asked that the others consider him a fellow citizen, not a ruler, and the business "our business," not his alone.

With everyone aware of the stakes—their jobs and their town were in peril—those who worked in the various Hershey businesses rallied to the cause. R.J. DeCamp could nitpick the factory's managers to save a nickel here or there, but he wasn't going to make any big moves that would suddenly improve the bottom line. All the chocolate company needed to do was produce more and sell more.

DeCamp was no more helpful to Hershey in Cuba. Sugar was a new business for the Hershey outfit and it was easy to see, in retrospect, that M.S. had created a huge problem as he built his island empire and played the futures market. But here too the fix would not be a matter of one man making a few bold suggestions. Especially not this man, DeCamp. When he got to Cuba, he set himself up in an expensive suite at one of Havana's most luxurious hotels. This set off an immediate conflict, as M.S. demanded he move out. M.S. won this fight, forcing DeCamp to live at Rosario, and made it clear he wanted to be free of the interloper as soon as possible.

Freedom came more quickly than anyone should have expected. Hershey chocolate sales increased by about 30 percent between 1921 and 1923. After a single down year due to the sugar crisis, the company was again profitable. One measure of this success: payments made by a newly devised profit-sharing plan for employees totaled more than 20 percent of their annual pay. In 1924 the figure would jump to 35 percent as sales reached almost $38 million. Satisfied that its investment was secure, National City pulled DeCamp out of the company and returned control to its founder.

Extra effort by everyone from the Hershey executive office to the loading dock had helped the company's quick recovery from Milton's misadventure in sugar. But Hershey also profited, once again, from a positive business cycle. In the postwar years the American economy grew at an astounding rate as mass production lowered prices and higher wages empowered consumers. The classic example was Ford, where the $5 per day plan reduced worker turnover and helped drive down the cost of each car. It also put upward pressure on overall wages, making it possible for millions to buy expensive items like cars. By 1929 industrial production in America would be double what it had been before the war.

Efficient manufacturing methods, which Hershey also adopted, were just part of the equation that boosted business in the Roaring Twenties. Smart managers had also embraced a new discipline, taught at business schools, that combined sales, advertising, and distribution into one big job called "marketing." Modern companies used marketing to train the public to expect quality and fair prices from prominent national brands. This was especially true for a vast new category of consumer products—packaged specialty foods—that hadn't even existed a few decades earlier. Treats like cookies, soda pop, and candy were a big part of this trend, and Hershey was right in the middle of it.

Evidence of Hershey's marketing success can be found in one of the first studies of brands ever done. In the early twenties, two professors at New York University surveyed more than a thousand people to discover the power of product names. In chocolate Hershey was first; other category leaders were Kellogg in cereal, Ford in cars, and Ivory in soap. Hershey came out second in cocoa, still trailing Walter Baker's company in Massachusetts. But, as the authors of the study noted, Baker had a one-hundred-year head start in the cocoa business, and since the 1870s the company had advertised "continuously and persistently."

In contrast, the Hershey company tended to promote the idea that it had earned its place in the heart of the consumer by simply offering a quality product at a fair price. Let William Wrigley put signs on every one of the country's 62,000 street, subway, and elevated cars and a flashing sign in Times Square (he did both these things); M.S. Hershey said he didn't need such unseemly hucksterism. He had quality.[5]

Except for some billboards, Hershey didn't use a great deal of paid advertising to sell chocolate bars. But that doesn't mean he was silent. While it spent comparatively little on consumer-oriented advertising for chocolate, the company made a great effort to promote everything else—the town, the school for orphans, the park and resort facilities—that bore the Hershey name. Much of this was done indirectly, as the company told its story to journalists.

Year after year, out-of-town writers were welcomed to tour Hershey and they returned the kindness with glowing reports of a happy people and contented cows. (By 1923, the three thousand people of Hershey were outnumbered by cows five to one.) No mention was made of the prejudice experienced by some Italians in Hershey, a problem that would be widely acknowledged in later years. And none of these articles even hinted at the fact that some workers were not happy with the wages paid by Hershey and the favoritism practiced by his managers.

In the early 1920s, some workers at Hershey were beginning to consider organizing a union to challenge a hiring and pay system that was open to cronyism and abuse. A machine operator named Ignazio Romanucci con-

tacted the revolution-minded Industrial Workers of the World to discuss organizing the factory. He had experienced enough bigotry to wonder if he
was being treated fairly and to be wary, in general, of American-style capitalism. But he concluded that the Wobblies, which had been involved in
several ferocious strikes, were too radical for Hershey. And many years
would pass before the idea of starting a union at the chocolate factory attracted real support.[6]

Meanwhile the press would continue to describe the Hershey company
as an ideal employer and the town as a bucolic paradise. If a little extra
sweetening was needed, the reporters could always turn to the orphans at
the industrial school, each of whom had been saved from poverty by M.S.

For the most part M.S. occupied the background in these stories, appearing to be a kindly and devoted benefactor who said he was shy about
publicity. Since he hungrily devoured what was written about him, this attitude was a pose. But it was good for business. For one thing, people prefer to buy candy from a nice man. For another, his reputed shyness and his
emphasis on service to others connected Hershey chocolate to an ideal
that is much bigger, and much more important, than any consumer item.
The name Hershey came to represent small town America at its wholesome best.

The *Hershey Press* contributed to this image building with a steady
stream of articles that explained why the company town was a utopia. A
typical piece, headlined THE IDEAL COMMUNITY, claimed that the town of
Hershey was "one of the healthiest centers in the United States" and "has
never had a criminal case."

The health claim is impossible to test, but the point about crime was exaggerated. Criminal incidents occurred in Hershey, even if they didn't become active cases for investigation. For example, when members of the
so-called Crusty Gang were arrested for burglary, the paper noted that M.S.
gave them "a good lecture" and then let them go. Later, in February 1924
the *Press* noted a Ku Klux Klan cross burning at the corner of Cocoa and
Chocolate Avenues. The Klansmen were reported to have come from elsewhere, and there is no record of an investigation into the incident, which occurred while townspeople attended a dance celebrating Washington's
birthday. At the time the Klan was at the forefront of a rising national anti-
immigrant movement that was often focused on Catholics such as the Italians of Hershey. The Klan was also a growing power in much of the South
and Midwest, where it controlled the Republican party in some states.[7]

Of course, Hershey wasn't unusual in its overweening effort to put the best face on everything. Hometown boosterism was in fashion, and excessive claims were considered an acceptable, even charming little sin. Fortunately no one had to stretch the truth when it came to the biggest news Hershey would ever make. On November 9, 1923, *The New York Times* revealed at the top of its front page that M.S. had invested his entire fortune in the industrial school's effort to save orphan boys. Other rich men had given more to charity, but none had focused their wealth on a single small institution serving such worthy children.

The article offered some good news alongside ominous page-one reports on Adolf Hitler's beer hall putsch in Munich. It noted that the bequest had been made in secret five years earlier and that it was confirmed with some reluctance. It painted M.S. as a visionary who had raised worker pay with profit sharing long before Henry Ford instituted his famous bonus system. It also explained that Milton had been "a poor boy" and that he had directed that the earnings of his corporations be used to improve the business or be paid to the school trust for the benefit of an endless number of poor boys.

After the story was out, a *Times* writer named James C. Young visited Hershey — he called it "the town of smiles" — to research a longer article that appeared about a week later. He toured the community, visited the factory, and went to High Point to conduct a long interview with the Founder, who spoke so softly that Young could hear the ticking of a clock in the background.

In this piece, the typically quiet M.S. spoke about his life and philosophy in greater detail than he ever had before, or ever would in the future. Some of what he said was Hershey boilerplate. He reiterated the importance of making quality goods that sold at fair prices. But when he turned to matters of human nature and the meaning of wealth, he showed himself to be an unusual kind of capitalist, one who saw that too often America failed to keep its promises.

To his mind, most people were capable of learning and doing almost anything. "The trouble with this world is a lack of opportunities," said Hershey. He called for a "leveling . . . in the matter of opportunity" because "it is the place where a man starts, more than where he ends that counts." To illustrate this point, he noted that early childhood can determine a boy's fate, and that many of the inmates in American prisons had been youngsters "who never had a chance."

With his industrial school and the trust he created to fund it, M.S. had attempted to improve the starting point for hundreds, and eventually thousands, of boys—he called them "the little fellows"—who would otherwise enter adult life many steps behind. His compassion for these children showed as he compared orphaned girls, who are "useful in the home," with boys, who "are likely to be looked upon as a nuisance. The more spirit they have the bigger nuisance from that standpoint. So I want to help them."

M.S. was prepared to help the little fellows beyond their school years. He created a community where they might live as adults and an industry where they could find work under better conditions than were found elsewhere. Hershey was troubled by the friction between workers and industry, and he laid much of the responsibility for that on the bosses. "In many of our big industries they spend a lot of time rubbing up the machinery and the brass doorknobs. Here we are trying to rub up the human element, and we do not have brass doorknobs. Almost every problem of business depends on the human side.

"What business needs is a better understanding of the worker," he continued. "I believe we are improving, going a long way ahead all the time, but so much is yet to be done that we cannot mend our ways too fast."

These were the kind of words that made other great industrialists cringe. But they were not the most radical of Milton's statements. He saved those for the subject of wealth, and its purpose. M.S. had come to believe that his money should be used for the greater good. He had placed his business in the school trust to make sure he could continue saving boys and to keep it out of the hands of those who might move the factory and deprive his community of jobs. Finally, he said, he didn't believe that the rich should be allowed to simply pass their wealth on to heirs. "The inheritance of great fortunes is a bad thing," he said. "Let us not put any curbs on the creation of fortunes, but we should limit their inheritance, I believe."[8]

Then, as now, important articles in the *Times* inspired imitation. The day after it appeared, newspapers around the world published the news of Hershey's great gift. And for months and years to follow, newspapers and magazines across the country played up the story of the chocolate millionaire who gave his fortune to orphan boys.

The only criticism in any of these reports came from child welfare experts who wondered if the terms of the trust, which allowed only institutional care for white orphan boys, were too restrictive. For example, two weeks after the endowment was made public, Homer Folks of the National Conference of Social Work noted that the number of orphans in America was declining and that "home care is better." Few others rose to question M.S. Hershey's choices, and Folks's opinions did not change things in Hershey.

Critics might find fault with M.S. Hershey's methods, but no one publicly challenged his intentions. Although his own comments on the gift were always brief, M.S. made it clear that he had been moved by long-standing concerns about the purpose of wealth. "When a man gets very rich, he either gets very selfish or his money worries him," he said. By divesting himself, M.S. had simplified his own life and set in motion a force for good that would long outlive him.

Added together, the stories painted a picture of an exceedingly generous man who, unlike the giants of the Gilded Age, got rich without exploiting workers, destroying competitors, raping the environment, manipulating stock, or purchasing politicians. If it's a rule that behind every great fortune lies a great crime, M.S. Hershey was the exception. He was the good millionaire and, as he moved ahead with plans to increase enrollment to a thousand boys, reporters could write only the most glowing accounts.

Typical was *McClure's* magazine, which published a profile that consumed all or part of eleven pages and contained half a dozen pictures, including one of Milton, at age seven, wearing a little black suit and holding a straw hat in his right hand.

McClure's reported that M.S. planned to expand the school from its enrollment of 124 to 1,000. And the magazine quoted Hershey at length as he explained his philosophy for training orphan boys. "We do not expect to turn out a race of college professors," he said. Instead, "we want to help the boys of the masses to become good American citizens—farmers, artisans and some of them perhaps businessmen ultimately—leaders in the mercantile, industrial and social life of their communities."

Like so many other journalists, the writer for *McClure's* made sure to tell the rags-to-riches story of M.S. Hershey's life and he offered a breathless description of the town. But Edward Woolley went beyond most reporters to compare the life of a working-class Hershey family with that of those in other small towns and big cities. In the Pennsylvania utopia, rents were remarkably low and the houses were surprisingly modern. This allowed people to live comfortably while saving to buy houses for themselves. (This process was aided by Hershey's annual profit-sharing checks.) These pleasant circumstances meant that at a time when fewer than half of Americans owned their own homes, three-quarters of the families in Hershey, including many who got by on meager incomes, did. Woolley explained, "I found numerous families of plain factory workmen living in trim little houses, some of them which had cost $5,000 or more. These are the same general class of people who in most industrial cities live in disreputable tenements or tumble-down shanties, surrounded by hideous litter and filth."

Considering Woolley's description of Hershey as a working-class paradise, it's a wonder he didn't inspire ten thousand readers to move there. Of course, short of going to Hershey, anyone who wanted to feel connected to the place and its noble cause could just buy a chocolate bar and know that the company's profit was going to the orphans. It made people feel good spending their nickels.[9]

The good feelings associated with M.S. Hershey and his product moved some people to write to beg him for money or some other kind of help. Others tried to get close to him in other ways. Mrs. E.L. Cook of Washington, D.C., sent a note asking if he might like to correspond "with a jolly widow." A mother in Indiana said she had eaten a Hershey bar every day that she nursed her baby and credited the chocolate with the child's good health. Mrs. P.R. Martin had lost a previous child in infancy and was so profoundly affected by the two different experiences that she wanted advice on how to tell the world about the miracle of Hershey-infused breast milk.

These letters confirmed Hershey's fame, and his place in the public imagination, but they didn't reflect the true value of his reputation. That can be seen in the loyalty consumers showed to his product. The goodwill that people felt toward Hershey helped his company defeat many competitors, including a well-financed newcomer called Eline's Chocolate, which was founded by the Wisconsin family that had made Schlitz beer prior to Prohibition.

Like Milton Hershey, Alfred Uihlein and his brothers saw a great milk supply—their home state was already famous for dairies—as the key to success in chocolate. They built an enormous factory where every office had a fireplace and the lobby was paved with Italian marble. They also recruited experienced people from throughout the industry. Hershey's sales and printing managers went to Eline's, along with a chemist and about twenty salesmen.

To get the brand established, Eline's gave away thousands of samples. But America's taste for chocolate was really a taste for Hershey's, and retailers were comfortable with a reliable brand and the various incentives offered to make sure it got prime display. Eline's would never overcome these disadvantages. As one salesman said, "We gave away plenty, but by God it would not sell." The Milwaukee-based chocolate company closed in less than a decade. The Uihleins lost roughly $17 million. But they had maintained their breweries and when Prohibition ended they were able to go back into their main business and thrive. Those who had left Hershey to work for the Uihleins were not welcomed back.[10]

In this period no other brand of solid-chocolate bar arose to challenge Hershey, and as the one big national player in this category the company enjoyed unrivaled access to America's 450,000 candy retailers. The chocolate bars themselves, decorated with the Hershey name in bold letters, were each little advertisements, beckoning consumers from the shelves of candy shops, drugstores, groceries, and gas stations. And every once in a while the company would attach itself to some public event with great effect. This happened in 1928, when Richard Byrd took Hershey chocolate with him to Antarctica. Byrd's expedition was a big story and his loyalty to Hershey bars, which nourished him along the way, was widely publicized.

But while the plain Hershey bar held a place in the American heart, the late twenties brought a flurry of competitors, mainly bars of chocolate mixed with other ingredients, like peanuts or raisins. Because the equipment needed to manufacture candy was relatively cheap, it didn't take much capital to get into the business. And low-overhead newcomers forced others to keep their prices low. Despite the low prices, U.S. candy sales were so brisk they totaled $1 billion a year, which was half the value of the auto business and more than soft drinks, ice cream, and all other confections combined.

By 1928 more than 260 small and medium-size competitors pecked away at Hershey. A few brought out bars backed by heavy advertising campaigns that became worthy challengers—among them were the Clark Bar, Baby Ruth, Mounds, Oh! Henry, and Milky Way. The Curtis company of Chicago spent more than $200,000 a year advertising Baby Ruth, and the Mars company, which was located in the same city, spent almost half that sum promoting Milky Way.

By offering new tastes, Hershey's rivals captured three-quarters of the new candy bar business. But with his own sales and profits continuing to rise, M.S. didn't respond with much urgency. In the entire decade he offered just one new bar—a peanut and chocolate confection called Mr. Goodbar, which debuted in 1925. The name was coined by M.S., who, because his hearing had started to fail, misunderstood a worker who said, "That's a good bar."

Mr. Goodbar was not an immediate success. In fact, ever since the development of the Kiss and the almond bar, Hershey had been unable to really excite consumers with a new product. Instead, much of the growth in Hershey's business came from selling bulk chocolate to bakers and other candy manufacturers. The Reese company, which started making peanut butter cups in 1928, purchased its chocolate coatings from Hershey and the two coexisted peacefully. The same was true for Williamson Candy, producer of Oh! Henry, and Mars, maker of the Milky Way. By 1929, Mars would be spending millions of dollars annually for chocolate produced by Hershey.

M.S. was even able to get along with the Klein Chocolate Company, which was founded by a defector from the Hershey ranks. William Klein and his siblings made competing items at a factory in nearby Elizabethtown, which was served by the Hershey trolley. But Klein, who once served Hershey as an industrial spy, always got along well with his old boss. He even sold Hershey his excess cocoa butter. "They did business as friends," said John McLain.

One of the few companies that couldn't find a comfortable niche in a business where Hershey wielded most of the power was one that used the same family name. Milton's salesmen first noticed Hershey Brothers chocolates in Pennsylvania candy stores in 1919. Jacob, Isaac, and Eli Hershey were not related to Milton, but came from the same area and had operated the Hershey Creamery in Harrisburg since before Milton built his factory in the Lebanon Valley. They had the legal right to market milk products—even chocolate-flavored ice cream—with a Hershey label, but when they got into making cocoa and chocolate candy, they dabbled in copyright infringement.

Soon after he heard that a new chocolate named Hershey was on the market, M.S. summoned a young office man named Charles Ziegler to a conference at High Point. It was Ziegler's first meeting with the boss and he would recall it in detail. In the end Hershey assigned him to investigate what the brothers, whose manufacturing plant was in Pittsburgh, were up to.

"I want you to go out and find instances of confusion and infringement and of unfair competition," said M.S.

Ziegler followed up complaints about the Hershey Brothers in Boston, New York, Binghamton, Norfolk, and Richmond. He found that the brothers were selling chocolate bars and a bite-size chocolate drop candy that were nearly identical to Hershey's products. The brothers also used packaging and lettering that made their candy look like Milton Hershey's. Ziegler found that retailers sometimes substituted the imitations for real Hershey chocolates and in other cases they were fooled by salesmen into thinking they had ordered from Milton when they were actually buying from Jacob, Isaac, and Eli.

In Harrisburg, just a few miles from Hershey, Ziegler was surprised to find an elaborate display of the brothers' "Hershey's Kisses" in a confectioner's window. Ziegler asked a police officer to stop traffic for a minute so he could step into the street with his camera and take a picture. As he raised his camera one of the Hershey brothers, apparently on a sales call, happened to step out of the shop and was caught on film.

Milton's side began the battle to stop the brothers with a long letter signed by lawyer John Snyder. It warned them that they might be committing fraud and risked reprisals. When the brothers didn't stop, M.S. sued. In a settlement they agreed to abandon the name, if not the chocolate business.

In the spirit of the agreement the brothers Hershey changed their company's name to Eatmor Chocolate. But they continued to put the family name on labels and Milton's men would have to chase the brothers and their salesmen around the country trying to enforce the agreement. They thought the job was done in 1926 when a federal judge upheld his trademark and barred half a dozen imitators from using the name. But then in July 1929 came a telegram from a Hershey company rep in Omaha:

Advise last week a gentleman purporting to be the President of the Eatmore [sic] Chocolate Company, accompanied by another man, introduced himself at the Fairmont Creamery in Omaha as the president of the Hershey Chocolate Company.

When this party was pinned down, he admitted he was not the president of the Hershey Chocolate Company, but represented the Eatmore Chocolate Company of Pittsburgh.

This brings up again the old trouble we had two or three years ago when the Hershey Brothers were representing themselves as Hershey's. Please advise Mr. Snyder.

Seven more years would pass before the battle with the scrappy and elusive brothers would end. This happened when Eatmor of Pittsburgh finally went bankrupt. M.S. bought the brothers' chocolate-making equipment and their trademark, Eatmors, which they had attached to the candy that resembled Kisses. The last flicker of the brothers' resistance to Milton's power came in February 1936. At that time Hershey headquarters sent an alert to salesmen. Someone was selling a Kiss-like product in the Southwest in a package that looked just like the Eatmor container and calling the candy Eaties. Records show Hershey took no action this time, and Eaties soon disappeared from the market.

With the war finally won, Milton showed no animosity. In fact, throughout much of this conflict, he employed a fourth Hershey brother, Paris "P.N." Hershey, as a manager in the department that procured and processed milk for the chocolate factory.[11]

As aggressive as he had been with the Hershey brothers, Milton's fairly casual approach to his other competitors suggests that his attention was focused elsewhere. It was. In the mid-twenties, M.S. would build a new junior-senior high and donate it to the public school system. A big house next to his mother's old place would be turned into a small hospital, complete with X-ray department and operating room. Hershey Park would be outfitted with several new kiddie rides. Ice-making machines would turn the Convention Hall into the Ice Palace for winter-time skating and hockey, and the industrial school would get a new center for elementary education called the Fanny B. Hershey Memorial Building.

While all of his projects in Pennsylvania boomed, M.S. resumed his adventure in Cuba, where he had installed an engineer named P.A. Staples to manage things. Still certain he had to control his own supply of sugar, Hershey quickly bought a plantation called Finca El Conde and before the decade was out he would purchase three more mills: Central Carmen, Central San Antonio, and Central Jesus Maria. He also began using labor from Haiti and Jamaica—these workers would accept lower pay. The practice eventually got him in trouble with Cuban authorities, but for years it aided his recovery from the sugar futures debacle.

Proud of what he had built, in the spring of 1923 M.S. conducted a tour of his Cuban holdings for some New York–based financiers. A report on this visit described Central Hershey as "the most American thing on the island." Near Santa Cruz the visitors were enthralled by the view they got from the crest of a hill, where they could see the Caribbean on one side and Hershey's plantation on the other. At Rosario they took in the mansion, the tropical gardens, and the renovated mill.[12]

Visitors were always welcomed at the Hershey properties, which were promoted as tourist attractions. Pamphlets distributed by the company offered package tours—train fare, lunch at the hotel in Central Hershey, golf, and a factory tour—for a grand total of four dollars (less if you didn't play golf). If a visitor couldn't get enough of Hershey Cuba in a day, he was welcome to stay overnight in one of the new hotel's rooms, each of which came with a private bath.

An observant tourist might catch a glimpse of the Founder during the long months he spent at his Cuban colony each year. On a typical morning at Rosario he rose early to have Cuban coffee and something to eat in his mansion's octagonal dining room. He would follow this morning meal with a cigar, which he smoked as he walked to the mill. (Tomas Cabrera had arranged for a supply of coronas, the premium grade favored by European royalty, which came with Hershey's picture on the band.)

When he got to the mill Hershey would rest the half-burned cigar on a windowsill while he went inside. He did this on purpose, knowing it would be snatched and smoked by one of his workers. Later in the day he would spend time in his garden, often sitting on a bench beneath a big ceiba tree, shaded by its umbrella-shaped canopy of green. At the end of the day M.S. would climb a spiral staircase to his private room at the mansion, where a door opened onto the roof. From there he could survey the plantation, the mill, and the moon and the stars.

The routine was a bit different when Milton was at Central Hershey. There he stayed in rooms above the mill offices, since the hotel was too noisy, and by day he enjoyed conducting experiments on sugar. M.S. worked in a special facility called the pilot plant, where he lost himself in the work. He'd have lunch delivered, and eat it while perched on a sugar bag. Then he might not rest again until the early hours of the morning, when he would call the hotel and have them wake up the cook to prepare him a chicken sandwich, which he would enjoy with a couple of bottles of beer.

The results of these experiments were not impressive. M.S. wanted to make a sugar that tasted like maple syrup. But after achieving the goal once, he could never repeat it. He also hoped to be able to cut out certain steps in the refining process, but never succeeded in doing it. However, these failures didn't appear to affect him much. In Cuba, he seemed to have always been in a good mood as he moved from place to place, drinking coffee with workers and dabbling in parts of the business he enjoyed.

The image of M.S. Hershey that emerges from this period is that of an old-fashioned *patron*, the type of wealthy man who could be found running things in communities across Latin America. He was charitable with those he considered to be deserving. For example, in 1924 he began to build an orphanage/school like the one he operated in Pennsylvania, and over time this place would help more than a thousand Cuban boys. The first to be enrolled were boys whose parents had been killed in a 1923 accident on the Hershey Cuban Railway, when two trains approaching a blind curve collided head-on. Generous in his approach to charitable activity, M.S. was controlling in his approach to business and would not share power with anyone. He squeezed wages and resisted workers' attempts to form unions. In 1925 newspapers in Havana reported regularly on a long campaign by five hundred employees of his railroad to gain recognition for their union and request wage increases. According to these accounts, M.S. ignored their demands, provoking angry threats. By January 18, 1926, *Heraldo de Cuba* was warning that a strike was imminent. The next day *El Diario* carried the American's reply: "Mr. Hershey will not submit to direction from labor union delegates and if he is obliged to satisfy the wishes of the workmen then he will end his business in Cuba and carry on no more improvements."

The "improvements" Hershey had created in the region had brought jobs and economic activity that eased poverty in a wide region of coastal Cuba. This fact made it difficult for editorial writers to choose a side in the labor dispute, but one paper urged the workers and the government to give Hershey's threat serious consideration. After some of the union advocates were fired, others tried to appeal to him directly, suggesting he had been misinformed by the "little bosses" who had charge of the railway.

The conflict between the railway workers and Hershey took place against a backdrop of widespread labor organizing and the formation of Cuba's first Communist party, which, as one analyst put it, "filled the Cuban bourgeoisie and foreign capitalists with justified alarm." Militant railroad workers led the labor movement, and the Hershey battle was just one part of their national strategy.

In March government arbitrators failed to broker a solution to the Hershey standoff. Electric plant workers seconded the demands of the railroad men. But when a strike was called at Hershey and another regional railroad, only some of the workers responded. The mill continued to operate and trains rolled. Eventually the stalemate was solved when Hershey gave the men a 10 percent raise—but he stopped the annual profit-sharing plan. The men who had been fired were never allowed to return to their jobs.

M.S. Hershey's tough approach to the Cuban railway workers reflected his overall attitude toward sharing his wealth. He reserved every decision about how and where to invest his fortune and would not be pressured into anything. Individuals might be helped in special circumstances, but he preferred to do things for the community at large. He built public schools to serve both the Cubans and the children of Americans who came to work for him. He brought American cattle, poultry, and vegetable crops to Cuba. In November 1927 he even put on a country fair, much like those held every year across the United States, which drew huge crowds from as far away as Havana. Visitors saw new tractors at work, prize vegetables, thoroughbred horses, and milk cows from Pennsylvania. The Cuban president opened the fair with a speech, but his horse was excluded from a breeders' competition because the contest was restricted to local entries.

As Hershey's sugar empire entered a long period of stable labor relations and rising production, P.A. Staples, the head of the Cuban operation, found the ideal outlet for what would be millions of pounds of excess production. Staples began selling sugar to the Coca-Cola Company in 1928, beginning a relationship that would last through World War II. Ties between the two big consumer icons would be strengthened as Hershey Chocolate supplied Coca-Cola with theobromine, a flavoring and stimulant derived from cacao bean shells.[13]

Difficult as some of his problems were in Cuba, M.S. Hershey rarely seemed personally troubled by them. His associates from this time describe a man who was generally relaxed, optimistic, and deeply interested in his businesses. An old man, Milton was completely comfortable in the successful life he had created for himself. Once William "Harry" Lebkicher died in February 1929, at age eighty-four, there was no one left in the country who could recall a time when M.S. wasn't rich, powerful, and famous.

Although he would turn seventy-two that year, M.S. showed little sign of slowing down. He still walked every day in his ten-acre garden at Rosario and played golf on the nine-hole course built at Central Hershey. He usually played alone, accompanied by a caddie, and if there were any other golfers on the course, they let him play through.

When he wanted more excitement, Milton went to Havana where the Nacional casino allowed him to play on credit. As time passed, this habit became quite expensive. One of his bankers in Cuba, W.S. Lambie, would recall that M.S. would draw as much as $50,000 per month to play at the casinos. His notoriety as a betting man spread as far as New York, where he was known to be one of the biggest high rollers of his era.

Financiers were not bothered by Hershey's withdrawals from the Cuba accounts. His gambling didn't seem to have any effect on his businesses, and it may have been safer for him to satisfy his appetite for risk at the casino than in the futures market. Besides, the Hershey entities had been separated in 1927 so that that no matter what happened in Cuba, the chocolate company back in Pennsylvania, which was the major source of profits, was protected.

The reorganization of the company, worked out by John Snyder and National City, had created three distinct corporations. The chocolate company, renamed the Hershey Chocolate Corporation, would make and market Hershey brand consumer products and function most reliably as a cash cow for the industrial school trust. A second firm, called Hershey Estates, would operate services such as electric power, water, and sewers, as well as the myriad businesses—trolleys, retailers, real estate, Hershey Park, a lumber mill, a quarry, etc.—that served the town of Hershey. The third company, called simply Hershey Corporation, managed all things Cuban.

As the three firms were created, National City arranged to sell a limited amount of stock in Hershey Chocolate to outside investors. The sale, which came at a time when investors clamored for new issues, was orchestrated by Stanley Russell, an officer of National City who often worked directly with M.S. As he put together the offering, Russell frequently visited Pennsylvania for working dinners with the Founder. Milton greeted him warmly, making sure to share some whiskey before the meal. "He was always considerate," recalled Russell. (Although it was still in effect, Prohibition was quickly losing favor as the public realized it had spawned rampant bootlegging and attendant violence.)

When the negotiations ended and the sale was set, M.S. went to New York with John Snyder to finalize things. (People at National City considered Snyder, who often chomped an unlit cigar, to be a difficult man. But they acknowledged that he had Hershey's interests at heart.) Russell took them to an office once used by National City's president, Charles Mitchell. M.S. sat at a big desk as Russell outlined the details of the deal. When he was finished, "Mr. Hershey thought a few minutes and said, 'That's satisfactory,'" recalled Russell. "My experience with Mr. Hershey was that when you got down to the final deal there was no haggling. When he was satisfied, he was satisfied." [14]

The reorganization of the empire left the industrial school with a majority interest in all three of the new companies. It also inspired Stanley Russell to develop a grand scheme that had the power to change the fate of Hershey chocolate, the town, and the school in a most dramatic way.

As a vice president at National City, Russell had watched with great interest as the Postum Cereal Company, started in a small barn in Battle Creek, Michigan, in 1895, acquired more than a dozen companies on the way to becoming the giant General Foods Corporation. By consolidating many different brands, the new firm was able to achieve economies of scale for shipping, sales, and distribution. In short, the whole was much more profitable than the sum of its parts.

After examining the Hershey operation, where freight costs were a major expense, Russell began to imagine creating another entity like General Foods. It would be a holding company for a grand collection of consumer products that would be sold and distributed by a single workforce. Shipments of soup could be consolidated with crates of coffee and delivered together to customers.

To test the idea Russell traveled the country to meet with the heads of Campbell, Heinz, Swift, and others. "The response I had was amazing," he would later recall. "They all had the same idea" for putting together a conglomerate and then selling it for a windfall profit to a public that was voraciously hungry for new issues.

It's no wonder that men of industry were contemplating stock deals. Since the end of the brief recession of 1920–21 the U.S. economy had been on a tear. The automobile, radio, and countless new electric necessities from toasters to refrigerators drove a household buying binge that raised both wages and prices. The explosion of consumer spending marked a historic shift in public attitudes about money and status. As one historian noted, the change could be seen in the slogans used by Ford. In 1919 the company urged people to "Buy a Ford, save the difference." In 1923 the message was, "Buy a Ford, spend the difference."

In the mid-1920s economists began to talk about a new era in which permanent prosperity would replace cycles of growth and recession. Credit for this development was given to new technologies, the skills of professional managers, and America's vast resources. The big winners were those who played the stock market, where prices kept going up. This trend was accelerated as the middle class, eager to join the American version of the Dance of the Millions, poured their savings into "investment trusts," the precursors of today's mutual funds.

The investment houses that made commissions on stock trades, and those business owners who took their privately held firms public, benefited enormously from the clamoring demand for stock. A fad for mergers and holding companies emerged as investment banks pasted together related companies and then sold stock in the new giant entities. In 1928 alone, Wall Street would conduct 201 mergers involving more than 1250 companies. This was more than double the volume of 1919.[15]

National City's Charles Mitchell was perhaps the most prominent proponent of this deal-making. Nicknamed Sunshine Charley, Mitchell rode the bull market to make a million dollars a year and turned his bank into an international powerhouse with one hundred foreign offices. More than anyone else, Mitchell made the securities business a salesman's game as he goaded his account officers and conducted contests to reward the ones who sold the most stock. He also led the rush to easy credit, making National City the first to grant personal loans unsecured by any hard assets. Any man or woman with an adequate salary could get $1,000 at 6 percent with a year to repay.

As a good and loyal National City man, Stanley Russell pursued his big deal with Mitchell-style verve. He put Hershey Chocolate at the center of the equation, planning for the bank to quickly buy enough stock to control it. National City would then purchase the other firms that would make up the conglomerate. While he could only imagine what a share of stock in this giant profit machine might fetch, Russell had to believe that the commissions alone would run into the tens of millions of dollars.

By June 1929, as hucksters fanned out across the nation to promote stock purchases on installment plans, Russell was about ready to implement his scheme. He felt so confident that he went to Europe first for a vacation. But when he returned he got an unpleasant surprise. William Murrie called from Hershey to say that a representative from National City's toughest competitor, a Chicago investment house called Dillon, Reed and Company, was in town inquiring about buying a large block of stock. Clarence Dillon, the firm's founder, had made millions putting together companies in trusts that then sold stock to the public.

Worried that the dream project nurtured for two years was about to be destroyed by Dillon's man, Stanley Russell dragged Sunshine Charley out of a meeting to get his permission to negotiate for the purchase of half a million Hershey shares owned by the industrial school trust. Ever the optimist, Mitchell didn't need to be persuaded. He said yes immediately. Russell then raced to Pennsylvania Station to catch the 4:00 P.M. train to Hershey. Murrie met him at the station around seven o'clock and took him to his home. M.S. soon joined them.

"He had a date at nine o'clock with the Dillon Reed fellow," explained Russell. "I talked to him like a Dutch uncle. I had a pleasant relationship [with M.S.]. I said, 'You have done business with the National City Bank for many years. Now is not the time you want to break it.'"

Although Russell may have considered him a Dutch uncle, M.S. did not give him the answer he wanted. Instead he left for his appointment with Russell's competitor. Murrie started pouring scotch and sodas. It was one of the hottest nights of the summer and the two men drank until Murrie's wife suggested they stop. Sometime around midnight John Snyder called them. Hershey was ready to meet again.

The four men—Murrie, Russell, Snyder, and Hershey—sat on a porch at High Point and hammered out the points of a stock sale. National City would pay half a million dollars for a six-month option on half a million shares. If National City could line up all the other companies that would be part of the conglomerate, then the option would be exercised. National City would get control of Hershey Chocolate. If the deal fell apart, Hershey could keep the option payment. When all the talk was over, Russell said good night to Hershey and Snyder and followed Murrie back to his house, where the two men had a bit more scotch and soda before retiring for a few hours' sleep.

Early the next morning, Russell went to a Hershey company office to dictate a memo on the option, got M.S. Hershey's signature on the paper, and wrote a check for $250,000 to seal it. The second half of the option was paid when the paperwork was approved by his bosses in New York. Then Russell raced to sign up other firms. He got agreements from Colgate-Palmolive and Kraft and formed the Quality Products Corporation, which could be the holding company for the various brands. Half a dozen other firms waited in the wings.

As he pieced together Quality Products, all the economic signals seemed to confirm that Russell was on to something good. In August the Ford company reached the two million mark for the Model A, just seven months after it produced car number one million. In the same month Russell's boss at the bank described the stock market as "a weathervane pointing into a gale of prosperity." And well-regarded economists, noting a 20 percent rise in corporate earnings, declared that old rules no longer applied and the stock market mania was based on sound fundamentals, not speculation.

At National City, Charley Mitchell had established a highly competitive culture that drove men like Stanley Russell to seek ever bigger achievements. Until 1927 the company had dealt only in bonds, but even though it came late to the stock market party, National City quickly became the biggest investment house in the world, reaching $2 billion in assets in 1929. Much of this had been earned on the sale of new securities sold in initial public offerings.

In late September Russell was poised to add to the pile and earn himself Charley Mitchell's praise, when the market began to wobble. The Dow Jones Industrial average dropped 13 percent in the month, and broker loans, which allowed buyers to purchase stock with minimal cash, soared. Two weeks later Mitchell tried to talk the market up, suggesting the price drop had "gone too far." Investors disagreed and the volume of sales set one daily record after another. True panic set in on October 24. Police surrounded the stock exchange, just in case, and in a last-ditch attempt to prop up prices Mitchell joined a group that tried to stop the hemorrhage with big purchases. This provided only a momentary respite. Black Tuesday, October 29, turned the crisis into a crash. The Dow, which had been valued at more than 380 in August, fell to 230.07.

No one could say for sure how much money was lost in the market during the last week of October 1929. Estimates ranged between $30 billion and $60 billion. One certain casualty of the crash was Quality Products Corporation. No one would be in a mood to buy new stock for many years to come, and Stanley Russell, who had been so flush with scotch, the summer heat, and hope on the porch at High Point, put his plan away. "If the market had lasted another ninety days, it would have gone through," he would say later. But it didn't last, and the option he had acquired on Hershey stock lapsed. Hershey Chocolate kept the $500,000, and the school trust retained complete control of the firm.

Years later, M.S. Hershey would call the market crash, and the collapse of the Quality Products scheme, "the best thing that ever happened." A merger, he told the board of his trust, would have placed the chocolate company under "outside control" and "made a big difference to the town." [16]

THE END OF INNOCENCE

11   F. Scott Fitzgerald wrote that the "Jazz Age," as the twenties were called, "leapt to a spectacular death in October 1929." But like the reports of so many investors committing suicide by jumping out of windows, Fitzgerald's analysis was exaggerated. The October Crash was not a brief, decisive event but rather the shove that started a boulder rolling downhill.

Three years would pass before the Dow Industrial Average reached its bottom of 41 points. At this time Charley Mitchell testified before a U.S. Senate committee and admitted to violating various banking rules. Congressional investigators branded him a "bankster" who had hyped stocks and exploited investors. Although he escaped criminal charges, Mitchell would eventually have to pay his way out of a federal civil suit and resign from National City Bank.[1]

Bad as things got for Sunshine Charley, they were far worse for almost everyone else. Initially those hit hardest were investors who had bought stock on margin—meaning they had borrowed much of the money to make trades—and suddenly found themselves liable for huge sums. In Hershey a number of the chocolate company's executives were in this position and could have lost their homes. M.S., who did not play the stock market, stepped in. "He did not let them lose their property," recalled Henry Stump, who worked at the Hershey Trust Company (another of Milton's enterprises) at the time. "He lent them the money."

The pain felt by investors spread gradually through the rest of the economy. In 1930, more than 26,000 businesses across the nation went bankrupt. In 1931, the figure was 28,000. The companies that remained carried almost $6 billion in debt and the value of the goods they produced was roughly half the total in 1929. By the start of 1933, 9,000 banks had closed their doors. Unemployment was 25 percent.[2]

Behind the numbers were millions of people who lost their jobs, savings, homes, and even their children as they were forced to give them up to agencies that could feed and clothe them. In big cities, breadlines stretched for blocks while in the Great Plains farm families were forced off the land by the terrible combination of plummeting prices, debt, and drought. Everywhere people learned that dandelions were edible.

Amid all the suffering, President Herbert Hoover declined to use the federal treasury for much more than a bailout program for a few major industries, in the hope that their recovery would produce jobs. Hoover believed that any bolder act would undermine the "sense of responsibility and individual generosity" of the American public. "I am confident," he announced, "that our people have the resources, the initiative, the courage, the stamina and the kindliness of spirit to meet this situation in the way they have met their problems over generations."[3]

Unfortunately, the "situation" that confronted Americans in the Great Depression was unlike any seen before. Financial risk taking, and the habit of credit, had become so widely dispersed that Wall Street's crisis reached into every corner of the economy in ways that previous panics had not. People may have possessed the spirit and character Hoover described, but very few had the resources to employ them. "No money, no banks, no nothing," was how the humorist Will Rogers described it. One exception was M.S. Hershey.[4]

Like the movies and other inexpensive entertainments, chocolate was more resilient than other businesses. Hershey sales did decline during the Great Depression. In the worst year, 1933, the total was just under $22 million, a little more than half the figure for 1929. But profits remained strong, because the price of Hershey's raw materials fell dramatically.

Hershey also benefited from the vertical integration of his company. By producing much of his own milk and sugar, he was able to keep supplies steady. But in the case of sugar, the company would have to fight to preserve its advantage. In the early 1930s, politically powerful American sugar refiners pushed for higher tariffs on foreign competitors, including Cuban producers. They were aided by politicians from states where farmers who grew sugar beets complained that they couldn't compete with the cheap labor on sugarcane plantations in the Caribbean, South America, and the Pacific.

Faced with a threat to its independence from the sugar giants, Hershey mounted a counteroffensive. In testimony before government officials, P.A. Staples, still Hershey's top executive in Cuba, argued that the island was a reliable source for a much needed commodity and that domestic sugar companies, who were unable to meet the nation's demand, were seeking unfair advantage. Although he didn't say it, Staples was also defending his company's right to bypass the big producers to maintain its own reliable, low-cost supply.

At the time, Hershey executives rarely referred to their company's status as, in effect, an orphan-owned concern. But Staples played this card in the tariff battle, noting that the "juvenile" stockholders in his company should "not be discriminated against." In the end, Hershey won and the tariff was not increased. However the island's sugar companies, including Hershey, would face years of uncertainty. U.S. refiners would continue to seek higher tariffs and stricter limits on shipments from Cuba to America.[5]

With adequate raw materials Hershey Chocolate could maintain production because, even during the Depression, consumers could afford a nickel bar of chocolate. In fact, the potential market for cheap candy was stronger during hard times, because people couldn't afford much else. To give consumers some novelty, and sales a little help, Hershey added a chocolate bar called Mild and Mellow to its lineup in 1933. In 1934 a bar called Not-So-Sweet was introduced and the factory began making a version of the British Aero Bar, under a license granted by Rowntree of Great Britain.

These new products helped Hershey recover from the Depression well ahead of the overall economy. A graph of the company's income from 1929 to 1936 shows the turnaround was abrupt and it brought sales back to the 1929 level in exactly the same amount of time—three years—that they needed to hit bottom. Through it all, Milton Hershey led with more strength than anyone should expect from a man approaching eighty. He even tried a new marketing technique, commissioning a short film called *The Gift of Montezuma* that promoted chocolate to theatergoers.

The film opens with two tuxedoed men standing in what looks like the library of an exclusive Manhattan club. They discuss the "utopian concern" headquartered in Hershey, Pennsylvania. With a $1,000 wager on the line, they fly to the Lebanon Valley in a biplane to see if M.S. Hershey, the generous industrialist, can really make a profit while doing good. After landing they tour a perfect town of neat homes and beautiful gardens.

They discover a factory that is like a "giant clockworks." Scenes from inside, backed by music scored with a march-of-progress urgency, suggest the height of machine age efficiency. In the end, the skeptic has to agree that M.S. has achieved the dream of the enlightened capitalist, making money while making everyone happy.

The Gift of Montezuma reflected perfectly the confidence of the Founder in the last season of his life. As M.S. had aged into a white-haired man with a prosperous paunch, people began to describe him as unshakable. Although he had blamed himself for the sugar crisis, for example, he never panicked. Instead he was invigorated by the challenge. A man who understood and used social symbols instinctively, he had dropped his usual reserve and humbly asked his employees and the townspeople to consider him their equal and lend a hand. They did.

When the Depression arrived, and the outside world threatened life in his perfect town, it was Milton Hershey's turn to act on behalf of the people. His first move was also powerfully symbolic. In April 1930 he gave his mansion, High Point, to serve as the clubhouse for the newly formed Hershey Country Club. (When it opened, he gave away one hundred memberships.) For the rest of his life, Milton's home would be just two rooms on the upper floor of the beautiful house on the hill. The rest of the place, which he had once shared with Catherine, would serve those townspeople who could afford memberships and the tourists drawn by one of the best golf courses in the country.

But M.S. was not going to wait for the eventual recovery of the U.S. economy to rescue his company, town, and school. Instead, he embarked on an extensive building program that would employ hundreds of workers full-time for more than six years. In that period M.S. would create several town landmarks, including a luxury hotel, a sports arena, a modern office building, and a massive new school. And he would pour more cash into a downtown community building that he had begun to build in 1929.

Six stories high and faced with warm-hued Indiana limestone, the Community Building was designed to resemble an Italian Renaissance palace—complete with murals, bronze statues of swans, and a white marble fountain—and would have been an imposing home for an elite club in midtown Manhattan. It included a gym, a library with 12,000 books, lushly decorated common areas, a swimming pool, more than 130 dormitory

rooms, and a small new hospital. The most impressive room in the building was an ornate theater that seated almost 2,000.

The Community Building would serve the people of Hershey daily and
become the town's social hub. But it did not have the same impact on the
valley's landscape as two big structures M.S. began to build on the highest
point of property he owned, a rise called Pat's Hill that overlooks downtown Hershey from a point roughly one mile to the north. One would be a
sprawling new junior-senior high for the industrial school; its eighty-foot
clock tower would be visible from much of the surrounding countryside.

The other big project on the hill was the grand Hotel Hershey, a sprawling, Spanish-style building with 150 guest rooms and a circular dining
room with thirteen huge windows outlined in stained glass. The hotel had
been something that M.S. Hershey had planned to build from the moment he bought his properties in the Lebanon Valley, and for years he and
Catherine had talked about the design. Anticipating construction, he built
a trolley line to the site in 1910, but other demands for his time, money,
and attention had delayed the project. Over the years, as he dabbled with
the design, he explained that while other millionaires played with yachts,
his hobby was the hotel.

When he finally had his dream fulfilled, M.S. made sure to use roof tile
purchased from California, and he salvaged weathered timber from an
abandoned dam to make railings and woodwork. As with his other projects,
he used all-Hershey labor, instead of hiring local subcontractors, and that
meant hundreds of jobs for men who might otherwise have been unem-
ployed. When the hotel opened in 1933, it became yet another source of
jobs and revenue.

Like the Community Building and the junior-senior high school, the
Hotel Hershey was a more or less traditional structure, even if it did seem
more suited to the California coast than the Amish countryside. But with
his two remaining construction projects, M.S. would play with more futur-
istic designs.

On Chocolate Avenue rose a big new office building that would be one
of the strangest structures in America. Called the Modern Office Building,
it was built without windows, so that executives, clerks, and secretaries
could labor in a perfectly controlled environment, where lighting, temperature, humidity, and mood were subject to strict control. The building was
equipped with the most advanced business machines from Burroughs, Ad-
dressograph, and Pitney-Bowes, and a careful observer would have been

able to discern a worker's rank by the type of desk—metal or walnut—he sat behind.

A booklet published for visitors explained that the design of the Modern Office Building would eliminate the "psychological effect of one employee feeling that he has not so desirable a location as another." This was because a windowless space deprived everyone of a good view. A similar approach was used in the allocation of space, the pamphlet claimed, so that status was taken out of the equation. "The offices vary only in size to suit the needs of the individual occupant."

Nothing at all in the building suggested individualized quarters. Every office was carpeted with the same green pile. Walls were colored tan and ocher. Two-inch-thick cork ceilings muffled sound. And each room was equipped with a clock and a set of little colored lights called "weather indication signals." White signaled that the skies were clear. Red meant rain; green, snow. Every day, at ten minutes before quitting time, the lights were adjusted to let everyone know if they needed galoshes or umbrellas for the trip home. If the building worked as its owner planned, the staff would make that trip "feeling less enervated and more happy," said the booklet.

Although the company promoted it as a "contribution of Science to business," it is impossible to say whether M.S. got the result he wanted from the Modern Office Building. Some of his employees likely felt *more* "enervated," not less, as they worked in a monotone environment deprived of even a glimpse of sky or earth.

However, the last big construction project of the period—a big new sports arena for Hershey Park—was an engineering marvel that delivered all that was promised, and more.

In addition to keeping Hershey workers busy, building this new arena would solve the problem of overflow crowds at events like hockey games— the local team won its minor-league championship in 1934—at the existing two-thousand-seat Ice Palace. The new facility would seat seven thousand for hockey and ten thousand for concerts and other stage events. But the size of the arena did not make it special. What made it unusual was the design and method of construction, which were devised by a young pioneer in the art and science of structural engineering named Anton Tedesko.

Tedesko had emigrated from Austria to Chicago just in time for the Great Depression and the collapse of the U.S. construction market. He brought with him a new concept for making domed buildings out of re-

markably thin shells of concrete. The technique was employed in a temporary building that was used as a dairy barn at the 1933 Chicago World's
Fair and in the construction of New York's Hayden Planetarium in 1935.
But these were both small structures and Tedesko wanted to test the design
on something bigger.

Late in 1935 a concrete company executive arranged for Tedesko, then
just thirty-two, to meet Paul Witmer, the man in charge of construction in
Hershey. Witmer listened to the younger man's ideas and was sufficiently
impressed to present them to his boss. M.S. was at first taken aback by the
size of the project the Austrian had in mind—the arena would be much
bigger than a football field—but he was persuaded. Within weeks the design was completed, and construction began on March 11, 1936.

No one in North America had ever constructed a thin concrete dome as
big as the one that would rise on the site at Hershey Park, and both
Tedesko and Witmer were excited by the project. To make the dome,
workers would first build a 100-foot-high wooden scaffold that would move
along tracks. They would then climb the scaffold to construct a metal arch
that was designed to hold and distribute weight like a suspension bridge.
The concrete skin of the dome would be applied to this metalwork. Because the structure depended on a very precise balance of stresses, the
pour would begin, simultaneously, at the two ends where the arch met the
ground. Once this process started, it would have to go on continuously,
timed so that the two crews reached the peak of the dome at the same moment. Otherwise the structure would collapse.

In the beginning Tedesko wondered if the workers he met in Hershey
were up to the task. Not one of them had experience with such a complex
or delicate project. But eventually he found a reliable foreman who organized a group of 250 men. Using the skills they had, and methods taught
to them by the engineer, they built the scaffold out of yellow pine and
then they began welding together the first steel latticework section.

On July 2, crews began pouring concrete for the first span and kept
pouring, twenty-four hours a day, for almost three days. When they were
finished, the scaffold was lowered and Tedesko anxiously waited to see that
the concrete had settled perfectly. Workers then rolled the scaffold into
place for construction of the next section of iron latticework. Following
this process, they built five arches in five months. When they were finished, the scaffold was dismantled and the wood was saved for use in the
construction of houses. Beneath the futuristic-looking dome, bleachers

were built for seven thousand souls, and four ice-making machines, capable of producing 140 tons of ice per day, were installed.

The first game at the Sports Arena was played on December 19. Boys in red ushers' uniforms led ticket holders to seats that were tiered to form a bowl above the ice. The *New York Times* writer who came to see the game described the many "outstanding features" of the arena, including unobstructed views, a modern sound system, and scoreboards, and declared it "magnificent." The arena "fulfills the fondest dream of the sponsor of the entire community, who unfortunately was unable to attend the dedication because of a cold," wrote Thomas Deegan. The Hershey team, defending champions of the Eastern League, defeated the New York Rovers, 3–2.[6]

M.S. Hershey was defying the Great Depression. His building program generated jobs. His company and town were prospering. (In contrast, the ideal city of Pullman, annexed by Chicago, had become just another run-down neighborhood.[7]) Who could find fault with him? *Fortune* magazine could.

Three years into its existence, *Fortune* had established a reputation for in-depth explorations of business and finance that went beyond numbers and a firm's public relations claims. *Fortune*'s perspective was sophisticated and analytical. It was in many ways a product of the times. During the happily Roaring Twenties, everyone was having so much fun there wasn't much reason to ask hard questions. But after the Crash, as more people began to understand the political and social failures of the time, much of journalism was more skeptical. At the same time, many important novels looked soberly at the structural problems of society. Aldous Huxley's novel *Brave New World* challenged naïve beliefs about progress. James T. Farrell's *Studs Lonigan* explored the dispiriting effects of the Depression. And with his dystopian novel *It Can't Happen Here*, Sinclair Lewis moved his readers' attention from the stifling banality of *Main Street* to the terrifying prospect of American fascism.

In a piece published in January 1934, *Fortune* used Hershey's status as a town untouched by the Great Depression to justify a sharp examination of a progressive millionaire's version of the ideal American place. Of course the magazine reported dutifully on the full employment at the factory and the cradle-to-grave amenities enjoyed by residents. But the article's author also snickered at the "sweet and oppressive odor of charity" permeating the town and the shameless promotional efforts behind the Hershey mystique. A caption below one illustration in the magazine quoted a company press agent whose prose grew more purple with every line:

> Even those who have not seen Hershey in its entirety can realize its incredible beauty. Like a dainty bouquet of mignonette a glance is sufficient to stir the heart. And every added observation . . . serves to drug the senses even more. Hershey is like such a bouquet; it is beautiful in part, as a single sprig of mignonette, but astounding and bewildering as a whole.

More astounding and bewildering, reported *Fortune,* was the status and wealth of the Hershey Industrial School, which had grown to serve 650 boys. Added together, the stock, real estate, and other holdings of the school's trustee, the Hershey Trust Company, were worth $65 million. *Fortune* found nothing wrong with the idea of a big endowment serving poor children. But it did see trouble in the way M.S. Hershey had constrained the trust, requiring that it preserve its capital in perpetuity and spend its income in one place—the industrial school—and for one purpose—the care of orphan boys.

So-called perpetuities established in the style of Stephen Girard, who founded a school trust in the 1800s, inevitably run into problems, noted *Fortune,* as times and circumstances change. For this reason, most major philanthropic funds grant flexibility to future trustees. This might be important for Hershey, considering that the nation's orphan population was shrinking, and child welfare agencies were moving away from the use of asylums to care for those who remained. In fact, modern thinking about the care of needy children emphasized providing in-home services so a child could remain with his extended family, leaving institutions for only the most difficult cases. But under its existing rules, difficult cases were excluded from the Hershey orphanage. As the school's own literature explained, it would not accept those "who are unable to follow our courses because of mental ability or boys who are unfit companions to others, and we do not keep boys who are afflicted with enuresis."

It was possible to argue that the Hershey Industrial School skimmed the best from the population of needy boys and turned away those who most needed a rich sponsor and caretaker. As a result, the Hershey boys looked and acted more like prep-school students than orphans, and this was how some of the other kids who lived in the town regarded them.

"They were very, very fortunate . . . always well dressed, well fed, well taken care of," recalled Edward Tancredi, who grew up in Hershey in the 1920s. "They were taken care of like they were members of a millionaire's family."

The magazine also saw flaws in Milton Hershey's perfect town, where he gave much but also held on to authority. Where other philanthropists involved their beneficiaries in managing and maintaining the projects they developed, Hershey retained sole control and responsibility for almost everything he created. "Hershey has no mayor and no municipal government because it has never been incorporated," reported *Fortune*. "Its inhabitants lead their daily lives in a relationship so close to Mr. Hershey as to be patriarchal."

Any *Fortune* reader would have to wonder if M.S. Hershey was one part benevolent genius and one part misguided egotist. He could have let the industrial school trust have the flexibility to change with the times. He could have allowed Hershey to become a real town in which voters elected officials who could collect taxes and deliver services according to the will of the people. He could have paid his workers better wages, and let them decide what to do with the money. Instead, he had set up a series of social experiments, which he intended to continue forever, making his school a monument to himself and his utopia a place of well-fed if politically crippled citizens.[8]

The *Fortune* article ended with a plea for M.S. Hershey to alter the deed of trust to make it more flexible. Remarkably, the same points had been made in a private review of the trust by Central Hanover Bank of New York. The Central Hanover report, commissioned by Hershey and completed in November 1933, noted the school trust could eventually exceed $600 million and generate more income than any single orphanage could ever spend. At the same time, changes in society would likely affect the way needy children would be aided and educated. As a result, a huge fortune intended to help suffering children might sit idle, growing ever bigger like a prize pig that has become the farmer's pet.

M.S. Hershey had made some minor changes to his deed of trust around the time of the Hanover report. One required the school to serve as many boys as the trust's income would allow. But many of the restrictive clauses in the deed of trust remained, and Hershey did not respond to *For-*

tune's overall criticisms. Instead, he and his executives began a boycott of the magazine that would last for decades. Hershey didn't need the blessings of experts or writers to continue his various missions. He was certain of the course he had chosen and could safely ignore those outsiders who disagreed.

For a man who had often said he believed in change, M.S. Hershey exhibited a remarkable resistance to it. This trend continued when outsiders raised a different kind of criticism in the summer of 1934. The issue was the industrial school's approach to religion, which reflected M.S. Hershey's personal beliefs. Although devoted to the Ten Commandments and the Golden Rule, he was not a churchgoer and never joined a denomination. His charity included gifts to a variety of churches and national Jewish organizations. But he resisted every effort that local pastors made to bring him into their flocks.

Milton's studied neutrality worked for him as an individual, but it was difficult to apply to others. This became clear when the school refused to provide transportation so that Roman Catholic boys could attend mass or participate in sacraments, both of which were religious obligations. The Roman Catholic bishop of Harrisburg, Philip R. McDevitt, heard about this problem, wrote to M.S. and then visited him at High Point to see if he could change things.

At that meeting, the bishop and the millionaire replayed a misunderstanding that holds a more or less permanent place in American religious life. M.S. was certain he had all the bases covered because his boys got generic Bible lessons of the sort any Christian should appreciate. And the Catholics were not singled out by his policies. The school did not organize and provide transportation to *any* church.

For his part, the bishop tried to persuade him that it was logically impossible to offer "nonsectarian" religious instruction, and that what he was teaching was a Protestant brand of Christianity inadequate for Catholics. In the end, as the bishop would later write, this argument "made no impression on Mr. Hershey, who declared plainly and definitively that there would be no change in the policy of the school."

After the meeting at High Point, the bishop made it clear that the issue was not settled and that Hershey should expect a fight. In a letter to the school's superintendent, he complained of "a tyranny and intolerance that find no parallel." He recalled how Catholic nuns who wanted to build were denied land in Hershey and said that M.S. would prefer to replace all the churches in his town with a single community church devoted to "Hersheyism." (He didn't mention that Milton Hershey had sold a local Catholic parish land to build their church.)

Soon Roman Catholic newspapers all over the country were publishing the bishop's words. HERSHEY HOME DENIES CATHOLIC TEACHING screamed an eight-column, front-page headline in the *Catholic Union and Times* of Buffalo. HERSHEY SCHOOL IN REFUSAL TO ALLOW CATHOLIC BOYS TO PRACTICE RELIGION CHARGED, said *The Indiana Catholic and Record.*

As the story spread, Hershey salesmen and wholesale jobbers began to tell the home office about returns from retailers who were offended by what they had read, Catholic schools that had previously sold the company's candy returned boxes unopened. Students at Catholic colleges pledged to boycott Hershey products. A typical telegram from the field reported:

Catholic schools and seminaries are returning product to our jobbers and instructing them to substitute Nestle. Geo Ast candy co. had eighteen returns half pound bars this morning.

From California, to Iowa and upstate New York came notices of long-standing customers canceling purchases. Salesmen who were being confronted by angry customers asked their bosses back in Hershey for help answering the complaints. As the controversy reached a wider audience, the company won some support. A Protestant group based in Washington, D.C., even called on its supporters to buy as much chocolate as possible "to defeat the Roman plot."

But in the end, profit trumped principle. And for the first time since Giuseppe Donato made him pay for *Dance of Eternal Spring,* someone forced Milton S. Hershey to do something he didn't want to do. With a simple order from the Founder, the Hershey Industrial School agreed to transport Catholic boys to church on Sundays. The Catholic press reported the news, the boycott was lifted, and Catholics across America moved quickly to satisfy their taste for Hershey chocolate.

"In view of the statement regarding the Hershey industrial school which appeared in this week's *Catholic News* I no longer have any objection to giving Hershey our trade," wrote Sister Mary Helena of Holy Rosary

School in the Bronx. "Will you please send 8 boxes 'mild and mellow #93' and 2 boxes 'Mr Goodbar #82'?"

The next summer, M.S. would give each church in his town $20,000 to retire debt. But while this generous act may have reassured local believers that he wasn't against them, the damage that the fight with Bishop McDevitt did to the company's reputation would linger. Years later, some Catholics still believed that the Hershey name stood for religious intolerance. On March 31, 1940, Josephine Larkin of Milwaukee would write to the company asking, "Do you only do business with the Masons, or do you also have Catholic trade?"[9]

A wide-angle view of Hershey in the mid-thirties reveals a man and a place struggling to keep the outside world at bay. In its first three decades, Hershey, Pennsylvania, had become the closest thing to a principality that anyone in America could imagine. Prosperous, pretty, and self-contained, the town thrived no matter what was happening in the rest of the country. And for the most part, its inhabitants bowed to the rule of a single man, accepting in return comfort, security, and a sense that they lived in a place that was superior to all others.

Then came the turmoil of the Depression and the intrusions of the press and the Catholic Church. The demands these problems made on the Founder and his top managers only added to the pressures they felt as they labored to keep their core businesses going and carried out their great building campaign. During this time Milton S. Hershey was also forced to adjust to the realities of old age. His mother and Harry Lebkicher were long gone, and just days after the row with the Catholics ended, attorney John Snyder died. Milton's generation was passing.

With so much going on, M.S. apparently missed signs of a growing dissatisfaction in his workforce. In the last weeks of 1936, a call to arms called "The Chocolate Bar-B" circulated on the factory floor. The two-page newsletter aired complaints about low wages, erratic work schedules, and recent orders to speed up production. Signed by the "Communist Party of Hershey, Pa.," the paper argued that a union would be a step "in the right direction" for workers who were struggling to maintain their homes and care for their families. (Communist organizations were quite active in America in the 1930s, but never had more than 100,000 members nationwide.)

Workers at Hershey were having trouble getting by on their paychecks because the company had changed the rules. Where once employees enjoyed sixty or more hours of work per week, they were now restricted to forty or fewer. And if overtime was available, the rate paid was lower than it had been before. The result of these policies was that every job that existed in Hershey in 1929 was still there in 1936. But few if any of the workers earned as much money as they were accustomed to making before the Depression.

At first M.S. Hershey could justify the tight controls on hours and wages because they were required by the rules of the National Recovery Administration, an agency created by President Franklin Delano Roosevelt in response to the Depression. But the Supreme Court had found the NRA to be unconstitutional in 1935. That ruling, combined with overall improvements in employment and economic activity, had led workers across the country to demand that companies raise wages and restore work schedules. Having suffered through the bad times, they wanted to participate in the recovery.

In many industries—mining, shipping, auto manufacturing, textiles, etc.—employees organized unions and won better pay and improved conditions through negotiations and strikes. In this period labor groups occupied many factories with "sit-down strikes," which made it impossible for bosses to keep a plant running. In Flint, Michigan, the United Automobile Workers, aided by the Committee for Industrial Organization (CIO), took over a giant General Motors plant on December 29, 1936. After a seven-week occupation, marked by a battle with police, the union won recognition and a contract.

The Flint strike would one day be recognized as the most important such action in history. At the time it drew the attention of the nation's press to worker criticisms of labor practices. It also emboldened the CIO, which had recently been suspended from the more cautious American Federation of Labor, and inspired workers at many companies to examine more closely the terms of their employment. In the year to come, more than 4 million people would join CIO-affiliated unions, and gain increases in wages, improved working conditions, and new benefits such as health insurance and paid vacations.[10]

In Hershey, workers at the chocolate factory could reflect on the fact that from 1930 though 1936, M.S. had spent more than $10 million on new construction while he reduced the earnings of his rank-and-file employees and stopped paying annual bonuses. In the same time period, the Hershey Chocolate Corporation made more than $37 million in after-tax profits. This figure was roughly ten times the total annual payroll at the chocolate factory.

Over the long term, the Depression-era building program at Hershey would produce benefits for the community. But anyone looking at the numbers in 1936 could ask if the company had really needed to suppress wages in the way that it had. It would be impossible, of course, to prove that the company had used the Depression as an excuse to cut wages and build new facilities at the lowest cost. But it was obvious that more than $45 million had been available in Hershey accounts. And while workers and their families were forced to scrimp and do without, M.S. had continued to cruise the town in his chauffeured car and escape for the winter to the Caribbean.

"The Chocolate Bar-B" reflected the suspicion some workers felt about the company's wage policies and their resentment over the paternalistic attitude of the company. In Hershey, a man who had one drink too many after work might hear about it from his supervisor the next morning at the factory. A second offense could cost him his job. The company took a strong stand against other personal failings, especially infidelity, and tried to govern behavior outside the factory. For example, it forbade workers from carpooling, to protect the trolley's business.

Not everyone was comfortable living in a place where one man and his key executives attempted to control so much—jobs, trade, civic life, and social behavior. Under this system, favoritism in hiring and pay were rampant and no one felt completely secure.[11]

Many hiring and firing decisions at Hershey were based on personal factors. In some cases, M.S. Hershey protected his favorites. For example, he kept on a longtime worker named Billy Brinker, overruling William Murrie when he tried to dismiss the man. Brinker had a job for life, and in his old age labored in a greenhouse where, said M.S., "he's going to stay even if he does put the plants in upside down." On the other hand, an employee who did his job well but was deemed by the Founder to be immoral had to go. This last point was made clear when Bert Black, who had helped M.S. discover his chocolate recipe at the Hershey homestead, was suddenly fired after decades of loyal service because he had an affair with a woman who worked at the plant.

The notion that a good worker could be fired while an incompetent one might stay forever didn't sit well with men and women who believed they owed their boss nothing more than a fair day's work. Among those who questioned the company's policies were many of the Italian-American men and women who knew they had no social or cultural ties to managers, who were mainly Protestants from long established American families. As Hershey employee Edward Tancredi would later explain, he and other Italian-Americans had experienced enough prejudice to wonder if they were being treated fairly and to be wary, in general, of a system that denied them any power. (Prejudice in Hershey was prevalent enough that as late as the 1940s residents circulated a protest petition when an Italian-American family bought a home in an upscale neighborhood.)[12]

"Being lord and master they could do as they damn pleased," said Tancredi, describing Hershey's management. "Some people were really abused."

Ignazio Romanucci, who had reached out to the Wobblies in the 1920s, believed that the pay he received was unfairly low and that conditions at the plant were "terrible." Contrary to what many outsiders assumed, many chocolate-factory workers did perform physically demanding labor. In some departments machinery produced deafening levels of noise. In others, like the roasting rooms, temperatures reached well over 100 degrees Fahrenheit. But the thing that bothered Romanucci most was the attitude some managers showed toward the rank and file.

"We were considered part of the machinery while we were working," said Romanucci. "Just labor, that's what we were, dumbos."

These feelings made hundred of workers receptive to the CIO organizers who came to town in early 1937. After meeting at a firehouse in nearby Palmyra, several hundred formed a local of the United Chocolate Workers Union. Within weeks a reported 80 percent of the factory's workers joined, but not all paid dues.

When they first approached the company to negotiate, the union's representatives met little if any resistance. In March the Hershey Chocolate Corporation announced it would raise wages to a minimum of 60 cents per hour for men and 45 cents for women.

With the company and the union holding such agreeable talks on wages, the conflict that arose weeks later would be hard to explain. It began when Hershey laid off some of the union organizers as part of what was said to be normal seasonal cutbacks. Job security for those who lead the union had been a key bargaining point and part of the initial agreement signed by both parties. The company said this point didn't apply.

The union said it did. Its leaders and the company also disagreed over union demands for a full union shop and payroll deduction of dues.

Several weeks passed with the sides failing to resolve this conflict. In this time, factory managers speeded up production. Machine operator Romanucci would recall discussing the new tempo with a foreman. He asked why he wasn't being paid more to produce more. And then, as if he were reading a script written by efficiency expert Frederick Winslow Taylor, he said he'd gladly continue to work at the faster pace in exchange for more money. Management didn't take him up on this proposal.

In retrospect, it's hard to imagine that Hershey's managers understood either the hopes or the mistrust felt by a significant number of their employees. The workers' hopes revolved around their own version of a better way of life, a competing view of utopia in which they would have a say in what went on in M.S. Hershey's factory and town. Their fears were based on the absolute authority held by Milton Hershey and his executives. These workers remembered capricious firings—cocoa bean roaster George Bowman, for example—and the company's tendency to play favorites by paying different salaries to workers with similar responsibilities. This system seemed unfair, and the company's refusal to let the union protect the jobs of its leaders, exempting them from seasonal layoffs, inflamed long-standing resentments.

"Hershey considered himself an autocrat," in these matters, said Romanucci, and workers were ruled by "fear psychology."

The fear turned to anger at an April 1 union meeting held at the Palmyra firehouse. Paul Miller, a worker who attended the meeting recalled that some workers were "really wrought up" and a visiting adviser from a carpenters' union felt compelled to admonish them. If the man from the carpenters' union had cooled things at all, it didn't last. By the end of the night the chocolate workers had decided to conduct a sit-down strike the very next day.

At eleven in the morning on Friday, April 2, union president Russell "Bull" Behman stood on the street outside the Hershey chocolate factory and waved a red handkerchief at workers who were looking out the windows. The signal meant the strike was on, and as word passed through the various buildings, machines were switched off and entire departments fell silent. The effect was dramatic.

"All of a sudden everything just went dead," said Paul Miller, who worked in the department that made chocolate syrup.

As hundreds of workers simply sat down at their posts, others went outside to walk picket lines. Scores found their way to the roofs of the factory buildings along Chocolate Avenue, where they waved and shouted at those who gathered below them on the sidewalk.

When the lunchtime whistle blew, workers who wanted no part of the strike left the plant. They would not return until things were settled. Those who supported the strike—organizers claimed twelve hundred, Hershey executives set the number at four hundred—began to prepare for a long stay. The strike would be manned in shifts, so that people could spend time at home. Food would be supplied from a kitchen staffed by the union. Monitors inside would make sure workers respected M.S. Hershey's property. They banned smoking in areas that were supposed to be kept sanitary.

Photos from the first days of the sit-down strike showed mostly young workers, including many women, smiling and waving from windows and rooftops. They look like they are having fun. On Saturday the night superintendent at the plant, A.P. Heilman, would report that the strikers he saw inside "all acted like gentlemen."

The smiles that strikers flashed for the cameras reflected the less than militant attitude held by many who sat down on the morning of April 2. For them the strike was more like a family squabble than an angry revolution. They knew M.S. Hershey and, while they may have thought he was out of touch, they felt some affection for him. Ignazio Romanucci would long remember, for example, a Sunday when M.S. had decided to work with him for several hours: "He was so kind. Kinder than my mother. . . . I'll never forget that, how he was kind all day long."

Such positive personal experiences may have made the striking workers optimistic about the negotiations that began almost immediately after the plant was shut down. However, in William Murrie they faced an executive with a strong antiunion history—he himself had been a railroad strikebreaker—who could choose from a variety of negotiating tactics. Across America, companies were grappling with a wave of strikes that demanded a response. On the morning that workers sat down in Hershey, Chrysler was working out a settlement with the United Auto Workers granting the CIO affiliate full bargaining rights and ending a work stoppage that had cost the company $60 million. But Henry Ford was taking a tough stand, removing strikers from a plant in St. Louis and insisting that his company would "never recognize" any union.[13]

William Murrie and M.S. Hershey chose the Ford approach, rejecting the key worker demands. According to some sources, this was the only negotiating session Milton Hershey would attend. He then turned things over to Murrie.

Although M.S. backed out of direct contact with the strikers, he was obviously affected by what was going on. Nonunion worker Dionisio Castelli saw him at a foreman's meeting during the strike. "He was very unhappy. He didn't think his employees would do this to him," recalled Castelli. "But he wasn't there half the time. I guess he didn't know what was going on."

Henry Stump, who worked at the Hershey bank, would recall that the Founder came to the bank and brought him into a back room. There he pressed Stump for information about the union's membership. Although his brother was the union's secretary, Stump insisted he didn't know anything.

"You know. Your brother lives with you," he recalled Hershey saying.

"I don't know."

"You must know."

"I don't know."

Under pressure, Stump agreed to infiltrate the union. He paid a dollar to join the local and then got a list of members to show to Hershey. Later the company would develop its own roster of union members and rate their level of involvement. Next to the name Vladimiro Cini, for example, was the note "needs watching." Beside Alex Wallace's name were the words "very bad radical, active CIO picket."

One of the more aggressive union representatives at the negotiating table was the local business manager, John Loy, who informed William Murrie that his members would hold the plant until their demands were met. Not to be outdone, Murrie said the strikers would have to leave the factory before the company would bargain in earnest. The two sides then settled in for what promised to be a long test of wills.

Similar standoffs between unions and corporations were occurring at factories across the country. In the course of 1936, CIO-supported unions had conducted more than four hundred sit-down strikes and won a total of $1 billion in additional annual wages. No single year in history would produce greater advances for unions in America, and the men and women inside the chocolate factory may have believed they would have a success similar to the one enjoyed by the General Motors strikers in Michigan.

However, there were big differences between GM in Flint, and the chocolate company in Hershey. The General Motors plant was a far more dangerous place to work and the company there took an especially hard line when dealing with employees. This meant that a greater percentage of the auto plant's workers were open to the union's criticisms of the company. It was also important that GM employed 80 percent of the city's workers, all of whom had something to gain if the sit-down strike succeeded.

In contrast, the Hershey Chocolate Corporation was regarded as a mostly benign employer, and many of the factory's three thousand workers felt some affection for M.S. Hershey. And while the chocolate plant was vital to the local economy, it did not employ anywhere near 80 percent of the area's workers. Other Hershey enterprises employed nearly two thousand people, who had nothing to do with the strike. And in the surrounding countryside there were thousands of farmers who earned a good part of their income selling milk to the factory. None of these people had any reason to support the strikers.

With the factory closed, and no outlet for the milk their cows produced, area farmers lost money every day. They were natural allies for the anti-union employees of both the factory and of Hershey Estates, which had not been approached by CIO organizers. On Monday, April 5, the fourth day of the strike, these two groups met in an auditorium at the Hershey Industrial School building on Pat's Hill. A committee of twelve was chosen to talk to the strikers about the lost milk sales. The head of the committee, farmer George Sanders, threatened violence if the problem wasn't resolved.

The strikers tried to accommodate the farmers. They agreed to let the company operate its creamery, so the farmers could have their milk processed for sale to other buyers. The hope that arose when this arrangement was announced lasted less than a day. The next morning Hershey milkmen failed to make pickups at nearly all area dairies. The company explained that the creamery's tanks were already full.

On the night of April 6, several thousand farmers, loyal workers, and townspeople marched by torchlight through the town of Palmyra in support of the Hershey Chocolate Corporation. Accompanied by marching bands and fire trucks, they followed a route that passed by a house where M.S. Hershey and William Murrie watched from the front porch. When the parade reached an old school where the union had established an office, some of the marchers talked of storming the place and dragging out its occupants, while others suggested the whole crowd go to the chocolate plant and remove the strikers. Neither idea was acted on.

The next morning, a Hershey milkman stopped at the Brightbill family dairy farm with instructions. They were to join other farmers in town at the Sports Arena, where the next step in the contest with the strikers would be considered. At about the same time, the strikers raised the CIO flag above the Stars and Stripes that usually flew over the factory.

By eleven o'clock more than three thousand Hershey company loyalists and farmers, including many entire families, were conducting a rally at the new arena. According to *The New York Times*, speakers appealed to the crowd's patriotism and affection for M.S. Hershey. One farmer said, "They want a closed shop, do they? Well, we'll open it."

Representatives for the group at the arena were instructed to deliver an ultimatum to the strikers—leave the plant by noon or face forcible eviction. While this message was carried to the factory, another parade was organized. Most of the arena crowd joined the march, which passed by taunting strikers at the chocolate factory and past the windowless Modern Office Building, where William Murrie and other executives stood on the steps and waved their fedoras. Among those they greeted were several dozen women in long cloth coats who called themselves the Loyal Hershey Housewives Brigade.

As a few of the marchers detoured to High Point behind a banner reading "We Pledge Our Loyalty to Mr. M.S. Hershey," the main parade wound back to the arena, where families stopped to eat picnic lunches and listened to music piped through the sound system as they waited for the deadline. Much of the talk was about the strikers' intransigence.

"Our income was being shut off by their behavior," recalled Viola Brightbill, whose family had gone to the arena. "Our feeling was that they weren't grateful. They weren't satisfied with what they had."

The noon deadline was extended to 1:00 P.M. Before that hour was reached, one leader of the antiunion group announced to the arena crowd that the strikers had agreed to vacate the plant. In fact, John Loy and Bull Behman had met with William Murrie and agreed to end the strike. They had also asked Murrie to intervene with the farmers and loyalists to prevent violence.

For a moment, it appeared that a violent clash had been averted. But then someone else rushed into the arena and shouted for men to come to the factory. Some of the men in the crowd grabbed billy clubs, which had been manufactured and provided by a Hershey subsidiary that made wood products. Others, who had brought their own bats, hammers, and pitchforks, retrieved them from where they lay. Waving antiunion placards and American flags, they went to Chocolate Avenue.

Henry Stump would later insist that the events that transpired next were planned by William Murrie and, perhaps, by M.S. Hershey himself. "They had strikebreakers that were supposed to come in but I don't remember them coming in," said Stump. "Hershey Estates guys were told to do it." Company officials would deny this, and claim that loyal workers, townspeople, and farmers had acted spontaneously.

All that is certain is that thousands of people came by car or horse and buggy or on foot to stand outside the factory. After a number of taunts and insults flew out from the plant, the farmers and loyal employees stormed the factory. The strikers were caught by surprise. According to John Loy and *The New York Times*, some who had agreed to vacate the factory were making their exit when men swinging weapons came crashing through the doors.

Striker James DeSantis was on the second floor of the factory when eight or nine men came in a window. Later he would say they were not loyalists or farmers but strikebreakers "from Philly" who were armed with iron bars, which they flung at him and two other men, who immediately ran. The three found their way to the basement and escaped out a rear window, where they joined a number of strikers who were fleeing across open land.

Elsewhere in the plant, women strikers were shepherded to back doors while some of the union men, who were themselves armed with knives, bats, and other weapons, stood against the tide of people spilling into the plant from outside. One of the antiunion men was cut on his stomach by a striker wielding an ice pick. But for the most part it was the union members, outnumbered four to one, who suffered injuries. They were attacked by men who used hammers and crowbars to open locked doors, turned fire hoses on the sit-down strikers, and then clubbed them. Once the fight inside the plant was settled, the strikers were marched to the door with their hands above their heads.

The three leading union organizers, Bull Behman, John Loy, and a CIO man named Miles Sweeney, were severely beaten. Sweeney had been "crowned by a coffee pot then struck by a baseball bat," reported one newspaper. John Loy lost several teeth. Some of their injuries were inflicted as the men were led out of the factory and past the gauntlet of screaming men and women. They were kicked, beaten, and pelted with stones and lumps of coal. In an article about the women who supported the antiunion fighters, writer Betty Brooks described their reaction as the wounded strikers came out of the building.

> Fearlessly some of them stood at the scene of eviction cheering and screaming while each blood-covered striker was pushed forcefully from the building—his hands high above his head. "Get him! Get him!" they shrieked. . . . Recognizing each striker as he ran the gauntlet, they booed or stood silent as their former friends and neighbors were hurried by.

When it was all over, and the antiunion crowd had stopped to sing the national anthem, twenty-five men were nursing injuries, many of them severe enough to require a visit to the hospital. The company regained control of the plant and announced that it would move quickly to resume production and accept shipments of milk from area farms. Within hours of the battle, the farmers had returned to their dairies and, according to the *Times*, "there was a general feeling on the part of the man on the street tonight that the farmers had done themselves proud."

Outside Hershey, reactions were not so positive. The governor of Pennsylvania called the riot "a disgrace" and blamed it on a local sheriff who "was not an unbiased law enforcement officer in this case." Declaring that "mob rule will not be tolerated," he ordered the state police to find and arrest those most responsible for the attack on the strikers, but investigators were never able to identify them.

On the day after the battle at the factory, people in Hershey studied newspaper photos of the fighting to determine where their friends, neighbors, and acquaintances stood. Union members held a rally in the Italian neighborhood. Loyalists gathered at a theater in the Community Building, where the pastor of the Derry Presbyterian Church called on people to "stand by Hershey because Hershey has stood by us." According to one newspaper, seventy-nine-year-old M.S. Hershey, shocked by recent events, was in seclusion. Other sources reported that when the riot broke out, the Founder, who was watching from High Point, cried.

On the surface, the sit-down strike and riot of April 1937 could be seen as another case of Hershey settling its own problems in its own way. Respectful even in rebellion, the workers who shut down the plant had maintained its machinery, so crews were able to resume production soon after the riot. Sales were not affected in any appreciable way. By year's end the company was able to introduce yet another new product named, ironically, Bittersweet.

M.S. Hershey surely took comfort in every little sign that life was returning to normal. For example, in the summer of 1937 he was charmed by a local Boy Scout troop who had asked to see him at High Point. After lining up before the Founder, the trembling leader of the group made their case. "We said we thought it would be nice to go to the first National [Boy Scout] Jamboree [held] in the United States," recalled Richard Bacastow. "We said we didn't have the funds to go. Could we arrange a loan?"

M.S. studied the boys and then agreed to the lend them fifty dollars, on the condition that they work it off on one of the Hershey farms. After the jamboree, the boys came back and reported for work picking peaches and berries. Sticking to his role in this little play, M.S. had his chauffeur drive him to the farm, where he checked up on his debtors. He released them a bit early, sending the message that he was satisfied with their efforts and they should enjoy the remainder of their vacation from school.

Good boys who kept their word were reminders that life could return to normal after the strike. But this process would take time. In the days after the battle, the National Labor Relations Board investigated and ordered the company to conduct a union election. The workers at the chocolate factory chose a loyalist organization called the Independent Chocolate Workers of Hershey over the CIO local by a margin of three to one. However, federal authorities would find that the winners in the election had been helped by management and were not members of a truly independent union. A second election in 1939 brought in the Bakery and Confectionary Workers, an affiliate of the American Federation of Labor. The first contract negotiated by the AFL union and the company gave the workers the overtime rates they wanted, paid vacations and holidays, and a proce-

dure for arbitrating grievances. For the first time in Hershey history, someone other than M.S. would wield a little power.

Few moments in the history of Hershey would affect the community so
profoundly. The strike and the riot brought an end to the town's utopian
innocence. Men who faced one another with fists and weapons raised
might return to work together, but they would never forget what had happened. The sound of women screaming for blood would echo for decades.

The events of April 1937 made it impossible for the people of Hershey
to deny certain social problems. Anti-immigrant (which largely meant anti-
Italian) sentiment was real in Hershey. And the division between those
who cherished the comforts provided by M.S. and others who chafed
under his control was long-standing. The difference was that these feelings
were now out in the open.

The conflict of 1937 also altered Hershey's reputation in the rest of
America. Now the sweet taste of chocolate, the good works for orphans,
and the pleasures of Hershey Park were joined in the public mind by images of bloodied men and a screaming mob.[14]

SOMETHING LIKE A GOD

On a Sunday morning we were working on a piece of equipment that was being installed where we made what they called the Aero Bar . . . and here comes this little fellow up through the room there. We were working in this department under the machines, and he comes by and he says, "Young fellow, what are you doing in here this morning? You should be in church."

"Mr. Hershey," I said, "well, this has to be done. If I wouldn't be here, I would be in church."

But here he was on his way to the laboratory, which he used to spend a lot of time in the laboratory fooling around with whatever. He had a little bag, Lord knows what he had in the bag, [and] was going down to the laboratory.

Edward Tancredi

 Edward Tancredi's name was on the Hershey company's roster of strikers, which was a sort of enemies' list, with the annotation "active CIO." He was also an Italian-American Catholic who never forgot that crosses had been burned near his family's home and that some landlords in Hershey wouldn't rent to immigrants. But even after the strike, the riot, and a host of other insults, he, like so many others in town, would speak fondly of M.S. Hershey and credit him with what was good and fair about the company and the place that bore his name.

The M.S. Hershey whom people would recall from the late 1930s rode around town in the backseat of a futuristic-looking, sixteen-cylinder Chrysler Air Flow—with a big shiny grille, curvy fenders, and balloon whitewalls—making sure everything was tidy. He was easily irritated by an unkempt lawn or an overturned garbage pail. Like everyone, Tancredi assumed that whenever an alley was cleared of litter, or an empty lot was mowed, it was "Mr. Hershey's" doing. Over time, he even came to believe that, if M.S. had been properly briefed, he would have done something to prevent the strike and the riot.

"I don't think the people that he had a lot of faith and trust in [were] telling him the truth, because had he known how the people felt and so on, he would have taken some steps to correct them rather than let them take the path that they did," said Tancredi. "But I think the people that used to report to him didn't give him the full story . . ."

In the aftermath of the strike there was no sign that Hershey was unhappy with his top managers. None of them were dismissed or demoted, and he never said publicly that he was displeased with any of them. Instead, in a *New York Times* report on the events of April 1937, Milton Hershey blamed "four or five" workers who "misled" the others, and he insisted that he could mind his employees' welfare better than they could themselves. Lila Snavely, who visited with him often, would report that after the strike M.S. spoke of the "ingratitude of labor."

Still, many people preferred to believe Milton Hershey had little to do with the events that transpired after the union men shut down the factory. To them, M.S. was benevolent and wise. This was obvious in September 1937, five months after the strike, when the Founder turned eighty and eight thousand people turned out to celebrate at the Sports Arena. Four different bands played. Cake and ice cream were distributed and M.S. allowed himself to wear a paper hat. His employees gave him a gold ring decorated with diamonds and engraved with the image of the cocoa pod baby from his early advertising.

Few in the enormous crowd knew that M.S. was, at that very moment, embroiled in a high-risk gamble in the cocoa bean market. Over the past eight years, the price of cocoa beans had declined to 4 1/2 cents per pound, which was half the going rate in 1929. The depressed market had devastated the economies of the regions of West Africa and South America that grew cacao, but it benefited Hershey and other buyers all through the Depression. (A highly specialized crop, cocoa was the one key ingredient in chocolate that Hershey never attempted to produce.)

When the world economy began to recover, chocolate manufacturers saw a surge in demand for their products and they subsequently made a run on cocoa. In 1936, importers in the United States bought 14 percent more cocoa and British buyers scooped up 25 percent more. Demand caused the price to rise to 9 cents per pound. Then in early 1937 speculators began to talk about problems with the crop in the Gold Coast Colony (now Ghana). This fear caused another 30 percent price hike in three weeks. Suddenly a pound of cocoa beans cost more than 12 cents.

With his factory requiring an enormous supply of cocoa beans, M.S. had no choice but to buy futures contracts at a premium. Then, as always happens with inflated markets, the bubble burst. Yields proved there was no trouble with the crop in West Africa and the supply was more than adequate to meet demand. The price of cocoa beans began to fall almost as sharply as it had risen. By summer it was bouncing around the 8-cent level. Hershey held contracts to pay a much higher price, which meant he was at a severe competitive disadvantage.

As his contracts rapidly lost value, M.S. faced a choice. He could endure the decline, buy his beans at the inflated price, and accept his losses. Or he could try to buy enough beans quickly on the spot market to make the market rise. He chose the second, riskier option, purchasing thousands of tons of beans at 8.3 cents. The buying campaign, which was financed with $17 million borrowed from National City, almost worked. Just before his big birthday party, the line on the cocoa price graph started heading up.

Unfortunately, others in the cocoa bean market found out that nearly all of the buy orders being placed were coming from one man. Without him, sellers would have been forced to accept even lower prices. Knowing that M.S. represented their only willing customer, they rushed to sell to him. Eventually he ran out of cash, and the price resumed its fall.

As a result of M.S. Hershey's cocoa gamble, his company suffered paper losses in the millions. Stanley Russell of National City would recall it as a time when M.S. "went haywire." But there was a difference between this commodities debacle and the sugar crisis. This time Hershey managed to stay profitable, and no overseer was appointed by the bank. And the beans, which would stay fresh if properly stored, eventually became an asset. When supplies became scarce during World War II, the value of this enormous reserve more than made up for the losses of 1937.[1]

After the cocoa bean crisis, the realities of old age settled on M.S. Hershey in a way they hadn't before. He stopped traveling internationally—his last visit to Cuba was in 1937—and withdrew further from his businesses. He became ill—one source reported it was a mild heart attack, another suggested a stroke—the night after his eightieth-birthday party, but quickly recovered. From this point on, however, he would be tended by nurses who served mostly as companions at his home, but also accompanied him on his travels around the eastern states.

One or another of these women was likely with M.S. when, after he recovered, he decided to travel by car to New York. Before he reached the city, he chose to spend the night at a hotel in Montclair, New Jersey. The next morning he dropped in on Stanley Russell, who lived in the town.

Over the years Russell had become a trusted adviser to M.S. Hershey and a friend to a man who seemed to have few human contacts outside of business. In the past Russell had aired his concerns about the school trust's relationship with the Hershey companies. He thought the trust should sell the stock it held and invest the money in other ways. M.S. had the power to make these changes, and on that morning in Montclair, Russell thought he had finally persuaded his friend to do so. Later he would recall what was said, word for word.

"I have been thinking about what you said," began M.S. "I think you are right. Let's go to work. Nobody knows anything about this, neither Murrie nor Staples. I wanted no one but you and me to know."

With the help of Hershey's auditor from the Arthur Andersen firm, two of Russell's associates at the bank analyzed the Hershey businesses and put together a plan to divest the trust of the stock. As Russell recalled it, he then met M.S. for dinner in a hotel suite in New York City and outlined a divestiture plan. After Russell left him that night, M.S. never acted on the plan. In fact, he never spoke to Stanley Russell again.

"I think only one thing stopped him from going through," Russell said. It was "the inertia of old age."[2]

Many men retire from business and seek the pleasures of new hobbies and entertainments. M.S. Hershey did not. Instead he just cut away those parts of life that he found trying, or annoying, leaving only the kinds of work and diversions that had always given him the most pleasure. At the top of the list was the development of new ideas. He spent long hours in a company laboratory, performing the same kinds of experiments that he conducted during the exciting days at the homestead, when he raced to perfect a milk chocolate recipe before his giant factory was completed.

At the moment when Milton Hershey returned to experimenting, America was enthralled with the health-giving power of newly discovered vitamins. (Vitamin A, the first isolated in a lab, was found in 1913. Others were found in the ensuing decades. In 1935, the first synthetic vitamin, C, was made.) Fruits, grains, and vegetables, which were rich in these nutrients, grew in popularity and food companies added vitamins in powdered or liquid form to their products to make them more appealing to health-conscious consumers.

In some cases, the focus on vitamins produced tangible results. Rickets was all but banished from the country after vitamin D was added to milk. But in other instances, it would be hard to say that anything more substantial than profit was achieved by enriched foods. Did Wonder Bread really build strong bodies? It was hard to say. Nevertheless, a vitamin craze swept the country. Vitamins were considered so important that when the University of Wisconsin, a center of vitamin research, commissioned a mural to decorate its new biochemistry building, the central figure in the piece was a scientist leading farm children with rickets from darkness into daylight.[3]

Ever conscious of what was modern and scientific, M.S. Hershey looked for ways to add what he called "vitt-a-mins" to his products and bolster his long-standing claim that chocolate was a nutritious food. Sam Hinkle, a Hershey chemist who would rise in the executive ranks, helped with attempts to mix turnips, parsley, celery, and even beets into chocolate.

Hershey's method involved dehydrating the vegetables first, grinding and then mixing them with milk, sugar, and all the other ingredients that went into Hershey bars and Kisses. In the beginning, Hinkle would try to talk him out of some of these combinations. "The mere thought of celery and chocolate mixed," he recalled, "gives the average skilled person, skilled in the art of mixing food, a feeling at once that it can't be good."

Hinkle's thoughts about food combinations, and his expertise in chemistry, didn't matter at all to M.S., and he made this clear. Soon the younger man was helping his boss create all sorts of concoctions, going ahead with mixtures that he knew were ill fated. "I often wondered," said Hinkle, "how Mr. Hershey could have been able to produce the fine milk chocolate which bears his name, and yet come up with some really terrible concoctions in his later life."

Whatever the results, M.S. pressed on, barking at whoever happened to be at hand. No one who was there would ever forget the time he used a wooden paddle to push bananas through a series of metal rollers and succeeded in creating a sweet-smelling mess. Amusing as these events were, no one laughed, or even smiled, until the boss showed it was okay. Usually he didn't. An exception occurred when helpers poured a huge quantity of milk into a large kettle and it splashed all over him. According to a man who was there, he smiled, licked some of the milk off of his face, and told them to keep on working.

The results of many of his ideas "tasted just about as bad as they sound," added Hinkle, but they always had to be tasted. This didn't bother the old man much. This was due in part to the fact that a lifetime of regular cigar smoking, combined with the normal loss of taste buds people experience with age, left him less sensitive to flavors and aromas.

Besides fulfilling his need to be useful and creative, Milton hoped his experiments would yield something nutritious to replace meat in the American diet, which he thought contained too many animal products. When he got close to his goal with a chocolate bar containing cornmeal, carrots, and raisins, he pressed one of his assistants to come up with another ingredient that would move the masses to buy it. When this assistant balked, Hershey grew impatient.

"Jesus Christ boy, you're a college man," he sputtered. "How the hell don't you know? You're a college man!"

When M.S. was in his eighties, he was likely to call anyone under seventy "boy" and tended toward outbursts of excited swearing. In old age the Founder was becoming difficult and the people around him sometimes struggled to keep him happy and treat him with respect even when he acted unreasonably. Bob Bucher, another employee in the lab, would long remember a Sunday morning when M.S. wanted to experiment with using a powerful hydraulic press to squeeze water out of milk. Unsatisfied with the effort his men were making, he shouted, "Damn it, get some pressure." Plumbers were called, and the pressure in the press was increased to a point that the other people in the room were afraid the machinery might just fly apart. The men called William Murrie, to see if he would intervene.

"Hell, let him go," was Murrie's reply. "Let him bust up the press, so long as he doesn't bust up the whole damn company."

In the end, the machinery was all right, but the experiment failed and Bucher decided that not even "the devil" could stop M.S. Hershey. "We had to be scared of him," he said. "We didn't know how to take him."

Undaunted by his failures with vegetables and hydraulic presses, M.S. pursued chocolate made with corn and other grains. He brought a pie crust into the lab and filled that with chocolate, and used various household items—ashtrays, for example—as molds to produce products with exotic shapes. Once he had the laboratory prepare a mixture of popcorn and flour, which was then used to make a cake. For a while he kept two men working full-time on a nondairy substitute for ice cream. A concoction based on rice flour came fairly close. For a time M.S. manufactured it in little batches under the name Victory Whip and sold it at the Hershey

Creamery. He stopped selling it after the dairy industry complained about the competition.

While most of Hershey's experiments were conducted on a small scale, there were times when he spent significant sums on fantasy products. When raisin companies began to advertise their product as a source of iron for better blood, M.S. bought two boxcar loads of raisins and two tank cars full of molasses (another vitamin-rich food) and set about making candy out of them. "He fooled around for about sixty days, experimenting with them. Finally he gave up," recalled John Hosler, a lab worker.

"'Hosler,'" he said, "'the raisins and molasses are all yours. It didn't work.'" Hosler was able to sell the raisins and recoup some of the cash Hershey had spent on them, but he wasn't able to make anything on the molasses.

Failures like the one with the raisins and molasses did not deter M.S. during this period. Instead, he broadened his interests. Milton Hunchberger, who worked for Hershey as a baker and candy maker, carried out many experiments that produced barely edible results. One exception was sweet potato fudge, which turned out well but was never produced in large quantities.

Hershey's methods during these experiments were similar to the trial-and-error technique he had employed at the homestead thirty-five years earlier. Hunchberger recalled, "He would say, 'Put in molasses' or 'put in a hundred pounds of 4X [confectioners'] sugar' and 'a couple of pounds of butter' until, in time, I didn't know what the formula was anymore and the price was excessive."

One recipe Hunchberger never forgot was for a type of muffin. He knew that if he followed the directions he received from M.S., the mix would come out wrong. He warned his boss, who said, "That's the way we learn." A few days later M.S. came back for a taste test.

"You don't think much of it?" asked M.S.

"No."

The old man ate some of what Hunchberger had made but said nothing. The next day the baker was called to have dinner with the great experimenter at the Hotel Hershey. He was told to make another batch of muffins and bring them along. At the hotel dining room he took an assigned seat with a group of executives and the waiter gave each man a muffin. After the muffins were eaten, M.S. went around the table asking, "What do you think of that thing the baker made?" The others said they liked it. Only Hunchberger disagreed, saying, "I don't like it. It is no good."

When all the men had spoken, Hershey turned back to the baker. "See what damned liars these fellows are. They know it is no good, but don't have enough guts to say."[4]

In his eighties Hershey practiced this kind of playful teasing—object lessons in status and practicality—more and more. It was as if he was trying to break down some of the barriers between himself and others by forcing them to treat him like any other human being. At the ice cream shop in the park he would sneak behind the counter to scoop a sample out with his finger and then delight in the scolding—"Keep your damn dirty fingers out of the ice cream!"—he received from a scooper who didn't know him. At the community center he would sit with a newspaper in front of his face, sometimes in a chair right below his own portrait, so he might hear what others were saying about him.

M.S. also enjoyed making gestures with his money. In the winter of 1938, he was hospitalized for six weeks with broken ribs suffered during a fall. Undoubtedly bored and restless during this long confinement, M.S. looked for things to do. He decided to keep track of the births in the hospital and started a savings account for each child born while he was there. Each of the fifty accounts was seeded with ten dollars from the Founder. After he got out of the hospital he showed similar kindness to a shopgirl who caught him sneaking sweets at a company candy shop. He rewarded her with a pay raise.

At the end of his life M.S. warmed up to the press as well. In the late thirties and early forties he submitted to more interviews than he had in the past. At last he had both the time and the inclination to reminisce. He gave the one and only radio interview of his life, letting the world hear his strangely high and soft voice. The program, *It Can Be Done*, was hosted by popular poet Edgar Guest and included a radio play about Hershey's life. At around the same time he reportedly went to Nebraska for a secret tour of Boys Town, traveling incognito to see what he could learn that might be useful back at the Hershey Industrial School.

While most of his eccentricities were, like this undercover mission, harmless, sometimes M.S. showed signs of losing perspective. One of the more egregious examples came after a doctor at the Hershey hospital admitted a polio-stricken boy from a nearby town who died the night he arrived. The next day M.S. complained because he didn't want "any diseased people in there." (This was strange, since M.S. had quietly paid for the care of many sick people in town.) Unlike others who shrank when M.S. spoke, the doctor stood up to the Founder, saying he would admit any patient who needed care. After a two-day standoff, he resigned, calling M.S. "a senile misanthropic millionaire."

Much of what M.S. did in his eighties might be viewed as self-indulgence or play. When, for example, he jumped behind the unmanned counter at a candy shop inside Hershey Park, he was having a little fun, not taking on a real job. But he was still concerned about the grand utopian experiment he had created—a business and town that supported his boys at the industrial school—and he took pains to remind Hershey's citizens that they were part of something important. In 1938 he wrote a memo to remind his workers that visitors could be "sold on The Hershey idea" if they were served with courtesy and efficiency.[5]

Of course, M.S. considered himself more than a cheerleader and inspirational figurehead. With his experiments he intended to create useful products and new businesses, and in one case he succeeded. For years he had wondered about what might be done with the excess cocoa butter produced at his factory. In the mid-1930s he focused on using it to produce soap, and by 1938 he had built a small soap factory that began turning out bars by the thousands. Some were packaged in brown wrappers that made them resemble thick, stubby Hershey chocolate bars. One customer wrote to complain that her child had mistaken the soap for chocolate and tried to eat it.

The cocoa butter soap was a challenging business from the start. For one thing, it didn't smell as good as others, and substantial effort was required to fix this problem. At one meeting of the company's board of directors, M.S. and the others were asked to test the aromas of several different bars that had been made with various perfumes. Knowing that the company had experimented with scents costing as much as thirty-five dollars per pound, Milton stopped after each sample to ask, "How much did you pay for that?"

M.S. had a cold and couldn't smell anything but he was worried that the others would pick the expensive perfume. He declared that the cheapest scent—it cost less than three dollars per pound—was the best, and that was the one that went into production. It took three months for the men who ran the soap business to discover that the cheap perfume tended to fade, allowing the cocoa butter fragrance to return. They subsequently experimented with more than three hundred fragrances before finding the right one.

In the meantime, M.S. Hershey turned himself into a human guinea pig in an attempt to prove that his soap had special healing properties. Using a knife, he scraped at the liver spots on his own hands until he had removed several layers of skin and they were bloody and raw. He made a thick lather out of his soap and water to coat the wounds, and then put on white cotton gloves to protect them. Days passed, his hands healed, and then he started the process all over again. Although his doctors told him to stop—he was risking serious infection—M.S. kept going until his skin was almost completely cleared of spots.

Milton's attempt to prove that his soap worked healing miracles was more a sign of his increasing eccentricity than a legitimate science experiment, and no one ever seconded his claim. Instead, when M.S. insisted that local barbers use a stinging cream made from the soap on their customers' freshly shaved faces, they yelped in protest.

After the problems of scent were resolved, and the idea of a healing cream was set aside, Milton focused his energy on selling the stock of soap that was piling up as he insisted his factory produce at full capacity. A fleet of twenty-four trucks, which were decorated with big signs, was used to distribute and advertise the soap locally. In New York, M.S. talked the Waldorf-Astoria into using his soap until guests made it clear they didn't like it. In Hershey he decided to give away six thousand bars at a hockey game. Although the arena manager implored him to hand out the bars *after* the final buzzer, M.S. insisted people get their soap on the way in. The inevitable happened: a referee made a call against the home team and first one and then thousands of soap bars flew out of the stands and onto the ice in protest.

Undaunted, Hershey came up with another promotional idea—a shop on the boardwalk in Atlantic City devoted solely to his soap. He put a tub and mechanical agitator in the shop window, filled it with soapy water, and left the agitator running all day to keep the tub filled with bubbles. Customers who entered the store were often served by M.S. himself, and he enjoyed telling them "Mr. Hershey will be pleased" by their purchases.

As always, Milton Hershey was more relaxed and mischievous when he was away from home. He would bet his nurses on almost anything, even the boxing matches that were broadcast over the radio. They rarely wagered more than a nickel, but if he won, he made sure to collect. At dinner he would say ridiculous things, trying to bait people into disagreeing. When they refused, he'd challenge them. "You know damn well you don't agree with me," he would say. "Why the hell don't you say so?"

During one stay in Atlantic City he suddenly told his nurses (by this time he had two whenever he traveled) that it would be a good idea to go to Saratoga Springs, New York, for the mineral baths. It just happened to be racing season, and for thirty days M.S. dressed up in a three-piece suit, donned a white brimmed hat and sunglasses, and went to the track to bet on the horses. Sometimes he brought the nurses with him. They went to the windows to place his bets, and he taught them a bit about his strategy, which often involved betting on the entire field in a race.

"Now, girls," he said, "I am not teaching you to gamble, but teaching you it is not safe to gamble." They couldn't help but notice that he played every race, and did quite well.

In the evenings at Saratoga he took his little entourage to various restaurants—they often picked which one—and then searched for a little after-dinner gambling action. But that year the authorities in Saratoga had cracked down on the illegal gambling parlors that served the summer crowds, and M.S. had trouble finding a place to play roulette. Finally he met up with a man who led a local gambling ring—the type of fellow whom M.S. would have run out of Hershey—and got a printed card that would gain him admission to one of the few secret casinos still operating. After that, he gambled every night.

In Saratoga, Atlantic City, and Hershey, the nurses who tended M.S. found themselves with an old man who was always ready to tease them and increasingly sentimental and willful. Despite doctor's orders, he ate what he wanted when he wanted it and that sometimes included champagne and caviar. And while he never ordered them about and always asked them their opinions, he could be a challenge to his caretakers.

"When he was about to play some trick, he looked like a bad little boy with his eyes looking sideways at you," recalled a nurse named Susan Spangler. "He would fiddle around for two hours finding excuses not to go to bed." When his nurses were running errands in downtown Hershey, if he could, M.S. would sneak away from them. And if they tried to make him dress a little better—turning down the brim of his hat, for example, which he always turned up—he'd resist them. "He looked like a man without a cent," said Spangler.

A few of those who knew him then believed that M.S. Hershey was lonely at the end of his life. He had no wife, no children, and apparently no intimate friends. It made sense to assume he was lonesome. Lila Snavely described him this way, and so did many others.

But M.S. didn't act like a lonely or unhappy man, and he didn't talk much about feelings of loss or isolation. He had made a conscious choice to never remarry, and to invest himself in building companies and communities, not personal relationships. And as the years had passed, M.S. Hershey appeared to be more content and more satisfied with the life he had made. In one of his rare moments of reflection, recalled by his associate Monroe Stover, Hershey's main worry was not that he wouldn't be comforted in the end, but that his successors would lack the nerve to continue building and developing his industrial paradise after he was gone.[6]

After M.S. relinquished day-to-day authority, his companies continued to build. In 1938 and 1939, a big outdoor stadium seating sixteen thousand for football was constructed near the Sports Arena and half a dozen new attractions, including a big Ferris wheel, were added to the park. In these same years the chocolate company began making a series of new products, including miniature candy bars, a candy called Biscrisp, and another named the Krackle bar.

In 1940 the Hershey Country Club hosted the Professional Golfer's Association Championship. The following year the club hired a superstar-to-be named Ben Hogan to replace Henry Picard, who had won the 1939 PGA Championship, as pro at the club.

Hogan's contract was unique in golf and it reflected both Milton's interest in the game (the one sport he truly enjoyed) and the Hershey company's low-key marketing style. Milton had built his own courses in both Pennsylvania and Cuba and played well into his seventies. Filling the pro's job at the Hershey club allowed him to buy himself a relationship with the best in the game.

In order to lure the taciturn Hogan to his club, Hershey didn't require him to perform the usual chores like giving lessons to members, which was something the pro abhorred. Nor did Hershey ask him to make public appearances to talk about chocolate products. Instead the contract committed Hogan to compete in a significant number of tournaments around the country as Hershey's representative. In exchange he would also permit the company to use his name and picture in advertising. It was a perfect deal for an aloof pro ill suited to socializing and for a manufacturer who merely wanted an association as Hogan became an iconic figure in his sport.

This almost shy style was apparent in the relationship between the two men as well. In September 1940 Milton watched Hogan play at a course near Atlantic City but left because he thought he was making the pro nervous and causing him to play poorly. That evening he told his two nurses to put on their best clothes for dinner. When they got to the restaurant, they discovered that Hershey had arranged for a special meal to celebrate his own eighty-third birthday and that Hogan and his wife would complete the little party.[7]

As they drew more attention to their brand with Hogan's name, new products, and new park attractions, the men in charge of Hershey saw chocolate sales reach a record $44 million in 1940, a robust recovery from the dip in sales during the strike year. By one industry estimate, the Hershey factory was now making three-quarters of all the chocolate consumed in the United States. In November 1941 the company was headed toward $55 million in sales when the U.S. military turned to Hershey to produce a nutrient-packed chocolate bar, called D Ration, that could survive in every conceivable climate and be packaged to stay dry even after submerged in water for an hour. Besides supplying six hundred calories, the bar would be enriched with vitamin B_1 to prevent beriberi in the tropics.[8]

While other companies struggled against wartime restrictions that made it difficult for them to buy new machinery, military contracts allowed the Hershey company to quickly obtain and install equipment to handle the thicker, stickier mixture that became the D Ration. Other manufacturers also suffered from federal controls placed on sugar, which made it impossible for them to produce enough chocolate to meet demand. In contrast, all through the Second World War Hershey would be allowed all the sugar needed to make millions of bars per week for the armed services. This patriotic duty helped to nearly double the company's sales in four years, to more than $80 million in 1944, the last full year of fighting.

Throughout the war, the chocolate industry would tussle with the government over restrictions on sugar. Eventually, with William Murrie leading the effort, they would manage to convince federal officials that chocolate was a food, essential to the well-being and morale of both the troops and the nation. This designation would end the restrictions on their use of sugar. With production at the Hershey factory rising due to the military orders and with so many men joining the armed forces, local women filled hundreds of jobs at the plant; they logged countless overtime hours as the plant operated around the clock, seven days a week. Along with the benefits of full employment, the community basked in its role as a bulwark for the military's morale and in the recognition it received from Washington. Before the war's end, the Hershey company would receive five citations for excellence, called Army-Navy E awards, from the Pentagon. Only one other military supplier, lens maker Bausch and Lomb, received more honors. Of course Bausch and Lomb didn't enjoy the other wartime honor that Hershey received: the Army Air Forces named a Pacific-based B-26 bomber *The City of Hershey.*

Only one other consumer product company, Coca-Cola, was as much a part of the war effort as Hershey. Like Coke, the Hershey chocolate that traveled with the troops was a sweet reminder of home and it became an icon of Americanism for the people who were liberated by U.S. forces. Soldiers handed out both products to local children and adults to show their good intentions and curry favor.

Coca-Cola followed the military, building temporary bottling facilities in the field at government expense. Coca-Cola managed to distribute 5 billion bottles of Coke to GIs during the war, while Hershey sent just 1 billion bars of chocolate rations overseas.

When the war ended, Coke turned many of these plants into permanent subsidiaries. In this way, Coca-Cola used wartime events to become a much stronger international brand. Hershey had the same opportunities, and through the efforts of friendly GIs much of the world had learned to like the peculiar Hershey taste. But the company did not show any global ambitions. Instead, after the war it would retreat from Europe and the Pacific and return its focus to the U.S. market.

During the war, M.S. had attended ceremonies when the military gave Hershey its awards, and he was often seen at the Community Building, at the bank, or in downtown shops. But he stopped going into the factory on a regular basis. When he was brought through the plant to see the new machinery and methods used to turn out as many as half a million D Rations in a day, he said it was "the finest thing I have ever seen accomplished here."

In his later years, Hershey allowed himself to take some pleasure in what he had built, and nothing pleased him more than the industrial school. During the Depression, a change in the deed of trust had opened admissions to boys as old as fourteen. (Previously no boy older than eight was accepted.) This new rule, combined with hard times, increased requests for spaces. In 1939, a record 1,018 boys lived in cottages and farmhouses scattered across the valley. Milton Hershey would devote much of his time to riding in his chauffeured car to the various homes and other buildings of the school, so he could see how the boys were being raised and educated. To the boys, he was something like Daddy Warbucks, a wealthy rescuer worthy of any desperate child's fantasies.

"He was right there when I first arrived at the school and they were giving me my clothes," recalled Lou Bocian, who enrolled in 1939, at the age of seven. "He put his arm around me and said, 'From now on, we'll take care of you. You're one of my boys.'"

A typical Home Boy, as they were called, Bocian's mother had died and his father was unable to provide for his six children. He would forever recall begging for food in the poor neighborhood where he lived as a child. He felt that the food, clothing, medical care, and housing he received at the school came directly from Milton Hershey himself and he was grateful.

But while the boys at the school were never again hungry or cold, their lives were not always easy. Their days were governed by a rigid routine and Buena Vista, the house where Bocian happened to live, was ruled by an unusually strict couple who were much more willing than most to use one of the paddles that were kept in the closets. "They were tyrants," explained Bocian many years later. "You couldn't walk on the grass and you always had to be alert to what they expected of you. They did things that would never be tolerated today. There were many times when I was black and blue." Many boys were unable to adjust to the home, he added. Some ran away.

Remarkably, Bocian didn't connect his bad experiences with his house parents with his benefactor. Like most of the other boys he was just thrilled when Milton Hershey stopped at the cottage to visit. "He'd come about every two weeks and watch us play. Once he took me on his lap in his car and I played with the steering wheel, pretending to drive. He was, to us, a very kind man whom we considered to be our foster father." Photos of these visits show Milton seated on the steps of a house in his business suit, with one boy on his knee and more than a dozen seated around him.

In his old age, as he spent more time at the school, Hershey did receive a large measure of love and attention from the boys he had made his heirs. They ran to him when he visited and prayed for him whenever he got sick. Bocian recalled in particular one of the regular Friday assemblies at the junior-senior high school that had been built near the Hotel Hershey. "He often came down from the hotel to these convocations, to hear us sing and listen to everything that went on. He might say a few words. There might be seven or eight hundred of us there. On this day, when he set foot in the place somebody started clapping and pretty soon all of us were yelling and clapping and we wouldn't stop. He started to cry. All he could do was wave to us."

Life still offered pleasure and purpose to Milton Hershey, even if it only involved visiting with his boys or serving as a good example. As one of the nation's senior industrialists, M.S. had allowed himself to be used as an inspiration for older Americans who were needed to replace factory workers and others drafted into the military. In late 1942, when he had reached age eighty-five, the *Philadelphia Inquirer* published an extensive profile of M.S. that showed him to be full of patriotic vigor. "I have often been asked—What is the best age for producing?" he is quoted saying. "I know only one answer, the age you are now."

Despite the bravado he displayed for the press and for the good of the war effort, an ailing heart and recurrent breathing problems had slowed Milton considerably. He spent more and more time in his two rooms at High Point. His bedroom, where pictures of his mother and father flanked the window, was furnished with two maple dressers, a matching bed, and assorted side tables and chairs. One dresser was filled with the talismans of an old man's life. The top drawer held, among other items, an assortment of hearings aids—he was never comfortable with any of them—along with a shaving kit, a cigar lighter, a nail clipper, and a set of brushes. Drawers below were filled with photographs and souvenirs from testimonial dinners and speeches.

Milton's other room, a combination study and parlor, was not so much decorated as simply filled with upholstered chairs, a big radio, and bric-a-brac. Scattered around were some of the seven pictures of Catherine, which he kept on display. In the center of the room was a folding card table where Milton often sat to read. The items on the walls included a picture of William Lebkicher and a framed engraving of the Ten Commandments.[9]

The nurses who tended Milton recalled a man who enjoyed reminiscing about the development of his business, his travels, and exciting moments in his life. Nurse Susan Spangler would recall that M.S. rarely said anything about his wife or his mother. But he told a vivid story about the historic blizzard of 1888, when snow halted transportation and trapped Hershey in New York City.

On most nights Milton's doctor, Herman Hostetter, stopped by the apartment to see his most famous patient. Their relationship was one of the few in which Milton Hershey met a man on even terms. Hostetter had asserted himself early in their relationship, when he discovered that M.S. had been throwing away his medication. "I won't waste my time with people who won't take the medicine," he had told him as he walked out. "Go ahead and die. I am done with you." Milton became more cooperative after this blowup, and the doctor would see him almost every night for eight years.[10]

These visits, which often ran past midnight, were as much social calls as medical checkups, and they always included big bowls of chocolate ice cream and glasses of cold milk. (Ironically enough, this man who had made millions promoting the purity of milk-based products had sworn off the stuff after getting sick on a meal of seafood and milk. He returned to drinking it only when Hostetter made it a prescription.) As doctor and patient enjoyed their snack, M.S. would muse about the past and fantasize about things he'd like to see built in his town. His memories of the distant past were clear, though he had trouble recalling the events of recent days, weeks, or months. As Hostetter recalled later, M.S. hoped his town would eventually get a new hospital. He also talked about the need for a place to house retired and disabled workers who were unable to live on their own.

In 1944, M.S. resigned his positions as board chairman for the Milton Hershey School Trust, the industrial school and the Hershey Foundation, which had been created to benefit the local community. He named P.A. Staples—"a good man to carry on"—as his replacement, and truly retreated into private life. Staples's appointment meant that William Murrie, who had been second to M.S. for the life of the company, would never get to run it on his own. It was the last momentous business decision of M.S. Hershey's life, and it may have made sense given Murrie's advanced age. But for the man who had made so many of Hershey's dreams come true, it must have been a blow.

• • •

The pleasures Milton Hershey enjoyed in this time were simple. He liked staying up late into the night and sleeping through the morning. (He said that if he rose early he was "bothered all day" but if he slept in, he would "only be bothered in the afternoon.") He listened to the radio and took walks out onto a flat rooftop at High Point, where, in the spring of 1944, a pool of water attracted a pair of ducks.

M.S. called the flat roof that covered one wing of High Point his "Atlantic City" and the walkway that led to it was his "Boardwalk." He stocked the pool with goldfish and considered it his responsibility to feed the birds. The menu included cracked grains and the bread left over from breakfast. A doting host, M.S. provided the mallards with a nesting box and made sure the rooftop puddle was always filled with cool water. The well-nourished couple produced eleven eggs. Three of the ducklings died from overindulging at the free banquet. A fourth disappeared in a thunderstorm, and the tragedy made headlines in a local paper. But before summer was over, M.S. saw the remaining duck children mature and fly

In September 1945, Milton Hershey celebrated his eighty-eighth birthday with a small dinner at the old homestead. Fourteen people, each of them connected to one Hershey enterprise or another, gathered in the downstairs room where Milton Hershey had been born in 1857. In one corner stood the simple, unadorned cradle in which M.S. had been rocked as an infant. At the table he was flanked by his ally of fifty-plus years, William Murrie, and his appointed heir, P.A. Staples. The meal, which included pheasant and various wines, was arranged by the manager of the Hotel Hershey. Coffee was accompanied by slices of birthday cake. By the time it was over M.S., who suffered from a faltering heartbeat and a persistent cough, showed the strain.[11]

With autumn at hand, and the days growing shorter, the rhythm of life in the Lebanon Valley began its familiar shift toward winter. Milton Hershey's apple orchards, 175 acres in all, would yield fifteen thousand bushels that fall. It would be one of the best seasons ever for peaches, as 20 acres of trees would give up more than six thousand bushels of the sweetest fruit ever grown on Hershey land.

On the night of Thursday, October 11, Dr. Hostetter went to High Point for his usual visit and noticed that M.S. had the symptoms of a cold, mainly a cough and a slight fever. The next morning the doctor was summoned by Milton's nurse and he ordered an ambulance to take him to the hospital. "All right," said M.S., "you're the boss."

At the hospital Milton Hershey was placed in an oxygen tent, but his condition worsened. As Home Boy Lou Bocian would recall it, the boys at the Hershey school learned of his illness and prayed for him.

On Saturday morning M.S. awakened for a moment, smiled at one of his nurses, and said, "You never thought that you would have to look at me in a cage like a monkey in the zoo, did you." Then he fell asleep. Hours later, as Dr. Hostetter was at his side, M.S. Hershey's heart gave out and he died. The official cause of his death was pneumonia.

Milton Hershey's death was front-page news in many papers. Most of these reports counted the industrial school and the town of Hershey as his greatest achievements. Pennsylvania Governor Edward Martin described M.S. Hershey in terms that would have made the utopian industrialist proud. Hershey's death "takes from our midst one of the great examples of what the free enterprise plan means," he said, adding that M.S. "amassed a great fortune but during his lifetime he gave it all for the benefit of those with small opportunities."

With no close family to request private services, M.S. Hershey's passing was handled almost as a matter of state. His open casket was placed in the lobby of the big junior-senior high school he had built on Pat's Hill, where it was surrounded by hundreds of bouquets, floral blankets, and wreaths sent from around the country. Many of these came from employees, managers, and those who did business with Hershey. Coca-Cola sent a wreath of roses with a cluster of orchids. The Automatic Canteen Company of America sent a basket of roses.

By one estimate, ten thousand people passed by Hershey's body as it lay in the rotunda. Twelve hundred attended a thirty-minute funeral service in the school auditorium, where the eulogy was said by the local Episcopal vicar. It's unlikely M.S. ever set foot in the vicar's church, and just as unlikely that the two men ever met. Perhaps for this reason, the Reverend John H. Treder's six-paragraph eulogy contained not one personal observation, or even a hint of the private M.S. Hershey. Instead he spoke in generic ways about the good deeds Milton had performed and then called on the community to uphold the spirit "of our founding father."

More than two hundred cars followed the hearse from the school to the cemetery, where an open grave waited beside a marble tombstone bearing the name Hershey in gold letters. Eight boys from the industrial school carried M.S. to a grave near the ones occupied by his mother, his father, and his wife.[12]

M.S. Hershey died with little personal wealth. His few possessions, mostly artwork and furnishings at High Point, were auctioned in December 1945 and the proceeds were added to a fund of roughly $900,000 that he established for the benefit of the public school system of Derry Township, which served Hershey. The highly profitable firm that M.S. had bequeathed in 1918 to the Hershey Trust produced roughly 90 percent of the milk chocolate consumed in America. It was a major player in the world sugar trade and the working heart of a community widely regarded as the ideal American industrial town.

Within a year, P.A. Staples would begin to change the Hershey businesses in ways that would have been difficult, if not impossible, to achieve while M.S. was alive. He would sell all the Cuban holdings, which he had never considered a valuable asset. And Milton's beloved trolley would make its last run in December 1946, falling victim to the automobile.

In the town, people would notice that litter hung around longer and the weeds in vacant lots were not mowed as frequently. "The only reason it wasn't being done was because the old man was gone," recalled Ed Tancredi. "The people that were left didn't have the interest . . ."

Some of the people M.S. left behind were at least devoted to keeping up the Founder's image. Students and alumni of the industrial school were especially grateful for his philanthropy. Writing in the school paper, they described him as "something like a god" and as a "fairy god father." One alumnus wrote, "I am certain his spirit will live on as if he were still alive." This last sentiment, expressed by a young man who confessed "I never knew him personally," was shared by workers, townspeople, and others who knew M.S. Hershey only as a figurehead. They associated everything good with Milton Hershey and, when a problem arose, many wondered how the Founder might handle it.

Only a few of the people who had known the private Milton Hershey talked about him as someone more complex than his public image. But about a decade after Milton died, one of these, Ruth Hershey Beddoe, wrote a letter to a professor who was researching an authorized biography of M.S. In it, she described the less than mythic facets of a man she had known since she had traveled with him in Europe as Catherine's companion.

"Milton was in many ways quite a man of the world, very hard and thoroughly spoiled," she wrote. "He would have made a good general, with his drive, his seeing everything clearly ahead, and knowing what to do. He didn't always know whom to get to do things. But the way he could call up loyalties and hold them would have been a big military asset."

Ruth Hershey Beddoe recalled a conversation she had with William Klein, who had worked for M.S. as a young man before going into business for himself. Klein had been treated well by Milton, and yet he said, "When you come to think of it, Ruth, the old man wasn't so hot."

Upon hearing this Ruth wrote, she "immediately stiffened up, straightened my chin and looked the other way. He changed the subject." But years later, the comment stayed with her, and she confessed that "I always wanted to know what he would have said, but I wouldn't let him say it."[13]

THE LEGACY

13 It didn't take long for Milton S. Hershey to be transformed from a human being into a sepia-colored myth. After all, he had outlived most of his peers, and without their recollections it was hard to preserve a true sense of him. Hershey's transition from man to legend was accelerated by the departure of his last, living original ally in business, William Murrie. He quietly retired in 1947, leaving the firm with no strong connection to the old days in Lancaster. In that year, sales reached a peak of $120 million and Hershey made 90 percent of the milk chocolate produced in America.

But while the ranks of those who knew the Founder thinned, his name and his image remained powerful. People even began to gossip about his personal life. Much of the speculation focused on the possibility that after Catherine's death M.S. had had a secret relationship with one of the industrial school's staff and fathered two children who were adopted by a local couple.

On the surface, the notion that M.S. had a mistress and two children is hard to accept. He was entirely devoted to Catherine and was never regarded as a ladies' man. And given his lifelong concern about public image, he doesn't seem the type to risk scandal. It would have been more in character for him to remarry and raise the children himself.

Nevertheless, this rumor persisted and amateur sleuths like Craig Stark, a member of the Hershey clan fascinated with genealogy, found hints that it may be true. Stark spoke with one witness who said that M.S. had frequently visited the home of the couple who had supposedly adopted the two children. The property had been in and out of the Hershey family for centuries.

In 2005, grandchildren of the same couple were able to confirm some tantalizing aspects of the legend. Two adopted girls did live on that property in the time when Milton supposedly visited. And years later, before dying, one of those women had hinted about having a blood tie to an important person. But the trail of evidence ended there. Milton's DNA isn't available for testing. And the secrecy shrouding adoption proceedings in the 1920s made it impossible for this family to reach a certain conclusion.

Although the mystery of the two children is not likely to be solved, no one needs be confused about the fates of the well-known creations Milton did leave behind: the companies, the town, the school, and the trust that supported it. Each one of these legacies grew and became ever more complex with the passing years. But without Milton to settle things, relations among these institutions and their supporters were often strained and confused.

Any effort to understand how the town, company, and school fit together has to begin with the fact that the school and its trust owned Milton's moneymaking enterprises and therefore their influence was felt throughout the empire. Everyone from the boardroom to the loading docks understood they were working for "the orphans" and this duty gave their efforts a little more meaning.

The boys themselves continued to regard M.S. Hershey as a true savior who remained with them in spirit. And for many years to come, the program Hershey had established would remain unchanged. John O'Brien, who arrived at the school in 1947, when he was just three, would forever recall the regimentation, social challenges, and hard farmwork.

"There was a *Lord of the Flies* element to it," said O'Brien, who had gone to Hershey after seeing his father, a coal miner in the small town of Snow Shoe, Pennsylvania, murder his mother. "When you went out to the farm you got the crap beat out of you by the older kids. But there were a lot of pluses, too. You learned discipline and a work ethic. You learned to endure things, to be tough. There was plenty of food, good clothing, and a pretty good education. And just about everyone ran into someone who took a real interest in them. For me it was the first set of house parents I had."[1]

In 1951, when John O'Brien was seven years old, the industrial school was renamed the Milton Hershey School. Eight years later, alumni gave the school a bronze statue of the Founder and a little boy. It immediately became the institution's most cherished icon.

In the post-Milton years, the school would grow to serve as many as 1,550 students who lived in scattered houses where small groups were overseen by house parents. Bans on the admission of nonwhites and girls would be lifted, and the school would become internationally famous for the quality of its programs. In 1970 the managers completed construction of Founder's Hall, an enormous (some said monstrous) building with a domed rotunda and an auditorium seating 2,700 people. The hall was constructed with nearly 1,500 tons of Vermont marble and features, according to the school, the second-largest domed rotunda in the world. Inside, where a fountain gurgles and tourists gawk, a mosaic depicts a dozen key moments in M.S. Hershey's life as if they were the Stations of the Cross. The life-size bronze statue of the founder standing with his arm draped over a boy greets those who enter the cathedral-like space. The first event in the huge hall featured the singing group Up with People.

During this time period, Hershey Chocolate (renamed Hershey Foods in 1968) built factories in Canada and California. In 1963 it acquired H.B. Reese Candy Company, a manufacturer of peanut butter cups and other confections. Minor efforts were made to develop business overseas, but in the view of many, the company's managers failed to move the company forward in a more substantial way because they felt overshadowed by M.S. Hershey. For a long period they even refused to adopt the type of modern marketing practices that their competitors used to build sales and increase profits.

While Hershey Foods cautiously pursued the same basic business, it was challenged in America by the Swiss giant Nestlé and by the Mars candy company, which became a dominant player in cocoa bean trading and aggressively developed foreign markets for its products. In 1973 Mars gained the lead in candy sales in America, passing Hershey for the first time.

Acting in part in response to Mars, Hershey Foods gradually became more modern and efficient. Under the stewardship of a Hershey Industrial School graduate named William Dearden, the company began to acquire new brands, develop new products, and follow new strategies, including national advertising. All along, Dearden continually reminded his executives corps that the company had a higher purpose than other corporations because it ultimately served the orphans of the Milton Hershey School.

Hershey Foods moved in and out of various side businesses, including pasta manufacturing and the Friendly's restaurant chain. Through acquisitions, licenses, and invention, the company also began to make and sell a

wide variety of products, including Kit Kat bars, Reese's Pieces, York peppermint patties, Jolly Ranchers, Mounds, and Almond Joy. Every move was
made with great caution, because executives didn't want to endanger the
value of the trust, and they were determined to generate enough profit to
run the school.

Hershey management was so cautious that one of the company's biggest
successes came to be seen as a matter of good luck, rather than active leadership. In 1981 a Hollywood filmmaker had approached Hershey's rival
Mars about using its M&M's candies in a few scenes of a new movie.
When Mars refused, the producers turned to Hershey. The deal allowed
for the star of the film, a little green alien named E.T., to eat Reese's
Pieces candies. Hershey got the option of featuring E.T. in its advertising.
Steven Spielberg's E.T. The Extra-Terrestrial made more money than any
movie up until that time, and sales of Reese's Pieces tripled.

Hershey Foods would grow from about $200 million in annual sales in
1970 to roughly $4 billion in 2005. It would gain back the top position in
U.S. candy sales, eventually capturing about 40 percent of the market. The
success of the executives who transformed the company after Milton
passed into memory would be so widely appreciated that officials of Wal-
Mart would seek their advice on managing the retail giant after the death
of founder Sam Walton.

Just as Wal-Mart fought rival Kmart, Hershey continually battled its
main domestic competitor, the privately held Mars. The struggle waged by
these two companies rarely got much press attention, although it was as
fierce as any corporate contest in the world. On one of the few occasions
that the public heard anything about it, Hershey got a lot of free publicity
with a heat-proof Desert Bar shipped to troops fighting the 1991 Gulf War,
but Mars won a government contract to supply candy to soldiers. Hershey
protested to the government and prevailed in the public relations arena—
grabbing most of the headlines—by challenging the quality of the Mars
product. But in the end the candy contract couldn't be broken and Mars
got the business.[2]

Except for the rare spat with Mars, Hershey Foods kept a fairly low profile. Its stock was solid, but it was never a flashy performer. This quality was
even most evident after 1980, when U.S. corporations entered a second
Gilded Age of soaring profits, hostile takeovers, inflated stock prices, and
astronomical executive salaries. In this environment, the Hershey companies stood out even more as conservative enterprises that served a serious

purpose beyond profit. As majority shareholder, the charitable trust that ran the Hershey School was interested in minimizing risk and pressed the company for consistent performance rather than quick profits.

As part of this strategy, Hershey continually monitored the competition and bought up smaller manufacturers when the time and the price were right. In 1996 the company spent $440 million on Leaf North America, seizing chocolate and nonchocolate brands, including Milk Duds, PayDay, Good & Plenty, and Jolly Rancher. In an era when manufacturers need leverage to maintain their prices when dealing with retail giants like Wal-Mart, Hershey would benefit from controlling so many of the public's favorite brands.

At the start of the twenty-first century Hershey CEO Richard Lenny would lead the development of a series of new products, including candies for dieters, chocolate mixed with cookies and pretzels, and many variations on old themes. By 2006, consumers could savor the company's chocolate mixed with toffee, strawberry flavoring, mint, and marshmallow.

The new products and acquired brands reflected the aggressive style Lenny brought with him to Hershey from his old workplace, Kraft foods. But some things about the company, especially its integrity and loyalty to the Hershey community, never changed. Executives tended to preserve these values just like they preserved the peculiar taste of Milton's recipe, which remained a sentimental favorite in America. Similarly, Hershey's link to charity and the brown wrapper with its bold lettering would continue to evoke warm feelings. In 2005, one hundred years after the Hershey bar was first produced along Spring Creek, it was the most popular chocolate in the country. Poetically enough, its century-old counterpart in Great Britain, Cadbury's original Dairy Milk bar, held the top spot in its home market, too.[3]

The American public's affection for the Hershey brand became enormously valuable for the other big company that M.S. had built in the Lebanon Valley, Hershey Estates. At the time of the Founder's death, "Ess-states" as locals pronounced it, managed a wide range of enterprises, including the hotel, local utilities, and the Hershey Department Store. But its most visible asset was Hershey Park, which would undergo dramatic changes. Once an oversized free playground for the town and its visitors, it was gradually transformed into a modern, Disney-style theme park with eleven roller coasters, water rides, and stage shows. The growth at this site would include hotels, restaurants, and a large new arena.

The rechristened Hersheypark provided more than one thousand jobs and drew millions of tourists and their money to the town each year. Hotels, restaurants, and shopping centers grew to serve this trade, and Hershey became a year-round vacation spot. But while the theme park pumped many millions of dollars into the economy each year, its growth required some sacrifice. Once free and open to all—townspeople considered it a public amenity—the park was fenced and began charging admission. Hersheypark also generated heavy traffic for local streets, placed demand on county services, and put intense pressure on real estate prices.

For Hershey Estates, which was renamed HERCO (Hershey Entertainment and Resorts Corporation), the theme park development made sound business sense and produced a good return on investment. In contrast, many of the company's other businesses—the utilities, the department store, and others—either lost money or produced only modest profits. For as long as M.S. Hershey had lived, the company had accepted these poor performances because the Founder took pride in providing for the people of his model town. He had counted profit and loss in a way that placed value on community pride and cohesion. His successors had no practical way to measure these assets. Confronted with their responsibility to generate profit for shareholders—the orphans of the Milton Hershey School—they began paring away businesses that represented the town's identity but failed to make money.

Between 1969 and 1980, HERCO sold its water, telephone, and electric companies. It closed the Hershey Department Store. The Cocoa Inn, a downtown landmark, was torn down and most of the Community Building, except for its theaters, was closed to the public. (In 1965 the smaller, separate foundation that M.S. Hershey created to support the community closed the free junior college.) All these losses affected the character of the town and the quality of life for its people.

In the absence of the Founder, the town of Hershey became more like every other place in America. Of course M.S. Hershey remained very real in the minds of those who knew him. As late as 1991, lifelong employee Monroe Stover even dreamed that Milton came back to earth, appearing like an angel. Not satisfied with that vision, Stover said he hoped for another dream in which his old boss would say, "Well done boys. Keep up the good work. You don't need me here. Good-bye."

But while some were obviously affected by M.S. Hershey the man, far more people fell under the spell of the powerful trust he left behind, which dominated the economy of the region. The companies it owned and the school it operated employed thousands of people and kept hundreds of smaller firms busy supplying everything from paper clips to construction services. Sometimes it seemed like nothing was too big for the trust to handle. For example, when HERCO ran into financial problems in the 1980s, the trust lent it millions of dollars to keep it out of bankruptcy.[4]

But as much as the trust and its holdings did to support the local economy, the fact that it operated in near total secrecy meant it generated as much suspicion as gratitude. Board meetings were held in private and records of their proceedings were not released.

In some quarters, this behind-closed-doors behavior bred outright resentment. Some people couldn't help but wonder if this secretive organization was actually fulfilling Milton S. Hershey's vision. Others developed an almost cynical point of view, believing that people who sat on the trust board used their power to benefit themselves and their friends. As might be expected, some of the students at the school and certain alumni felt antipathy toward the "townies" of the community, especially those who held seats on the board of the trust.

Critics of the board focused on a dramatic move the trust announced in 1963. At that time the core holdings and excess income of the school trust had grown to nearly $400 million. The revenues from this fund far exceeded the needs of the school as it existed, and so each year the value of its holdings continued to grow. Under these conditions it had become the fifth largest charitable education fund in America, bigger than the Carnegie Foundation and bigger than the endowments of Harvard and Yale.

For years the growing value of the trust had troubled members of the board. In the late 1950s they had started looking for ways to overcome the deed's restrictions. They considered M.S. Hershey's philanthropy and how it focused on education and the local community and decided that a medical school and teaching hospital would be consistent with his values. They also searched the law for a way around the restrictions placed on the trust. The established legal doctrine of *cy pres*, a French term meaning "as close as possible," permits courts to free trustees from an overly restrictive deed. In the summer of 1963 the trustees went to the Dauphin County Orphans Court and, citing the doctrine of cy pres, won permission to spend $50 million on the medical school and hospital.

In time, the Milton S. Hershey Medical Center would grow to include a children's hospital, the med school, and ten research institutes. It would attract a highly educated staff, many of whom settled in the town of Hershey. Their presence moved the community further from its original identity as a working-class utopia. Some long-term residents and Hershey school alumni would resent this change. In their eyes, the medical center would forever represent an unwarranted deviation from the school trust's true mission.[5]

In a material sense, the Hershey community gained much more than it lost during the decades after Milton's death. Certainly many who arrived in Hershey after 1970 were grateful to find a thriving local economy, a top-tier research hospital, and a society far more diverse and sophisticated than one might find in other small towns.

However, these newcomers had not lived under the informal social contract that had prevailed in Hershey for most of its existence. Even if they had never known him, many longtime residents believed they understood Milton Hershey's feelings, and his vision for their town. They acknowledged that he had created powerful institutions beyond the typical citizen's influence. But they felt that the system would work, as long as it was governed by benevolent men and women who adhered to M.S. Hershey's values. Monroe Stover, who lived in the town for seventy-five years and had sold soap with M.S. on the Atlantic City boardwalk, put it this way in 1989: "There are different kinds of dictatorships. The one we live under here in Hershey, if you want to call it that, is a philanthropic dictatorship. We would have a much better world if there were more of them."[6]

Aside from the medical center decision, which had its detractors, the members of the board of the Hershey Trust had generally held to the Founder's philosophy into the 1980s. This meant that when intramural conflicts arose, the sense persisted that everyone who cared about Hershey was pulling together in the direction that M.S. had set. His influence bound different factions together, the way blood ties bind the personalities in a big family. It discouraged radical change and encouraged the resolution of disagreements.

Unfortunately, one side effect of this stability was a certain amount of stagnation. Innovation was rare at the school, and alumni and school officials generally agree that by the end of the 1980s the education program was not very good. It did not offer much in the way of advanced instruction and had been slow to embrace new technologies. At the same time, enrollment had declined. In 1989 a regional accrediting agency gave the school a passing grade, mainly out of respect for its past. "They said the education we offered was terrible," recalled one school official.

In response to the accreditors and others, the school's managers began to make changes. Farm programs, which required students to work at school-owned dairies, were closed. Vocational education was reoriented to prepare students for jobs in growing fields such as health care and food services. The staff was overhauled. And a new central campus, worth more than $250 million, was planned to replace the scattered houses that had previously served as homes for students.[7]

The transformation of the Milton Hershey School was driven, in part, by the ideals and values of a new breed of leaders. Under Chairman Rod Pera, several seats on the board of the Milton Hershey School Trust were filled by nationally recognized experts in child care and education. They brought in a new president (headmaster), William Lepley, who had been the top education official in the state of Iowa. Lepley and the board he sat on saw in the Hershey Trust, which had grown to a value measured in the *billions*, a unique opportunity to create the best school of its type in the world.[8]

No private child-saving institution could match the Milton Hershey School's wealth or its independence. Because it could function without state funds, the school was free to provide any kind of program it chose, and could pay for it, too. Under Lepley, the school pursued what was called its "21st Century Initiative." The admissions office began seeking students with more diverse backgrounds, including those with better academic skills and the potential to go on to college. Standards were altered so that high-potential children from less-poor families—some had incomes more than twice the poverty rate—were brought to the centralized campus. Once there, they were assigned to houses where younger and older children lived together, which Lepley believed would approximate family life. They also adhered to a new calendar, which allowed for extended visits to their families every summer.[9]

• • •

The 21st Century Initiative promised to make the Hershey School a special environment for bright underprivileged children. Managers who supported the transformation of the school believed it was consistent with M.S. Hershey's ideals. To support this notion, they pointed to his forward thinking, his ambition, and his willingness to change and adapt in business.

But as each of the new policies went into effect, officers of the school's alumni association grew more concerned. For decades, the Hershey alumni association had been little more than a cheerleader for the school. But in this period the former students became critical of the direction the school was taking. With Milton Hershey's legacy at stake, not to mention billions of dollars, they began to write letters and contact school trust managers. They based their critique on their understanding of M.S. Hershey's life, his deed of trust, and the history of the school they developed during their own research. Some of these alumni were also affected by the long-standing townies/school tension. They feared that under Rod Pera, a townie, the school had been set on the wrong path. But Pera wasn't their only target. Critical alumni were also upset with trust board members, some of whom were graduates of the school, who had failed to expand the number of children the school served.

One of the most zealous of the alumni critics was a 1970s graduate named Joe Berning. A self-employed mechanic who lived near Hershey, Berning devoted himself to researching the Founder's philosophy and the school's history. Working from the basement of his home, which was decorated with photos of Milton Hershey and other memorabilia, he gradually filled more than a dozen empty motor oil boxes with documents and notes. Berning believed his research confirmed his belief that his alma mater was supposed to be as much a home as a school. It also stoked his fear that the type of child traditionally served at Hershey—very poor kids who had trouble with academics—would not qualify to attend the new Milton Hershey School.

To a person, the concerned alumni had come from difficult childhood circumstances and credited the school with their rescue. (Berning's mother had died, and his father had suffered a stroke, when the school accepted him, at age nine, in 1964.) In their student days they had lived in farmhouses, milked cows, and received vocational education, and they believed that these elements of school life had been good for them. They considered M.S. Hershey an almost saintly man and they regarded his deed of trust as a bit of scripture to be followed to the letter and reinterpreted at one's peril.

"I felt that outsiders who really didn't understand the place and didn't understand Mr. Hershey had come in and taken control," explained alumni Lou Bocian, who once sat on Milton's lap and pretended to drive his fancy car. "We use the word 'family' when we talk about the school because that's how we feel. I've got thousands of brothers and sisters who are part of that family. How would you feel if someone came in and wanted to change everything about your family?" [10]

For years the alumni said that the school was becoming more like an elite prep school and less like a home for orphans. They thought that hundreds of millions of dollars had been spent on unnecessary construction. They thought that the salaries paid to top school officials were too high (President Lepley's total compensation would surpass $400,000 in 1999). And they complained to the state's attorney general, who policed charitable trusts, alleging that some board members had profited from business arrangements with the school.

In fact, a board member named William Alexander owned a construction firm that did tens of millions of dollars worth of business with the school. And Rod Pera's former employer, a prominent Harrisburg law firm called McNees, Wallace and Nurrick, also did work for the school and Hershey Foods. But while these connections were unseemly in the view of some alumni, Pennsylvania Attorney General Mike Fisher found that no laws had been broken.

Although the state found that no crimes had been committed, the attorney general didn't address the alumni's most pointed criticism: the school's enrollment had declined as the trust's assets soared. These two trends were illustrated by a chart developed by John Halbleib, a Hershey school graduate who had gone on to become a lawyer at a nationally prominent firm. One line of the chart showed that between 1970 and 1998 enrollment dropped from fifteen hundred children to fewer than eleven hundred. The other line showed the estimated value of the trust rising in this time frame from $187 million to more than $5 billion. The trust was more than twenty-five times larger, but it served fewer students. In comparison, the famous Girls and Boys Town of Nebraska, with an endowment of just $210 million, served about five hundred more kids than the Hershey school.[11]

The conflict between the Hershey alumni and some members of the school's board was at times marked by anger and acrimony. This was especially true when a spate of sexual abuse cases seemed to show that the new housing strategy, which put younger and older students together, had failed. The conflict reached a peak in 1999 when the board proposed to spend $25 million a year running a training institute for teachers who would come from around the country and perhaps the world.

"They were going to have this big institute that would teach people the best practices for working with children," recalled alumnus John O'Brien. "The problem was, there wasn't anything great being done at the school that they could teach to anyone. All the money and potential that were there had given people an entitlement mind-set." This was especially true for the school's leaders and staff, added O'Brien. "They began running things with the adults as the priority, not the kids, and the focus was maintaining control, not preparing needy kids to be good citizens and leaders."

The first legal move against the planned institute came from Craig Stark, a member of the Hershey clan who had put years into studying his family history and putting together what he called the National Hershey Association. Stark filed papers in the Orphans Court to stop the board from using funds for the teacher institute. Soon the alumni association and the state of Pennsylvania also rose to oppose the institute. Led by the state attorney general, who insisted there were better ways to help children with the trust's money, they defeated the plan.

In his order barring the diversion of funds, Judge Warren Morgan found that the institute would detract from the main purpose of the trust, which is "to care for as many children as the income would permit." Many members of the board, including William Lepley, disagreed with this view. They saw the institute as an extension of the Hershey school mission, a way to serve a broader population without leaving the local community. Faced with a court order, however, they had no choice but to abandon the plan.[12]

For the first time, outsiders had managed to change the course set by the board of the powerful Hershey Trust. In the process, the alumni had shed light on the workings of the trust and brought attention to the spectacle of a $5 billion fund, which grew larger every day while children who lived in poor and even violent circumstances waited for help.

Not content with a momentary victory, the alumni continued to press Attorney General Fisher for more structural changes in the way the whole

Hershey system was run. Executives from Hershey Foods and HERCO had often held seats on the board of the trust. The alumni saw a potential conflict of interest, and so did the attorney general. In early July 2002 this arrangement was ended in an agreement Fisher made with the school trust. No one would be allowed to serve on the board of the trust and a Hershey company board at the same time. In the same document, the school agreed to seek students from poorer families (defined as those whose income was no more than 150 percent of the federal poverty rate) and those who struggled academically.

With the attorney general's intervention, the alumni had rolled back much of the 21st Century Initiative and changed the basic power structure of the trust in a way that seemed lasting and permanent. This appeared to be far more significant, in the long term, than the defeat of the planned teacher-training institute. But dramatic as it may have been, in a matter of days this turn of events would be overshadowed by an even bigger confrontation—one that would have pained the Founder himself—over the future of everything that carried the famous Hershey name.[13]

WHAT WOULD MILTON DO?

14 The alumni and others who challenged the Hershey Trust over spending and policies at the school may have thought that they understood its workings. At times members of the board reinforced this idea by leaking juicy details from key meetings. But in the spring of 2002, no one said a word about the historic choice that the trust was poised to make. It was just too big, too sweeping an idea for anyone to risk it. Besides, there was an enormous amount of money at stake.

Months earlier, staff for the state's attorney general had discussed with the board the possibility that the trust's holdings were out of balance. The stock market was reeling from the collapse of two major corporations— Enron and WorldCom—in scandals that drew attention to the risks inherent in securities. As strong as Hershey Foods was, the state officials said, the trust might be taking a risk by keeping half its value in Hershey Foods.

By the time the meeting was over, the people on the board were already reflecting on the effect a sale would have on the trust, the school, Hershey Foods, and the local community. They knew that a buyer might cut jobs— Hershey Foods had 6,400 local employees—or even move the company away. On the other hand, the board's duty was to the orphans who were Milton Hershey's heirs. They couldn't take for granted that Hershey Foods would be forever profitable. After all, Enron and WorldCom had been considered solid companies until they imploded. Who was to say the same couldn't happen to Hershey Foods?

"If we sold control of the company, we could get a premium, a higher price than the market was paying for a share of stock," recalled trust board member Anthony Colistra. A former leader of the alumni association who had criticized parts of the 21st Century Initiative, Colistra was also superintendent of a local school district. He had joined the board in 1997 hoping to contribute his expertise as an educator. After listening to the discussion of the trust's lopsided holdings, he was in the majority who voted to investigate the sale of Hershey Foods.

Through the winter and early spring of 2002, the trust board's investment committee considered the possibilities. They discovered that the sale of the trust's majority stake in Hershey Foods might yield a windfall of $10 or even $12 billion. Of course locals would no longer run things at Hershey Foods, but in one move the school would make itself much richer and, possibly, much more secure.

Not surprisingly, executives at Hershey Foods opposed the sale. For decades the trust's position as majority owner had made the company immune to takeover attempts. While the food industry was consolidated into ever larger entities, Hershey had stayed independent and operated on its own terms. Through the decades, leaders of the company had enjoyed the security of knowing they could not be deposed in a buyout.

Independence also suited the company's relationship with the town. Some local plants, most notably the company's century-old birthplace on East Chocolate Avenue, were inefficient. But as long as control of the company was kept in friendly local hands, Hershey Foods could continue to operate there and forgo a little efficiency for the sake of tradition, local workers, and the community.

For these reasons and others, Hershey Foods CEO Richard Lenny offered the board an alternative to an outright sale. He suggested the company buy a large block of stock back from the trust. This would improve the balance in the trust portfolio but maintain Hershey Foods' independence. Sure, the trust would have to give up the enormous profit it might earn if it allowed outsiders to take over the company. But it would also protect local jobs and businesses that depended on things staying the way they were.

In May 2002, the board rejected Lenny's recommendation. Instead, the trust would seek an outside buyer. As spring turned to summer, investment advisers and brokers who stood to make many millions of dollars on a sale began looking for a match. As various giant corporations sent their representatives to Pennsylvania to go over the books and inspect facilities, two possibilities emerged. In one scenario, Cadbury-Schweppes and Nestlé would divide Hershey among themselves. The other prospect involved a merger with, ironically enough, the William Wrigley Company, which had been founded by Milton's nemesis. In either case, M.S. Hershey's company would be swallowed whole or in part, by a former competitor.

While momentum was building behind the biggest change in the history of Hershey, the public remained in the dark. In fact, in May and June 2002 the big issue in town was a strike called by the chocolate workers' union over the company's plan to increase employees' share of health care costs. After a six-week standoff, during which the union vilified CEO Lenny, the workers agreed to lower wages, the company backed off on the health care issue, and, on June 9, peace returned to the Lebanon Valley.[1]

Somebody talked. Given all the consultants, lawyers, executives, and board members who knew that Hershey Foods was for sale, a leak had been inevitable. (For this reason Tony Colistra had jokingly warned others on the board that someday "Vesuvius was going to erupt.") Still, when *The Wall Street Journal* broke the news, it surprised people on the inside of the deal almost as much as it surprised the rest of central Pennsylvania. They had hoped to complete the sale before anyone on the outside ever knew it was in the works.

On Thursday, July 25, under a two-column-wide headline on its front page, the *Journal*'s story announced that "the sweetest place on Earth may be about to lose its sugar daddy." The report noted that the company's share of the U.S. candy market—roughly a third of total sales—would make it very attractive to investors. The only downside foreseen by the *Journal* might be seen in the local community, where jobs and vital business might be lost: "Reaction is apt to be far more grim in Hershey, the company town Mr. Hershey founded . . . where the street lamps are shaped like Hershey Kisses and streets bear names such as Chocolate Avenue and Cocoa Avenue."

At noon on the day of the *Journal*'s report, a small group of community leaders who gathered for lunch at a Friendly's restaurant in Hershey was grim. They were shocked and disbelieving and certain that, for efficiency's sake, any buyer would move the company's headquarters, close local plants, and eliminate hundreds if not thousands of jobs. Hershey, as Milton created it, would disappear.

"We felt that the entire community was being betrayed," recalled Bruce McKinney, the former CEO of HERCO and a former trust board member. "There was no debate about the fact that it was a very bad idea."

McKinney was joined at Friendly's by former Hershey Foods chairman Richard Zimmerman, who had also served on the trust board, and by a local plastic surgeon, Tom Davis. The trio had been meeting regularly to organize the upcoming celebration of their town's centennial. For months they had been reflecting on M.S. Hershey and his remarkable three-part legacy: the town, the companies, and the school.

"Mr. Hershey had intentionally brought all these things together in one place," recalled McKinney. "The sale of Hershey Foods would have ripped apart the legacy."

None of the men at Friendly's that day would have disagreed with McKinney's forecast. Those who had been on the trust board understood the principles behind the proposed sale. A mixed portfolio of assets is safer. But they were sure that the trust could diversify without losing control of Hershey Foods. And there are exceptions to every rule. In this case, Hershey stock had a long history of growth. Its thirty-year record made it one of the top stocks in the country, with annual returns averaging more than 17 percent. It was hard to imagine a better place to put money.

As they talked, the men at Friendly's barely touched their food. They were too upset, and too focused on the crisis at hand. Before they were done, they agreed to organize the community to stand against the sale. In a matter of days, the sale opponents would be fighting on three fronts. First, the powerful and the prominent in town could be called upon to exert their individual influence on the board. Second, the press would be invited to cover protests that would build public support. Third, the trust would be challenged in Orphans Court.[2]

On the day after the news of the sale broke, the Harrisburg *Patriot-News* devoted hundreds of column inches to the possibility that Hershey Foods might be sold. Attorney General Mike Fisher, a Republican who was starting a campaign for governor, was showered with citizen complaints about the sale. Scores of people came to McKinney and the others with various bits of information. One person called to report seeing luggage with Nestlé company tags arriving at the nearby airport. Others revealed what they knew about the positions of various trust managers and corporate officials.

Dr. Davis and a local lawyer named Kathy Taylor organized a rally at a downtown park that was attended by more than five hundred people, among them senior citizens, chocolate factory workers in hairnets, and Hershey school alumni. Ric Fouad, president of the alumni association, was the main speaker at this event. A 1980 graduate, Fouad had spent much of the previous year pressing the attorney general for reforms at the school. He had become a fierce critic of the trust board—he thought they wasted money and served far too few children—and was comfortable attacking the sale proposal.

"How dare they!" roared Fouad as the crowd cheered. Fouad described M.S. Hershey as "a man who did the Lord's work, who cared about the children, who cared about the community."

When the speeches were over, the crowd marched in ninety-degree heat to the offices of the trust, which just happened to be at High Point, M.S. Hershey's former home. The people streamed past guards who had been sent to keep them off the grounds. They assembled near the doors and chanted for the trust's president, Robert Vowler, to come out and answer their questions. No one answered their calls.

Remarkably, the protest group included both former members of the trust board—widely regarded as the "wise men" of the community—and Hershey School alumni who had previously criticized them. The campaign against the sale made allies of these onetime antagonists, and captured the attention of the national media. Soon after the *Journal* announced that the company was in play, print and broadcast reporters from around the world arrived in Hershey and nearly all of them seized on the obvious angle:

"Bitter chocolate"—CBS News
"The Sweetest Place on Earth has turned into a pretty sour place."
    —*The Financial Times*

"Choc horror"—*The Guardian*

It was no accident that the press lined up with those opposed to the sale. From the very beginning of the controversy, the antisale forces had purposely sold the issue as a David and Goliath tale. The message was crafted in part by John Dunn, a former Hershey Foods marketing executive who threw himself into the task. Dunn was available for this work because he had been encouraged to retire when CEO Lenny came to Hershey. Not surprisingly, he and others who had lost their jobs in the management shuffle were delighted to put their time and skills to use fighting for what they regarded as the traditional values of their old employer.

Eager for the town to make a big show for the press, Dunn went to a local printer, whose business would be ruined if Hershey Foods left town, and got him to produce thousands of little white lawns signs bearing words of protest. "The Hershey Trust—An Oxymoron," said one. "Don't Shut Down Chocolate Town," read another. Because the sale might be completed at any moment, the printer took another job off his press and made the signs overnight. The next morning Dunn had a wooden pallet loaded with signs put in the back of his pickup truck. As he sped home, perhaps a little distracted, Dunn had to slam on the brakes when a boy ran out into the street. The pallet slid forward in the bed of the truck, crashing into the cab wall and producing a big dent.

Dunn drove the rest of the way feeling a bit rattled, but soon recovered. As the first of his signs began to appear, they became very popular. In many neighborhoods every single lawn sprouted one. So many people came to his home to get signs that he just left them outside, with a basket for donations. Thousands were picked up, and the basket was filled with coins and bills.

Along with the signs for lawns, Dunn and others, including local union chief Bruce Hummel, produced sandwich boards and posters that they carried to rallies and tacked to trees and light poles. Like many people in the town, Hummel had a multilayered relationship with the Founder's legacy. As a boy he had been educated at the Milton Hershey School. "If it weren't for Milton Hershey," he would say, "I'd probably be dead." Later Hummel became a Hershey Foods employee, and then head of the chocolate workers' union. All these experiences had led Hummel to believe in the status quo at Hershey and to defend it any way he could. This included criticizing William Lepley and Rick Lenny, two of the most powerful men in town, as outsiders who may not "understand what Milton Hershey's ideals were."[3]

Privately, most opponents of the sale expressed themselves with anger and outrage. But in keeping with local tradition, their public appeal was polite and took advantage of the playful image of the company and town. Many of the antisale posters featured a drawing of a cheerful-looking Hershey's Kiss and the scolding words "Wait 'til Mr. Hershey finds out!" Taken together, all the posters and placards that decorated the neat homes in Hershey gave newscasters a charming, Rockwellian image of genial small town protest.

Calculated as the campaign may have been, it was not false or cynical. No one could deny that in this moment of crisis, people who were more accustomed to arguing with one another had come together in an inspiring effort to maintain the balance of company, school, and community that M.S. Hershey had set when he was alive. Hershey was an unusual, perhaps even unique American place and everyone in town—alumni, factory workers, retired executives, and everyday citizens—was determined to keep it as it was.

"It may sound corny, but I fell in love with Hershey and thought it was worth fighting for," recalled Tom Davis. He had first seen the town in the 1970s, on his return from service in Vietnam, when he came to complete a residency at the medical center. On that visit he was most impressed by the American flags that decorated Chocolate Avenue. "The country wasn't that welcoming to vets, at the time," he explained. "But this town was."

After living there a few years, Davis came to believe that M.S. Hershey had created one of the best places on earth. Unlike other industrial utopias, like Torrance, California (Llewellyn Iron Company), and Indian Hills, Massachusetts (Norton Company), Hershey retained the identity and sense of optimism established at its beginning. Davis felt devoted to its preservation.

Others in town expressed similar feelings. They felt secure and happy in Hershey. It was the kind of hometown people loved. These emotions were all the more appealing when contrasted with the trust board and its position. Represented by the president of the trust, Robert Vowler, the board members had defended their decision to seek a sale while trying to reassure people that they would find a buyer who would promise to keep the company in Hershey. "We would have to be convinced," Vowler told the press, "that they're going to be good corporate citizens."

Placed side by side, the words of the trust president and the feelings of the opponents left the public and the press with no choice at all. Almost anyone with a heart warmed to the remarkably polite rabble-rousers who marched down Chocolate Avenue demanding the trust consider "What Would Milton Do?" Similarly, almost anyone who wanted to please the public—especially the *voting* public—was far more likely to come down on the side of the alumni, factory workers, homemakers, and wise men of Hershey.

So it was hardly a surprise when Attorney General Fisher announced that he would challenge the proposed sale in court. Although his own staff had prompted the sale by urging the trust board to rebalance its holdings in the first place, in mid-August he filed a petition demanding that the Orphans Court intervene. He sought to require that the company get the court's approval before handing over Hershey Foods to an outside buyer. Fisher's opponent, Ed Rendell, the popular Democratic mayor of Philadelphia, also opposed the sale.

At every turn in the public debate over the sale, Fisher was backed by the allied opponents from the town. Whenever possible, they invoked M.S. Hershey's affection for all of his own creations, and credited him with making the progressive vision of utopia real. The members of the trust board countered with their own arguments about what Milton would do. They noted the times when M.S. had considered selling to outsiders, and the fact that the Founder had focused his wealth on the orphans first. Their care was primary, went the argument, so a sale of the company would honor the Founder if it made those children more secure.

The historical record on M.S. Hershey was far more complicated than either side in the sale debate wanted to acknowledge. He was not a miracle-working saint. He was profoundly ambitious, and more than a little egotistical. Both these qualities are required of any man who would build so much and acquire so much power.

However, M.S. was also sincere in his desire to do good. He was committed to his orphan heirs, and generous to them in every way possible. He was a true utopian dreamer who took pleasure in building the perfect company town and rigging it to run on its own, like the perpetual motion machine of his father's fantasies.

But while the opponents of the sale insisted that M.S. would never agree to sell his chocolate company to outsiders, in fact he had done just that. If not for the stock market crash of 1929, Hershey Chocolate would have become part of a larger, diversified food conglomerate. Sure, he later said he was glad the deal was aborted, but his sigh of relief didn't erase the fact that he had been ready to let the company go. When you then recall that M.S. again flirted with selling out in the 1930s, it becomes clear that he was open to change and could imagine an end to the grand social experiment he had begun when he first bought land for his factory.

Perhaps he understood that it would be impossible for anyone to guarantee that life in a place like Hershey would continue unchanged in perpetuity. Certainly he knew that his descendants would have to find a way to live in harmony. No deed of trust can cover every possibility. No great man can lead forever by his example.

As so often happens, money became the source of discontent. The fortune Milton left behind grew so large that the mere thought of it affected relationships and events. The attorney general's office worried about making the money safe. The board of trustees worried about maximizing its value. Hershey school alumni obsessed over how it was being used. And the townspeople trembled at the thought that those who controlled it would abandon them.

The fear and anger produced by this possibility were real. Tom Davis would recall that a trust manager who attended his church felt so ostracized by old friends that he asked to meet some of them to discuss the problem. At that session, held in Davis's home, "We told him that he and his wife *were* being shunned. We said we're trying to do that because we don't like what you are doing and you have to think about it."

Anonymous opponents of the sale used more troubling tactics against Robert Vowler. They posted his home address on a Web site. In the information age, this represented a threat, and the trust responded by assigning an armed guard to Vowler's home. His family would have this protection —a constant reminder of conflict—until the whole matter was settled.[4]

On the morning of September 3, John Dunn and other protesters stood outside the Orphans Court in Harrisburg carrying signs and singing a Hershey's chocolate jingle. Inside, Attorney General Fisher argued to block the sale, citing the harm it would do to the region. Trust lawyers presented an investment expert who explained that, without a sale, the institution's portfolio would remain "twice as risky as the portfolio of a [typical] college or university."

The very next day, the judge barred the trust from going forward with the sale without his approval. His remarks, which included criticism of the basic "intelligence" behind the sale, were harsh. Wall Street, which had bid up Hershey Foods stock in anticipation of the sale, reacted by knocking it down by about 5 percent. The order from the Orphans Court wasn't necessarily the last word. The trust could appeal. In the end the managers might even prevail. But the attorney general had made it clear he would make the process difficult.

Faced with these issues, the board gathered in a hotel meeting room which was, poetically enough, in sight of the historical battleground at Valley Forge. Several big tables were pushed together and for eleven hours the seventeen men and women debated whether to sell Hershey Foods to the Wrigley Company, which was offering more than $12 billion in cash and stock. William Wrigley Jr., the grandson of Milton's gambling foe, addressed the group and promised to keep factories in Hershey open. He then met separately with Rick Lenny to discuss the mechanics of a sale.

In the hours of argument that followed Wrigley's presentation, "each person took as much time as they needed to speak and got off their chests how they felt," recalled trust president Robert Vowler. "The Wrigley Company heard us well with regard to what we said about the community," he added. But as good as Wrigley's proposal was, the effects of the six-week controversy showed. Three board members who had once supported the sale, Anthony Colistra, William Alexander, and Vowler, said they had changed their minds. All three had been subjected to intense pressure from critics. Vowler had even received death threats. In the end, the board voted 10–7 to reject Wrigley's offer. Vowler would say that the Wrigley deal—$5 billion in cash and $7.5 billion in stock—didn't solve the problems of the trust's portfolio. It would have remained lopsided, with a huge portion invested in the new Wrigley/Hershey combination.

When he heard about the trust board's decision, Bruce McKinney went outside and rang a bell to alert his neighbors. Soon people were playing music, toasting, and dancing in the street. The next morning another crowd gathered to celebrate downtown, and drivers passing by honked their horns to express their joy.[5]

The news of the decision thrilled those who had fought the sale, but it didn't end all the turmoil. Empowered by their success, the sale opponents demanded the trust board be revamped. Under pressure from the attorney general and the Orphans Court, the board was purged of all those who had supported the Wrigley deal at that meeting in Valley Forge. The board was reconstituted with fewer members, eleven instead of seventeen. Those named to fill the vacant seats were all locals, unlike the experts who had been dismissed. The new board would work with a new school president, because William Lepley moved up his retirement, planned for the following summer, to December 1, 2002.

Although some of his critics would blame Lepley for much of the conflict that took place in Hershey during his tenure, in fact he had been brought to the school to enact the very changes that took place. He had been hampered in this effort by the school's peculiar mission. The school was founded to serve kids in great need, but not those with significant psychological problems. Poor, neglected kids who are well adjusted are hard to find and this complicated efforts to build enrollment. At the same time, an ever more critical group of alumni had made it difficult for Lepley to break from traditions that may have become outdated.

"I discovered that the biggest enemy of doing good there was the insularity of the culture," said Lepley, long after he departed Hershey. "It's the most unique opportunity for helping kids in America. But it is still a missed opportunity."[6]

If Lepley and the old board had prevailed, they may have been able to use the increased wealth of the trust to enlarge the school and even build satellite facilities away from the town of Hershey. The problem posed by the unspent riches and unserved children would have been solved, and Milton Hershey's philanthropy would have been expanded. Children across the country, and perhaps around the world, would have been saved.

Those who won the fight over the sale saw things differently. They believed that the philosophy of the Founder had been heeded in the end. He had created the three-part legacy of the companies, the town, and the school. They had kept it together. It was what Milton would have done.

Hershey school president William Lepley was eventually replaced by John O'Brien, who had come to the school as a three-year-old in 1947 and became an alumni activist in the 1990s. O'Brien said he found "a traumatized culture" at the school and "a place where mediocrity was acceptable." All the money had led both staff and students to expect big rewards for little or no effort, said O'Brien. "The kids were expecting to be given things like laptop computers when they were too young to handle them." One result, he noted, "was that a lot of street-smart kids sold their laptops within a couple of weeks of getting them."

Under O'Brien, admissions would favor kids from poorer families, summer family visits would be reduced in length, and efforts would begin to increase enrollment to two thousand children. To accommodate this growth, plans were developed to build a second campus, near the hill occupied by the Hotel Hershey.

While O'Brien's appointment reassured some alumni, many of the structural problems that bred suspicion about the trust, and ultimately led to the crisis, remained. In the summer of 2003 the attorney general, the court, and the trust reversed some of the reforms that had been adopted during the turbulent times. For example, Hershey company officials were let back on the board. People like Tom Davis liked this idea because they believed the executives would protect the town. Alumni like Ric Fouad objected because they saw potential conflicts of interest. They would continue to monitor and criticize the management of their alma mater.

Although the managers of the Hershey School resented the outspoken alumni, it is not unusual for the graduates of private schools to continue to show an intense interest in the places where they were educated. In 2004, for example, some alumni of the prestigious St. Paul's School in Concord, New Hampshire, complained loudly about mismanagement and excessive salaries at their alma mater. The difference between the conflict at St. Paul's and the one at Hershey was that the school in Pennsylvania was supposed to rescue children who were in danger. And with every news account of child abuse and every new scandal in the nation's foster care system, they felt justified in asking why the Hershey School wasn't saving thousands more children.[7]

Beyond the issues of power and control, the big question of how to use the revenues of the enormous trust remained unanswered. As of 2005, three years after the sale to Wrigley was stopped, the value of the fund had reached $8 billion. This, combined with the reversal of reform, appalled some leaders of the alumni association. They asked a Harrisburg court to grant their group the status to sue the trustees. When they won, the school appealed.

The feud, which would continue for most of 2005, would have surely pained the Founder. He had devoted his life and fortune to the invention of Hershey—the companies, town, and school—and had adjusted the balance of power to make sure that harmony reigned.

Perhaps the only thing about Milton Hershey that is absolutely certain is that he believed in progress. As an industrialist, a philanthropist, and a social engineer, he was always moving forward. For this reason, the advances made by his companies, especially Hershey Foods, were true to his spirit. Similarly, his town's development as a genial, affluent, and stable community was just what he wanted. But it's hard to imagine he would be pleased to see that his school trust, while building impressive facilities and a monument like Founder's Hall, served no more children at the start of 2005 than it did in 1963.

In his rare moments of open reflection, Milton Hershey showed his greatest affection for the "little fellows" whom he hoped to save. The children he intended to rescue came from fractured families. They were challenged by school work. They knew loneliness, hunger, and want. In short, they were quite similar to the boy Milton Hershey had once been. His father had neglected him when he was young, never providing him real security and comfort. His mother had struggled to feed her children. Milton had never been a good student.

As an adult, Milton fulfilled his father's dream of success and acclaim by building a great industry. With the creation of his utopian town he heeded his mother's admonitions about serving something higher than the accumulation of personal wealth. Then, when it came time to consider his legacy, he invested his fortune with a poignant flourish. He would save himself symbolically—by rescuing little boys in the straits he knew as a child—over and over again in perpetuity.

If there is any real evidence of Milton Hershey's genius, it may lie in the fact that this child-saving mission would have continued no matter who won the fight of 2002. Under one outcome the trust might have been made richer, but it and the school were never in peril. The big difference is that now the attorney general, certain alumni, and the general public have become focused on the school's management. People are putting pressure on the trust's managers so they might make more progress on behalf of kids, with Milton Hershey's money. The Founder would be pleased.

NOTES

Many of the sources used for this book are held by the Hershey Community Archives, Hershey, Pennsylvania. This archive is a repository for the papers of Milton S. Hershey and records of his companies, the Hershey School, and the Hershey Trust. It holds many valuable manuscripts, most notably the unpublished books of Samuel Hinkle and Paul A. Wallace. The Wallace manuscript, which was researched and written under the auspices of the Hershey company, is accompanied by all of the Wallace records, including transcripts of interviews, letters, and subject and date files.

The abbreviation HCA is used throughout these notes for Hershey Community Archives. Books self-published by Joseph Snavely are held by HCA and by Lancaster County Historical Society, Lancaster, PA.

INTRODUCTION

1. Jack Sherzer, "Five Hundred Rally Against Proposed Hershey Sale," Harrisburg *Patriot-News*, August 3, 2002, p. A1.

2. David Morgan, "Hershey Sale Would Kill Jobs, Court Told," *Toronto Star*, Sept. 9, 2002. Enron and WorldCom were cited by Hershey Trust officials in "Behind the Decision," Harrisburg *Patriot-News*, July 28, 2004, p. A1.

3. Estimate of costs from Milton Hershey School president's office; see also Steven Pearlstein, "A Bitter Feud Erupts over Hershey Plant," *The Washington Post*, Sept. 2, 2002, p. A1. Other data from St. Paul's School, Concord, N.H.; the National Center for Education Statistics, *Digest of Education Statistics 2003*, table 358; and *Boarding School Review*. For largest endowments see also Martin Wooster, "The Milton Hershey School, The Richest Orphans in America," *Compassion and Culture* (Capital Research Center, Washington, D.C.), April 2004.

4. Potential buyers noted in Gary Strauss and Thor Valdmanis, "City of Hershey Tastes Fear," *USA Today*, Sept. 2, 2002, p. 1; Gerold Frank, "Back to Land Plan Evolved for Welfare of Employees," Jan. 7, 1934, clipping from unknown source, HCA, B2, F53.

5. Pearlstein, "A Bitter Feud Erupts," p. A1.

6. Charles Thompson, "Trust Felt Pressure to Diversify," Harrisburg *Patriot-News*, July 26, 2002, p. A15. See also Brett Lieberman, Ellen Lyon, and Jerry Gleason, "When Other Towns Have Lost 'the Company,'" Harrisburg *Patriot-News*, July 28, 2002, p. A20. For Tyco's layoffs at AMP, see "AMP Takeover Jolted Midstate," Harrisburg *Patriot-News*, July 28, 2002, p. A20.

7. Lois Fegan, "Hershey Wouldn't Sell, Former Executive Says," Harrisburg *Patriot-News*, August 12, 2002, p. B1. Governor Schweicker's opposition and alumni protest noted in Brett Marcy and Charles Thompson, "Governor Concerned About Sale of Hershey," Harrisburg *Patriot-News*, July 30, 2002, p. 1.

8. Jack Sherzer, "Stock Market Crash Prevented Hershey Founder's Merger Deal in 1929," Harrisburg *Patriot-News*, Sept. 11, 2002, p. 1.

9. Strauss and Valdmanis, "City of Hershey Tastes Fear," p. 1.

1. THE OAK AND THE VINE

1. An account of the marriage of Henry Hershey and Veronica "Fanny" Snavely appears in Joseph Snavely, *An Intimate Story of M.S. Hershey* (Hershey: self-published, 1957). Further detail is in Wallace interview of Lila Snavely.

2. Charles Landis, "The Philadelphia-Lancaster Turnpike," *Journal of the Lancaster County Historical Society* 20 (1916), p. 230; H. C. Frey, "The Conestoga Wagon," *Journal of the Lancaster County Historical Society* 34, no. 13 (1930), pp. 289–312.

3. William Riddle, *Lancaster Old and New* (Lancaster: self-published, 1900). Also useful is Uhler W. Hensel, "How the Pennsylvania Railroad Came Through Lancaster," *Journal of the Lancaster County Historical Society* 100, no. 3 (1998), pp. 75–113. For the telegraph, see William Sullenberger, "The First Commercial Telegraph Line," *Journal of the Lancaster County Historical Society* 38 (1934), pp. 48–54. For Buchanan, see Randall M. Miller and William Pencak, eds., *Pennsylvania: A History of the Commonwealth* (University Park: Pennsylvania State University Press, 2002), pp. 207–10.

4. "Sugar from Indian Corn," *Columbia* [Pa.] *Spy*, Sept. 18, 1857; "Columbia Rolling Mill," *Columbia* [Pa.] *Spy*, Sept. 12, 1857. See also *Lancaster Intelligence*, Sept. 14, 1857.

5. For Panic of 1857 in Lancaster, see John W. Loose, *The Heritage of Lancaster County* (Woodland Hills, Calif.: Windsor Publications, 1978), p. 66.

Also note that all estimates of historical values in 2005 dollars are calculated with various tools available at www.jsc.nasa.gov/bu2/inflate.html.

6. Peter Krass, *Carnegie* (New York: John Wiley and Sons, 2002), pp. 65–67. Sutter's Mill and California gold rush data from California Resources Agency, Sacramento, Calif.

7. Hildegard Dolson, *The Great Oildorado* (New York: Random House, 1959), notably pp. 28–35, 61–71.

8. Sale noted in Wallace card files, HCA.

9. Dolson, *The Great Oildorado*. Extensive descriptions of the oil boom are also found in Ron Chernow, *Titan: The Life of John D. Rockefeller* (New York: Vintage Books, 1999).

10. H. Frank Eshleman, "Lincoln's Visit to Lancaster in 1861; and the Passing of His Corpse in 1865," *Journal of the Lancaster County Historical Society* 13, no. 3 (1909), pp. 55–79.

11. Dolson, *The Great Oildorado*; Chernow, *Titan*.

12. Jokes and insights into Pennsylvania Dutch culture were provided by Professor Richard Beam, Center for Pennsylvania German Studies, Millersville State University. Details of Henry Hershey's oil-field adventure are in Wallace interview of Joseph Snavely.

13. Pennsylvania weather conditions noted here and throughout from online historical records of the College of Earth and Mineral Sciences, Pennsylvania State University. Reports on the Battle of Gettysburg appear in the *Lancaster Daily Inquirer*, July 1–6, 1863. For Nissley, see John L. Ruth, *The Earth Is the Lord's* (Scottsdale, Pa.: Herald Press, 2001), pp. 557–71. See also Caryl Clarke, "When Rebels Came Calling," *York Daily Record*, May 31, 2003; and John H. Mellinger, "An Autobiography," *The Messenger* (Salunga, Pa.), Sept. 1952. The story of M.S. Hershey's buried can is told in the Wallace manuscript, HCA.

14. Joseph T. Kingston, "History of the Fulton Opera House," *Journal of the Lancaster County Historical Society* 56, no. 6 (1952), pp. 141–60. Felix Reichman, "Amusements in Lancaster," *Journal of the Lancaster County Historical Society* 45, no. 2 (1941), pp. 25–66. John Andrews, "The John Wise Story," *Journal of the Lancaster County Historical Society* 59, no. 5 (1955), pp. 109–48. Also see online exhibit http://www.lancasterhistory.org/collections/exhibitions/wealth/panwise.html; the society maintains the John Wise Collection, 1808–1993; Wise is mentioned in Loose, *Heritage of Lancaster County*, p. 115. For Baum, see Linda McGovern, "The Man Behind the Curtain," www.Literarytraveler.com; Frank Joslyn and Russell P. MacFall, *To Please a Child: A Biography of L. Frank Baum, Royal Historian of Oz* (Chicago: Reilly & Lee, 1961).

15. Life at Nine Points and the perpetual motion machine are detailed in

Snavely, *An Intimate Story*, and Joseph Snavely, *The Hershey Story*, Hershey: 1950.

16. The Hersheys' poverty of this time is described by Ruth Hershey Beddoe in her interview with Wallace.

17. Wallace interview of Anne Pownall Webster. Sarena's death and the separation of Henry and Fanny Hershey are discussed in Snavely, *An Intimate Story*, and Snavely, *The Hershey Story*. See also Wallace interview of Mary Hershey Pautz and Wallace manuscript, especially pp. 23–34, 40–51.

2. HEROIC BOYS AND MEN OF INDUSTRY

1. For an understanding of the lyceum movement, see Carl Bode, *The American Lyceum: Town Meeting of the Mind* (New York: Oxford University Press, 1956). Twain's "Roughing It" is at http://etext.lib.virginia.edu/toc/mod-eng/public/TwaRoug.html. Twain's talk is described by Lancaster *Daily Evening Express*, Jan. 13, 1872, and in William R. Luck, " 'Roughing It' at the Fulton: Mark Twain Comes to Lancaster, January 19, 1872," *Journal of the Lancaster County Historical Society* 97, no. 1 (1995), p. 13. The Lancaster County Historical Society also maintains extensive records on the Fulton Opera House, including programs and newspaper advertisements.

2. Milton's experience at Royer's is reported in almost every article and manuscript written about him, including Joseph Snavely, *An Intimate Story of M.S. Hershey* (Hershey: self-published, 1957), pp. 10–11, and Wallace manuscript, pp. 47–50. See also Joseph Snavely, *Meet Mr. Hershey* (self-published pamphlet, 1939; copy in HCA).

3. For a complete history of Lancaster see John W. Loose, *The Heritage of Lancaster County* (Woodland Hills, Calif: Windsor Publications, 1978). Another source of Lancaster history is Gerald Lestz, *Lancaster County Firsts and Bests* (Lancaster: John Baer and Sons, 1989). The architecture of the time is described in Willis L. Shirk Jr., "The Bruner Family and Their Homes," *Journal of the Lancaster County Historical Society* 98, no. 1 (1996), pp. 12–28. The tale of the ten-hour house is told in Warren T. Metzger, "Mishler's Ten-Hour House," *Journal of the Lancaster County Historical Society* 12 (1908), p. 47.

4. Kevin Phillips, *Wealth and Democracy* (New York: Broadway Books, 2000), pp. 40–43, 280–85. See also Theodore Dreiser's *The Financier* (1912; reprint, New York: Plume, 1988), chapter 59.

5. Figure for worker deaths from Maury Klein, *The Flowering of the Third America* (Chicago: Ivan R. Dee, 1993), p. 88; for Westinghouse, see p. 131. Carnegie's life is revealed in its entirety in Peter Krass, *Carnegie* (New York: John Wiley and Sons, 2002). The industrial giants and financial power of Pennsylvania are described in Randall M. Miller and William Pencak, eds., *Pennsylvania: A History of the Commonwealth* (University Park: Pennsylvania

State University Press, 2002), pp. 229, 372–79. Henry Hershey's failure at Nine Points is in Wallace manuscript, pp. 48–50. Quote regarding champagne and beer from Wallace interview of Israel Shaffer.

6. Gary Scharnhorst and Jack Bales, *The Lost Life of Horatio Alger, Jr.* (Bloomington: Indiana University Press, 1985), and Stefan Kanfer, "Horatio Alger: The Moral of the Story," *City Journal*, Autumn 2000. Among Alger's titles were *Ragged Dick, Brave and Bold*, and *Tattered Tom*, which was about a girl who disguised herself as a newsboy.

7. For Wanamaker and the centennial see Miller and Pencak, *Pennsylvania*, pp. 221–22, 247; Klein, *The Flowering of the Third America*, pp. 28, 115–16, 129, 146–47; and William Leach, *Land of Desire*, (New York: Random House, 1993). The centennial is described in great detail in a series of articles in the May 10 and 11, 1876, editions of the *New York Tribune*, the source for the "wretched failure" of 1853. The Free Library of Philadelphia offers a detailed account of the centennial, including a quote from The Tastemakers, at http://libwww.library.phila.gov/CenCol/index.htm. "Emerson and The Atlantic" from Maury Klein, *The Flowering of the Third America*, (Chicago: Ivan R. Dee, 1993), p. 146.

8. Milton's Philadelphia experience is detailed in Wallace manuscript, especially pp. 53–60. See also Hinkle manuscript, pp. 4–9. M.S. Hershey letters and replies are held by HCA. Further detail is in Snavely, *An Intimate Story*, pp. 14–17. An example of Henry Hershey's candy display case is on display at the Hershey Museum, Hershey.

9. Daniel Webster, "Influence of Woman," *Godey's Lady's Book*, January 1852; for the cult of domesticity, see www.library.csi.cuny.edu/dept/history/-lavener/386/truewoman.html.

10. For Henry's cough drops, see Wallace manuscript, p. 58. Milton's failure and trip home are noted in Snavely, *An Intimate Story*, pp. 14–22; see also Wallace manuscript, pp. 57–67, and Hinkle manuscript, pp. 4–9.

3. WANDERING

1. "Leadville District History," *United States Geological Survey Bulletin 707*, Washington, D.C., 1922; see also Howard Lamar, *The New Encyclopedia of the American West* (New Haven: Yale University Press, 1998), pp. 242, 435.

2. Mitch Tuchman, "Supremely Wilde," *Smithsonian*, May 2004, pp. 17–18.

3. Lamar, *New Encyclopedia of the American West*, pp. 296–98. For crime, Indian wars, and other social conditions, see Crandall Shifflet, *Victorian America* (New York: Facts on File, 1996), pp. 16, 277–79.

4. Wallace manuscript, pp. 68–72; Hinkle manuscript, pp. 9–10; pp. 22–23. See also Wallace interviews of Paul Witmer, Paris Hershey, and Jennie Erb.

5. Donald Miller, *City of the Century: The Epic of Chicago and the Making*

of America (New York: Simon & Schuster, 1997), Ch. 1. Rudyard Kipling's *American Notes* of 1891 is available at http://www.hn.psu.edu/faculty/jmanis/-kipling/American-Notes.pdf.

6. Wallace interview of Paul Witmer. Joseph Snavely, *An Intimate Story of Milton S. Hershey.* (Hershey: self-published, 1957).

7. The development of consumer marketplace and mass-market product is noted in Maury Klein, *The Flowering of the Third America*, pp. 182–84; and Robert Kanigel, *The One Best Way* (New York: Viking, 1997), p. 28. Jefferson quote from his *Notes on Virginia*, http://etext.lib.virginia.edu/toc/modeng/public/JefVirg.html. Nineteenth-century retailing booklet is S.H. Terry, *The Retailer's Manual* (Newark: Jennings Brothers, 1869). See also Jagdish Sheth and Ronald A. Fullerton, *Research in Marketing* (Greenwich: Jai Press, 1994), pp. 246–49.

8. Klein, *The Flowering of the Third America*, pp. 38, 47, 182–84.

9. Candy shops and their offerings are listed in *Trow Business Directory* (New York, 1884–85). The problem of whiskey in candy noted in "Candy, Rye and Rock," *The New York Times*, March 19, 1884, p. 4. For Daniel Peter's discovery see Paul Richardson, *Indulgence* (New York: Little Brown, 2003), pp. 237–60.

10. Layout of streets and rail system as well as identification of various buildings from block maps held by the Map Room, New York Public Library, Atlas Shelf g1524.n4251.c6; buildings and other landmarks in 1880s New York identified in Harmon Goldstone and Martha Dalrymple, *History Preserved: A Guide to New York City* (New York: Simon & Schuster, 1975), pp. 117, 234–249. Details on elevated trains and various buildings from Gerard R. Wolfe, *New York: A Guide to the Metropolis* (New York: New York University Press, 1975), pp. 115–17, 235–51.

11. Alvin Harlow, *Old Bowery Days* (New York: D. Appleton and Co., 1931), pp. 387–92, 403–15.

12. LeRoy Ashby, *Endangered Children* (New York: Twayne Publishers, 1997), pp. 58–65; Allan Alexander Sr., *Jacob A. Riis* (Millerton, N.Y.: Aperture, 1974), p. 22. For perils of life in New York, see also Seymour Mandelbaum, *Boss Tweed's New York* (New York: John Wiley and Sons, 1965).

13. Hershey's quote about cities is in Charles Lobdell, "Hershey," *Liberty*, Sept. 13, 1924. For the Hersheys in New York, see Wallace manuscript, pp. 73–77; Joseph Snavely, *An Intimate Story* (Hershey: self-published, 1957), pp. 23–24; Hinkle manuscript, pp. 10–13. Henry's time in the Bowery is also noted in Wallace manuscript, pp. 130–31.

4. EDIBLE MUD

1. M.S. Hershey's start in Lancaster is told in Wallace manuscript, pp.

78–86; Hinkle manuscript, pp. 13–15; and Joseph Snavely, *An Intimate Story of Milton S. Hershey* (Hershey: self-published, 1957), pp. 24–25. "Black sheep" and the growth of the caramel company from John McLain in his interview with Wallace. For caramel process, see Wallace manuscript, pp. 95–98, as well as Wallace interview of Abe Heilman.

2. For dangerous conditions, see *Albert Reese v. M.S. Hershey* in *Pennsylvania State Reports* 163 (New York: Banks and Brothers Law Publishers, 1895). For Reading fire, see Wallace interview of Heilman.

3. D.W. Meinig, *The Shaping of America* (New Haven: Yale University Press, 1986) and Page Smith, *The Rise of Industrial America* (New York: McGraw-Hill, 1984) provide a comprehensive view of American economic history in this period.

4. Maury Klein, *The Flowering of the Third America* (Chicago: Ivan R. Dee, 1993). For corruption in politics and the case of J.N. Camden, see Ron Chernow, *Titan* (New York: Vintage, 1999), p. 210.

5. Pennsylvania's industrialists and wealth are noted in Randall M. Miller and William Pencak, eds., *Pennsylvania: A History of the Commonwealth* (University Park: Pennsylvania State University Press, 2002), especially pp. 370–78. For Carnegie's "gospel of wealth" and its effect on wealthy America, see Peter Krass, *Carnegie* (New York: John Wiley and Sons, 2002), pp. 241–49.

6. For a panoramic view and details of exhibits at the World's Columbian Exposition, see Bruce Schulman's "Interactive Guide to the World's Columbian Exposition," available at http://users/vnet.net/schulman/Columbian/columbian.html. Other sources include *The Book of the Fair*, the official publication of the exposition, and Erik Larson, *The Devil in the White City* (New York: Crown, 2003). Larson's excellent history is the source for Krupp's "pet monster" (p. 207) and details on the Ferris wheel (pp. 208, 305, 373).

7. Stanley Buder, *Pullman* (New York: Oxford University Press, 1967), pp. 63, 81–84; Richard Ely, *Pullman A Social Study*, Harper's Magazine, February 1985, pp. 452–56. Also see Margaret Crawford, *Building the Workingman's Utopia* (New York: Verso, 1995), pp. 42–43.

8. Lehmann appears in Joel Glenn Brenner, *The Emperors of Chocolate* (New York: Random House, 1999), p. 85. Lindt's invention is noted in Paul Richardson, *Indulgence* (New York: Little Brown, 2003), pp. 12, 225. For effects of chocolate, see Dana Small et al., "Measuring Brain Activity in People Eating Chocolate," *Brain*, vol. 124, no. 9 (Sept. 2001), pp. 1720–33.

9. The Cadburys and other European chocolate makers appear throughout Richardson, *Indulgence*. Quaker business practices are reported in Jim Boulden, "The Quaker Way," CNNfn television program, Dec. 16, 2000. A timeline of Cadbury family history and many other key facts appear at

www.cadbury.co.uk. For the Cadbury company town, see William Wilson, *The City Beautiful Movement* (Baltimore: Johns Hopkins University Press, 1989), p. 85, and Richardson, *Indulgence*, pp. 166–74.

10. Wallace interview of Clayton Snavely.

5. CATHERINE

1. "Chocolate Machinery Installed," Lancaster *New Era*, Jan. 25, 1894. A list of Hershey's first chocolate workers and note about their recruitment appear in Wallace files, HCA. For Taylor, see Robert Kanigel, *The One Best Way* (New York: Viking, 1997), especially pp. 9, 11, 17, 60.

2. For National Biscuit Company, see David Traxel, *1898: The Birth of the American Century* (New York: Vintage, 1999), pp. 45–46. For the rise of the management class, see Maury Klein, *The Flowering of the Third America* (Chicago: Ivan R. Dee, 1993), p. 11.

3. Wallace and Snavely both write extensively on Murrie and Blair. Anecdotes about Murrie are in Wallace interview of John C. McLain. Dances were noted in Wallace interview of Mrs. Art Zecher.

4. Mattie's death is noted in the Wallace manuscript, pp. 111–12, and in Joseph Snavely, *An Intimate Story of M.S. Hershey* (Hershey: self-published, 1957), p. 31. For Greeley, see Hiram Schenk, *A History of Lebanon Valley in Pennsylvania* (Harrisburg: National Historical Association, 1982), p. 367.

5. Hershey's acquisition of the homestead and life there are related in Wallace manuscript as well as in Wallace interviews of Mary Hershey Pfautz, Herbert Miller, and Mrs. Paul Copenhaver. Wallace describes Elizabeth Hershey on p. 178. See also Wallace interviews of Herbert Miller and John Moyer.

6. Harold Eager, *The Hamilton Club of Lancaster*, Lancaster, 1989, pp. 50–79. See also *Social Club File*, Lancaster County Historical Society, Lancaster. For Hershey's diamond jewelry, see Wallace manuscript, p.121.

7. For the 1894 banquet, see *The Hamilton Club of Lancaster, 1889–1989*, published by the club in 1989 and held by Lancaster County Historical Society. For the habits of wealthy bachelors, see E. Anthony Rotundo, *American Manhood* (New York: Basic Books, 1993), pp. 129–31. For bordellos, see Peter J. Betts, "A History of the Lancaster Law and Order Society," *Journal of the Lancaster County Historical Society* 69, no. 4 (1965), pp. 216–39.

8. For Milton's courtship of and marriage to Catherine Sweeney, see Wallace manuscript as well as Wallace interviews of Ruth Hershey Beddoe, John McLain, Sam Clark, Lila Snavely, and Katherine Shippen Chambers. Information about Catherine's family from *Biographical and Portrait Cyclopedia of Chautaqua County, New York* (Philadelphia: Gresham and Co., 1891).

9. Berill Champion letter on file at HCA. For the Cadburys and Bournville, see Paul Richardson, *Indulgence* (New York: Little Brown, 2003), pp. 166, 168,

172–74. For the garden city movement, see William Wilson, *The City Beautiful Movement* (Baltimore: Johns Hopkins University Press, 1989), p. 85, and Richardson, *Indulgence*, pp. 166–74.

10. Bournville and the Cadburys are described fully in A.G. Gorden, *The Life of George Cadbury* (New York: Cassell and Co., 1923). *Cosmopolitan* published its article on Bournville in June 1903. For statistics on wealth, see Kevin Phillips, *Wealth and Democracy* (New York: Broadway Books, 2000), p. 38. For the Lattimer strike, see Michael Novak, *The Guns of Lattimer* (Somerset, N.J.: Transaction Publishers, 1996).

6. EGO, ECCENTRICITY, AND SCREWBALLS

1. Sale of caramel company and data on candy sales and cocoa imports from Hinkle manuscript. Information on LaFean from biographical files in library of York County Heritage Trust, York. M.S. Hershey's attitude about the future of caramel was made clear in his comments to Frank Snavely—it's "a fad"—at the Chicago fair, as reported in Wallace interview of Frank Snavely.

2. Details of the sale from Wallace interviews of John McLain and Ruth Hershey Beddoe. See also Joel Glenn Brenner, *The Emperors of Chocolate* (New York: Random House, 1999), pp. 87–89.

3. Wallace manuscript, pp. 147, 150; Sidney Lawrence, "The Ghirardelli Story," *California History* 81, no. 2 (Spring–Fall 2002), p. 90. Hershey advertising materials held by HCA.

4. Wallace interviews of Mrs. Thomas Chambers, Mrs. Eugene Herr, Clayton Snavely, and W. Allen Hammond. See also William Gowers, "Syphilis and Locomotor Ataxia," *Lancet* 181, no. 1, pp. 94–95. Thomas Rolla, *The Eclectic Practice of Medicine* (Cincinnati: Scudder Brothers, 1907); Wilhelm Erb, *The Etiology of Tabes Locomotor Ataxia* (London: New Sydenham Society, 1900). 1899 advertisement Buffalo Lithia Springs of Virginia, HCA. Dr. Erb's warning about pneumonia from Ruth Hershey Beddoe interview, HCA. Information about symptoms of syphilis from Medline, the online medical encyclopedia of the United States National Library of Medicine, www.nlm.nih.gov/medlineplus/ency/article/001327.htm.

5. Wallace manuscript, pp. 161, 167. For "continuous market," see Wallace interview of John McLain. For William Klein, see Wallace interview of Ruth Hershey Beddoe. For chocolate making, see Brenner, *Emperors of Chocolate*, p. 101; Paul Richardson, *Indulgence* (New York: Little Brown, 2003), pp. 238, 241; and Sophie and Michael Coe, *The True History of Chocolate* (London: Thames and Hudson, 1996), pp. 250–59. See also Wallace interviews of Bert Black, Howard Shelley, and Harry Tinney.

6. Wallace interviews of Samuel Moyer, Edna Erb, and Jennie Erb. See also John Loose, "Evolution of the Government of the City of Lancaster," *Jour-*

nal of the Lancaster County Historical Society 95, no. 2 (1992); Lincoln Steffens, *The Shame of the Cities* (1904; reprint, Garden City, N.Y.: Dover Books, 2004); Randall M. Miller and William Pencak, eds., *Pennsylvania: A History of the Commonwealth* (University Park: Pennsylvania State University Press, 2002); Joseph Snavely, *Meet Mr. Hershey* (self-published pamphlet, 1939; copy in HCA); Wallace manuscript, p. 153; Maury Klein, *The Flowering of the Third America* (Chicago: Ivan R. Dee, 1993); Hiram Shenk, *A History of the Lebanon Valley in Pennsylvania* (Harrisburg: National Historical Association, 1982). Real estate transactions from ledger held by Milton Hershey School.

7. Hamilton's planned city is noted in Margaret Crawford, *Building the Workingman's Paradise* (New York: Verso, 1995), p. 2; she discusses the connection to labor issues throughout. See also William Wilson, *The City Beautiful Movement* (Baltimore: Johns Hopkins University Press, 1989), pp. 9, 11, 41, 126–46; "Liberty Hyde Bailey: A Man for All Seasons," online exhibition at Cornell University Library rare manuscript collection, http://rmc.library.cornell.edu/bailey/index.html; Anne Raver, "New World Plants Were a Marvel," *The New York Times*, Nov. 23, 2003, p. LI-10.

8. *Harrisburg Independent*, Feb. 19, 1903. See also Wallace manuscript, pp. 154–57. For data on gap between rich and others, see Kevin Phillips, *Wealth and Democracy* (New York: Broadway Book, 2002), p. 49. Report on Hershey from Joseph Solomon, "Where Happiness and Health Will Go Hand in Hand with a Great Enterprise," *The Business World*, June 1903, pp. 248–50. See also Maury Klein, *The Flowering of the Third America*, pp. 138–40; and David Traxel, *1898: The Birth of the American Century* (New York: Vintage, 1999), p. 319.

7. "Here There Will Be No Unhappiness"

1. Wallace manuscript, p. 171. See also Wallace interviews of Bert Black, Mrs. Paul Copenhaver, and John Schmalbach.

2. Wallace interviews of Donald and Robert Staley.

3. Wallace interviews of Edna Erb, Jennie Erb, Ed Forman, John Moyer, and Hoffer Bowman. Book-burning story told by Harry Tinney in his interview with Wallace. See also Wallace interview of Mary Hershey Pfautz.

4. Wallace interviews of John Habecker, Lila Snavely, Catherine Olfansky, Mrs. Leon Smith, and George Girth. See also Wallace manuscript, pp. 148–50.

5. Wallace interviews of John McLain, Lila Snavely, Sam Clark, and Mrs. Louis Smith.

6. Wallace manuscript, pp. 189–90. For corporations, see Roland Marchand, *Creating the Corporate Soul* (Berkeley: University of California Press, 1998). See also Kevin Phillips, *Wealth and Democracy* (New York: Broadway

Books, 2002), pp. 48–49, 312; Wallace interviews of Irvin Wagner, John Moyer, and Lila Snavely. For progressivism, see Robert Crunden, *Ministers of Reform: The Progressives' Achievement in American Civilization* (Champaign: University of Illinois Press, 1982).

7. For attitudes about "criminal rich" see text of "The Man in the Arena," speech by Theodore Roosevelt, given at the Sorbonne, Paris, April 23, 1910, www.nlm.nih.gov/medlineplus/ency/article/001327.htm. Joseph Solomon's article, "Where Happiness and Health Will Go Hand in Hand with a Great Enterprise," appeared in *The Business World*, June 1903. See also "Hershey the Chocolate Town," *Hershey's Weekly*, May 29, 1919.

8. Monroe Stover oral history, HCA. See also J. Bradford DeLong, *Slouching Toward Utopia* (Cambridge, Mass.: National Bureau of Economic Research, 1997); H.N. Herr, "Planning the Chocolate Town," *Lehigh University Alumni Bulletin*, 1937; Mary Davidoff Houts, Mary Davidoff, and Pamela Cassidy Whitenack, *Images of America: Hershey* (Charleston: Arcadia, 2000).

9. George Bowman oral history, HCA.

10. Houts, Davidoff, and Whitenack, *Hershey*, p. 37; Wallace interviews of McLain and John Wickersham.

11. Wallace interview of George W. Light.

12. Wallace manuscript, p. 199, and his interview of Wickersham.

13. Leo Donnelley, "After a Hershey Tryout," *Philadelphia Evening Times*, Oct. 12, 1908, p. 4; Deborah Wescott, *The Inspiration for Sweet Success* (University Park: Pennsylvania State University Press, 1998); Wallace interviews of Clayton Lehman and Ruth Hershey Beddoe.

8. BENEFICENT JOVE

1. Wallace manuscript, p. 216.

2. "It's a sin" quote from Wallace interview of Sam Clark; see also John Halblieb, "Milton S. Hershey," (unpublished manuscript, 2004, HCA), p. 7; "Report of the White House Conference on the Care of Dependent Children," January 25, 1909, Government Printing Office, Washington, D.C.

3. Leroy Ashby, *Endangered Children* (New York: Twayne Publishers, 1997), p. 80.

4. *Vidal v. Mayor Alderman and Citizens of Philadelphia*, U.S. Supreme Court, January 1844.

5. Trust company ledgers noting discharges at Hershey Industrial School, held by HCA.

6. The Hershey Industrial School Deed to Hershey Trust Company Trustee Milton Hershey and Catherine S. Hershey, Nov. 15, 1909, HCA, Arthur Whiteman oral history, HCA; Wallace interviews of Mrs. Warren Bowman and

Nelson Wagner; see also Wallace manuscript, pp. 209, 227; and J.R. Snavely, *M.S. Hershey Builder* (Hershey: self-published, 1935), pp. 80–81.

7. "Labor Madness," *Hershey's Progressive Weekly*, June 19, 1913; see also Wallace manuscript, p. 204. For Fairfield, see Margaret Crawford, *Building the Workingman's Paradise* (New York: Verso, 1995), pp. 83–87.

8. "Hershey the Chocolate Town," *Hershey's Weekly*, May 29, 1913, Hershey timeline, HCA; "Things to Be Seen in Hershey," *Hershey Press*, May 11, 1911; "Finest Young Bull in America," *Hershey Press*, Oct. 21, 1915; "The Record Year in America's Most Remarkable Town," *Hershey Press*, Nov. 4, 1915; "One of America's Best Employers," *Hershey Press*, Jan. 16, 1919; "Taft Lauds Boy Farmers," *Hershey's Weekly*, Dec. 26, 1912; "What Good Is Sugar?" *Hershey's Weekly*, Dec. 26, 1912; and Joseph Snavely, *An Intimate Story of M.S. Hershey* (Hershey: self-published, 1957), pp. 282–83. See also Wallace manuscript, pp. 205, 209. Sales figures come from list in HCA.

9. Ron Chernow, *Titan: The Life of John D. Rockefeller* (New York: Vintage Books, 1999), pp. 520–54; "Roosevelt the Unique," *Hershey's Progressive Weekly*, Oct. 24, 1912; "Republican Mass Meeting," *Hershey's Progressive Weekly*, Oct. 31, 1912.

10. For Elbert Hubbard and his credos, see Gina Kolata, "Vegetarians vs. Atkins: Diet Wars Are Almost Religious," *The New York Times*, Feb. 22, 2004, section 4, p. 12. See also Rosie Mestel, "Our Appetite for Dieting," *The Los Angeles Times*, March 16, 2004; Snavely, *An Intimate Story*. Ad from *The Fra, Exponent of the American Philosophy*, Aurora, N.Y., August 1913.

11. "Blood Money," *Hershey's Weekly*, Nov. 6, 1913.

12. Letters, Kraver's Bureau to John E. Snyder, Dec. 1911–Jan. 1912, HCA; "Jews Soon to Rule Entire World," *Hershey's Weekly*, Dec. 26, 1912; "Temperance Is Gaining," *Hershey Press*, Dec. 31, 1914; "Don't Kiss or Coddle Baby," *Hershey's Weekly*, Dec. 26, 1912; "Long Living Among the Hebrew Nations," *Hershey's Weekly*, Oct. 24, 1912; "Assassinations Un-American," *Hershey's Weekly*, Oct. 31, 1912; *Lebanon Valley and the State*, Hershey Press, Feb. 22, 1917; "Wisconsin's Marriage Law," *Hershey's Weekly*, March 4, 1915; "Hershey the Chocolate Town," *Hershey's Weekly*, May 29, 1913.

13. "The Assembly Line and the $5 Day," Michigan Historical Center online www.michigan.gov/hal; Douglas Brinkley, *Wheels for the World* (New York: Viking, 2003), pp. 161–75.

14. "Birdman McCalley to Try for Altitude Record," *Hershey's Weekly*, May 22, 1913.

15. The text of Omar Hershey's speech was published in *Hershey's Weekly*, June 5, 1913. See also John G. Hayes, "The Hershey Song; Roosevelt May Speak in Hershey," *Hershey's Weekly*, April 3, 1913; "Letter of Regret; Loving Cup Presentation" *Hershey's Weekly*, June 5, 1913.

16. Wallace interviews of John Myers, Ruth Hershey Beddoe, and Chris Papsin. For "God Save the Queen," see Wallace manuscript, p. 232. Wiesbaden grape cure confirmed in a letter to the author from the Archives for the History of Psychiatry in Leipzig, Germany.

17. Wallace interview of Beddoe; for the Battle of the Flowers, see Wallace manuscript, pp. 229–32.

18. Wallace interviews of Morris Koser and Beddoe.

19. Wallace interviews of John McLain and George Bowman.

9. A THIRD LIFE

1. "Things That Ruin a Town," *Hershey's Weekly*, Jan. 12, 1915.

2. Wallace interview of Ruth Hershey Beddoe; Wallace manuscript, p. 238; and "Mrs. Catherine S. Hershey," *Hershey Press*, April 1, 1915. The invoice for funeral expenses is in HCA. For death of Catherine Hershey, see Debra Wescott, *The Inspiration for Sweet Success* (University Park: Pennsylvania State University Press, 1998). Condolence letters, including Elias Hershey's, are held by HCA. See also Wallace interview with Joseph Snavely.

3. "The City and the Boy," *Hershey's Progressive Weekly*, July 31, 1913.

4. Wallace interview of Ida Gray.

5. George Bowman oral history, HCA.

6. "Donato's *Dance of Eternal Spring*," BBC Online, Sept. 11, 2002, www.bbc.co.ok/dna/h2g2/pda/A813926; "Mr. Hershey Gives Fountain to the City of Harrisburg, Donato on Stand in His $25,000 Suit," *Philadelphia Bulletin*, Nov. 22, 1915; "Harrisburg Is to Get Dance of the Eternal Spring; Hershey Not Angry at All, Sculptor Holds," undated clipping (accession 82.001), Hershey Museum, Hershey; "Hershey upon Stand in Phila. Sculptor's Suit," Philadelphia *North American*, Nov. 23, 1915; Donato letter to M.S. Hershey, dated July 2, 1934, is in HCA.

7. Wallace interview of John Myers.

8. Wallace interview of Clayton Snavely.

9. Peter Krass, *Carnegie* (New York: John Wiley and Sons, 2002), pp. 540–41; Kevin Phillips, *Wealth and Democracy* (New York: Broadway Books, 2002), pp. 310–11, 370.

10. For zoo acquisitions, see Hershey timeline for years 1909–1934, HCA. For monkey catching, see Wallace interview of Howard Shelley. The deaths of Bob and Mag were reported in *Hershey Press*, March 12, 1912, p. 1.

11. Jean Stubbs, *Cuba* (Oxford: Clio Press, 1996), pp. xvi–xix, 199–200; Oscar Zanetti and Alejandro Garcia, *Sugar and Railroads: A Cuban History, 1837–1949* (Chapel Hill: University of North Carolina Press, 1998), pp. 199–200; Allen Ryan, *A Reader's Companion to Cuba* (Orlando: Harcourt Brace, 1997).

12. Beveridge quoted in Allen Wells, "Did 1898 Mark a Fundamental Transformation for the Cuban Sugar Industry?" (paper presented at Latin America and Global Trade Conference, Stanford University, Stanford, Calif., Nov. 16–17, 2001).

13. Wells, "Did 1898 Mark a Fundamental Transformation"; Clifford James, "Sugar Crisis," *American Economic Review*, Sept. 1931, pp. 481–97; *Fortune* editors, *Understanding the Big Corporations*. (New York: R.M. McBride and Company, 1934), Ch. 10, American Sugar Refining.

14. For a description of Havana in this period, see Joseph Scarpaci, *Havana* (Chapel Hill: University of North Carolina Press, 2002). For Hershey in Cuba, see Wallace interviews of Tomas Cabrera and Mrs. Fernandez Chiron.

15. Joseph Snavely, *Milton S. Hershey Builder*, (Hershey: self-published, 1935), pp. 187–88.

16. Wallace interview of Angel Ortiz.

17. Thomas Winpenny, "Milton S. Hershey Ventures into Cuban Sugar," *Journal of the Lancaster County Historical Society* 105, no. 1 (Spring 2003), pp. 2–14; Hudson Strode, *The Pageant of Cuba* (New York: Random House, 1934), pp. 240–43. See also Wallace interviews of Francisco Rodriguez, Philip Rosenberg, and Joseph Snavely.

18. "Henry Ford and M.S. Hershey," *Hershey Press*, March 8, 1917. See also Wallace interview of Rodriguez. The outpouring of job applicants and other wartime events are noted in Hinkle manuscript and in Wallace's date files, HCA.

19. Douglas Brinkley, *Wheels for the World* (New York: Viking, 2003), p. 220; Zanetti and Garcia, *Sugar and Railroads*, pp. 199, 200, 258; Wells, "Did 1898 Mark a Fundamental Transformation"; Winpenny, "Milton S. Hershey Ventures into Cuban Sugar."

20. Damien Fernandez and Madeline Betancourt, *Cuba; The Elusive Nation* (Gainesville: University Press of Florida, 2000); Scarpaci, *Havana*, pp. 45; Wallace interview of Myers.

21. "Birth of a Nation Next Week," *Hershey Press*, May 16, 1918. For the Building 25 fire, see *Hershey Press*, Feb. 22, 1918.

10. A BETTING MAN

1. "Seeing Hershey Cuba with Mr. M.S. Hershey," *Banker's Life Bulletin*, March 1923, reprinted in *Hershey Press*, April 12, 1923; Hudson Strode, *The Pageant of Cuba* (New York: Random House, 1934), pp. 240–55.

2. Hershey's financial records held by HCA; see also Wallace interviews of Kathleen Musser, J.N. Sollenberger, and Herman Seavers. Anecdote about Lebkicher and his guardian from Wallace interview of Henry "Doc" Henny.

3. Katherine Shippen and Paul Wallace, *Milton S. Hershey* (New York:

Random House, 1959). See also Wallace interviews of Tomas Cabrera, Sollenberger, and Seavers; "Sugar Mill at Hershey Cuba Is Modern," *Hershey Press*, July 5, 1923; and Oscar Zanetti and Alejandro Garcia, *Sugar and Railroads: A Cuban History, 1837–1949* (Chapel Hill: University of North Carolina Press, 1998).

4. Wallace interviews of Stanley Russell and Cabrera. See also J. Bradford DeLong, *Slouching Toward Utopia* (Cambridge, Mass.: National Bureau of Economic Research, 1997).

5. George Hotchkiss and Richard Franken, *The Leadership of Advertised Brands* (New York: Random House, 1923); Merele Crowell, "The Wonder Story of Wrigley," *American Magazine*, March 1920.

6. Ignazio Romanucci oral history, HCA. See Wallace interview of Clayton Snavely for billboards.

7. "The Ideal Community," *Hershey Press*, Feb. 17, 1921; "Rowdyism in the Park," *Hershey Press*, July 3, 1913; "Cross Burning," *Hershey Press*, Feb. 28, 1924; "Klan Casts Shadow on Nation's Politics," *The New York Times*, Nov. 18, 1923, sect. 10, p. 1.

8. "MS Hershey Gives $60,000,000 Trust for an Orphanage," *The New York Times*, Nov. 9, 1923, p. 1; James C. Young, "Hershey Unique Philanthropist," *The New York Times*, Nov. 18, 1923, sect. 10, p. 4.

9. "Welfare Workers Criticize Hershey," *New York Herald*, Nov. 20, 1923; for "When a Man Gets Very Rich," see *Success* magazine, Oct. 1927, and HCA quote file; Edward Woolley, "How Hershey Pays Back His Chocolate Millions," *McClure's*, April 1923.

10. Letters in M.S. Hershey letters collection, HCA. See also Wallace interview of Sollenberger, as well as Monroe Stover oral history, HCA. For Eline's Chocolate, see Michael Reilly, "Schlitz Brewing Company: A Chronological History," 1995, available at www.chiptin.com/schlitz/history7.htm.

11. Mr. Goodbar and other production anecdotes from Hinkle manuscript. See also Wallace interview of John McLain. The conflict with the Hershey brothers is detailed in files at HCA: of special note are various letters to and from Hershey brothers; "Hershey Co. Enjoins Rivals' Use of Name," *The Interstate Grocer* (St. Louis), Feb. 6, 1926; and the settlement agreement filed with the District Court of the United States, Middle District of Pennsylvania, Oct. 1921.

12. Tour described in letter from Mario Lauzardo to J.G. Snavely, Oct. 30, 1956, HCA. See also "The Hershey Cuba Connection," *Lancaster Intelligencer Journal*, Sept. 9, 2003; and "Seeing Hershey Cuba." For Elwood P. Cubberley, see *An Introduction to the Study of Education and Its Teaching* (Boston: Houghton Mifflin), p. 444.

13. Wallace manuscript, p. 251; "The Hershey Exposition," *El Mundo* (Havana), Nov. 22, 1927; further information on labor in Cuba in Hinkle manu-

script; Thomas Winpenny, "Milton S. Hershey Ventures into Cuban Sugar," *Journal of the Lancaster County Historical Society* 105, no. 1 (Spring 2003), pp. 3–14. For the country fair, see Lauzardo letter and copy of fair program held by HCA. See Zanetti and Garcia, *Sugar and Railroads*; translations of articles on labor unrest from the Cuban newspapers *El Mundo, El Diario, Heraldo de Cuba, El Universal,* and *El Combate* from Sept. 1925 to May 1926 are held by HCA. For background on sugar in Cuba, see Christina Hostetter, "Sugar Allies" (master's thesis, University of Maryland, 2002), in HCA, and Wallace interview of J.W. Eric.

14. Wallace interviews of Eric, Russell, and W.S. Lambie.

15. For Ford slogans, see Maury Klein, *The Flowering of the Third America* (Chicago: Ivan R. Dee, 1993), pp. 173–75. See also "Report of the Committee on Recent Economic Changes of the President's Conference on Unemployment," (University of Michigan, Ann Arbor), 1929, and Kevin Phillips, *Wealth and Democracy* (New York: Broadway Books, 2000), p. 61.

16. Maury Klein, *Rainbow's End* (New York: Oxford University Press, 2001); Don Nardo, *The Great Depression* (San Diego: Greenhaven Press, 2000); Wallace interviews of Russell and Arthur R. Whiteman; Arthur Whiteman oral history, HCA.

11. The End of Innocence

1. Maury Klein, *Rainbow's End* (New York: Oxford University Press, 2001), p. 276; Conrad Black, *Franklin Delano Roosevelt: Champion of Freedom* (New York: Public Affairs, 2003).

2. Don Nardo, *The Great Depression* (San Diego: Greenhaven Press, 2000).

3. William Myers and Walter Newton, *The Hoover Administration: A Documented Narrative* (New York: Scribner's, 1936), pp. 63–64.

4. Samuel Eliot Morison, *The Oxford History of the American People* (New York: Oxford University Press, 1965), p. 950.

5. Allen Dye and Richard Sicotte, "U.S.-Cuban Trade Cooperation and Its Unraveling," *Business and Economic History,* Winter 1999, pp. 19–38; Allen Dye, "Cuba and the Origins of the U.S. Sugar Quota" (paper presented at Eighth Annual Conference of the International Society for New Institutional Economics, Tucson, AZ, Sept. 30–Oct. 3, 2004). Staples's 1934 statement on sugar tariffs and quotas is in HCA. See also *Fortune* editors, *Understanding the Big Corporations* (New York: R.M. McBride and Company, 1934), Ch. 10, American Sugar Refining.

6. A timeline of construction and descriptions of various projects are available at HCA. See also "Thin-Shell, the Concrete Barrel Roof," *Construction Methods and Equipment,* April 1937, pp. 44–47; Angelo Elmi et. al, "A Study of the Hershey Sports Arena," *The Literary Artisan,* Nov. 1939, p. 22; Edmond

Saliklis and David Billington, "Hershey Arena, Anton Tedesko's Pioneering Form," *Journal of Structural Engineering*, March 2003, pp. 278–95; "Building a Grand Hotel on Pat's Hill," *Hershey Chronicle*, May 21, 1998, p. 5; "Hotel Hershey," HCA online (www.HersheyArchives.com); Ivan Viet, "Anton Tedesko, 1903–1994," *National Academy of Engineering* 8 (1996), pp. 262–67; "Industrial High School," *Hershey Hotel High-Lights*, Nov. 10, 1934; *The Modern Office Building* (pamphlet published by Hershey Chocolate Company, 1937), in HCA; Thomas Deegan, "Arena at Hershey Opened for Hockey," *The New York Times*, Dec. 20, 1936, sect. 5, p. 1.

7. Stanley Buder, *Pullman* (New York: Oxford University Press, 1967), p. 226.

8. "Mr. Hershey Gives Away His Fortune," *Fortune*, January 1934, pp. 72–80. See also Edward Tancredi oral history, HCA.

9. "Hershey Home Denies Catholic Teaching," Buffalo *Catholic Union and Times*, Nov. 8, 1934; "Hershey School in Refusal to Allow Catholic Boys to Practice Religion Charged," *The Indiana Catholic and Record*, Nov. 9, 1934, p. 1; "Religious Care Assured at Hershey School," *The Brooklyn Tablet*, Dec. 1934, p. 1; "An Ad for Hershey," *America*, Dec. 15, 1935, p. 268; memo to Hershey Salesmen from Sales Department, Nov. 28, 1934, HCA; "Rome Fights Chocolate Man," *The Fellowship Forum*, Dec. 1934.

10. United Mine Workers of America official history, www.umwa.org; Victor Bondo, *American Decades, 1930–1939* (New York: Gale Research, 2002), pp. 117–22, 232–35.

11. "The Chocolate Bar-B" is in HCA. See also *Forbes*, May 1, 1937.

12. For Billy Brinker, see Wallace interviews of Israel Shaffer, Robert Bucher, and Abe Heilman. Author interviews with residents of Linden Road, Hershey.

13. "25,000 Cheer Lewis at Chrysler Rally" and "Will Never Recognize Any Union," both in *The New York Times*, April 8, 1937, p. 1.

14. Recollections of the strike and anti-Italian sentiment can be found in the oral histories and interviews held by HCA, including those of Rollin and Viola Brightbill, Rose Gasper, Edward Tancredi, Ignazio Romanucci, Dionisio Castelli, Victor Blouch, Henry Stump, William Cagnoli, and James DeSantis. Extensive news reports on the strike and related events are in File 97020 BX01, HCA. Other sources consulted for these events include Hickle unpublished manuscript, pp. 363–75, Wallace manuscript, pp. 320–40, Hartley Barclay, "Civil War in Hersheytown," *Mill and Factory* (New York), May 1937; Hershey Company list of union activists, HCA; "General Demands of the Sit Down Strikers," press release issued April 7, 1937, by Hershey Chocolate Corporation, HCA; strike timeline, HCA; "The Chocolate Bar-B" was published by the Communist Party of Hershey and is in HCA; "Farmers Drive Sit-Downers Out of Idle Hershey Factory After Battle with Clubs, Fists," *The*

Washington Post, April 8, 1937, sect. 2, p. 1; and "The News of the Week," *The Washington Post*, April 11, 1937. Finally, I consulted an array of articles in *The New York Times*, all from April 1937: "Farmers Oust 500 Sit-ins," April 8, p. 1; "25,000 Cheer Lewis at Chrysler Rally," April 8, p. 1; "Will Never Recognize Any Union," April 8, p. 1; "$87,000,000 Cost in Chrysler Strike," April 8, p. 4; "Fear Hershey Riot; Plant Shut Again," April 9, p. 1; "Earl Will Not Tolerate Mob Rule in Pennsylvania," April 9, p. 3; "Pleas for Vote Rejected," April 10, p. 1; and "Hershey Concedes Vote Negotiation," April 11, p. 1.

12. Something Like a God

1. Roger Southhall, "Farmers, Traders and Brokers in the Gold Coast Cocoa Economy," *Canadian Journal of African Studies* 12, no. 2 (1978), pp. 185–211; "Understanding the Cocoa Market," (pamphlet published by *New York Cocoa Exchange*, March 17, 1938); Wallace interview of Stanley Russell; Edward Tancredi oral history, HCA; Hinkle manuscript.

2. Tancredi oral history and Hinkle manuscript, p. 368.

3. "A Century of Change in America's Eating Patterns," *Food Review* (U.S. Department of Agriculture, Washington, D.C.), Jan.–April 2000, pp. 16–32.

4. Wallace interview of Milton Hunchberger and Wallace interview of George Horsdick and Hinkle.

5. For Boys Town visit, see *Quiz Kid of 84*, undated company press release, HCA, and Wallace interview of Lila Snavely. See also M.S. Hershey, *Team Work Sells the Hershey Idea*, 1938, HCA. For anecdote about sitting under portrait, see Herb Krone, Lancaster *New Era*, Feb. 8, 1950. "Senile" quote from Wallace interview of William Kishbaugh.

6. Anecdotes from Wallace interviews of Edmund Madciff, Lila Snavely, and Susan Spangler and from Monroe Stover oral history, HCA.

7. Curt Sampson, *Hogan* (New York: Broadway Books, 1997), pp. 65–67; see also Wallace interview of Spangler.

8. Joel Glenn Brenner, *The Emperors of Chocolate* (New York: Random House, 1999), pp. 8, 9; Christina Hostetter, "Sugar Allies" (master's thesis, University of Maryland, 2002), in HCA.

9. Author interview with Lou Bocian. Inventory of M.S. Hershey's possessions in HCA.

10. Wallace interview of Richard Light.

11. Herman H. Hostetter, *The Body, Mind and Soul of Milton Hershey* (Hershey: self-published, 1971; held by HCA); "Mallard Duck Storm Victim," *The Middletown* [Pa.] *Press*, June 23, 1945, p. 5; Hinkle manuscript, pp. 450–56.

12. "Hershey Rites Simple, Brief," undated clipping in HCA; "M.S. Hershey Dies, Stricken Ill Thursday," Lancaster *New Era*, Oct. 14, 1945, p. 1;

"M.S. Hershey, One of America's Gracious Giants of Giving, Reaches the End of Life," *Hotel Hershey High-Lights*, Oct. 20, 1945, p. 1; "Hershey Farms Apple Crop Looks Fair, Peaches at Best," *Hotel Hershey High-Lights*, Oct. 20, 1945, p. 1; copy of Rev. John H. Treder's eulogy held by HCA.

13. Letter from Ruth Hershey Beddoe to Wallace, June 11, 1954, HCA.

13. THE LEGACY

1. From author interviews with Craig Stark, descendants of the couple who may have adopted Hershey's offspring, and John O'Brien.

2. Hershey annual reports, available at HCA, and author interviews with former Hershey executives. See also Joel Glenn Brenner, *The Emperors of Chocolate* (New York: Random House, 1999), pp. 10–18.

3. Hershey Foods 2003 annual report, HCA; Hershey timeline, HCA; Brenner, *Emperors of Chocolate*, pp. 227–28, 243–54.

4. Monroe Stover oral history, HCA; author interview with Bruce McKinney.

5. "The $50 Million Phone Call," *Pennsylvania Medicine* magazine, May 1968, pp. 41–48.

6. Monroe Stover, *A Little Talk About a Big Man* (Hershey: self-published, 1989; held by HCA).

7. Author interviews with Ric Fouad and William Lepley. See also *60 Minutes*, CBS, Sept. 22, 2002.

8. Author interviews with William Alexander and Anthony Colistra. See also Sandy Marrone, "Rod Pera: Champion of Change," Harrisburg *Patriot-News*, Dec. 6, 1994.

9. Hershey School Board of Managers, *Milton Hershey School: Its Purpose, Goals and Strategies*, Feb. 8, 1990.

10. Author interviews with Joseph Berning and Lou Bocian.

11. Milton Hershey School Trust IRS filings, Girls and Boys Town IRS filing, supplied to author by the institutions.

12. Martin Wooster, *The Milton Hershey School: The Richest Orphans in America, Compassion and Culture* (Washington, D.C.: Capital Research Center, 2004); "The Great American Chocolate Trust," Dec. 9, 1999, Mayer Brown Rowe Web site www.mayerbrownrowe.com; also author interview with Lepley.

13. Ford Turner, "Milton Hershey Will Alter Policies," Harrisburg *Patriot-News*, Aug. 1, 2002.

14. WHAT WOULD MILTON DO?

1. Author interviews with William Lepley, Anthony Colistra, and William Alexander; "Hershey Foods Furor," Harrisburg *Patriot-News*, July 26, 2002, p.

1, as well as several other articles in that day's issue; Bill Sulon, "Strike at Hershey Foods Ends," Harrisburg *Patriot-News*, June 9, 2002, p. 1; Shelley Branch, Sarah Ellison, and Gordon Fairclough, "Hershey Foods Is Considering a Plan to Put Itself Up for Sale," *The Wall Street Journal*, July 25, 2002, p. 1.

2. Branch, Ellison, and Fairclough, "Hershey Foods Is Considering," p. 1. Account of Friendly's meeting from author interviews with attendees. See also John Helyar, "Hershey Sweet Surrender," *Fortune*, Oct. 1, 2002, available at www.fortune.com/fortune.

3. From author interviews with participants. See also "Hershey," *CBS Sunday Morning*, Sept. 1, 2002, and Helyar, "Hershey Sweet Surrender."

4. Author interviews with Robert Vowler and Tom Davis.

5. Author interviews with Vowler, Colistra, and Bruce McKinney and from videotaped recording of Vowler press conference, Sept. 18, 2002, provided by John Dunn, Hershey Community activist. See also Bret Marcy, "Trustees Were Blindsided and Besieged," Harrisburg *Patriot-News*, Sept. 22, 2002, p. 1; Bill Sulon, "Area Trustees Prove Key in Hershey Decision," Harrisburg *Patriot-News*, Sept. 23, 2003, p. A8; Helyar, "Hershey Sweet Surrender."

6. Author interview with Lepley.

7. Author interviews with Ric Fouad and John O'Brien. See also Stephanie Strom, "Turmoil Grips Elite School over Money and Leaders," *The New York Times*, Nov. 21, 2004, sect. 1, p. 24.

ACKNOWLEDGMENTS

Milton S. Hershey was a man of few words and even fewer letters. He didn't like to write, and he didn't keep much of the correspondence that passed through his hands. These habits make him a difficult subject to capture. I knew early in the hunt that I would need many guides. I was fortunate to find them.

The Hershey Community Archives is not just a deep and broad resource for information about Hershey the man, the place, the companies, and the school. It is one of the best sources available for records on American business and society in both the Gilded Age and for the period from World War I through the end of World War II. Archivist Pamela Whitenack generously shared the holdings she oversees as well as her time and counsel.

While Pam and her staff contributed almost daily assistance, many others responded to requests for information and insight with real generosity. Joseph Brechbill, Ph.D., opened the records of the Milton Hershey School and explained significant aspects of the school's story. Amy Bischof of the Hershey Museum freely shared her understanding of the man and the place while conducting an insider's tour of the collection.

Further aid and advise were provided by researchers Craig Stark, David Rempel Smucker, Ph.D., and Michelle Dally. Vital insight into local culture and custom were shared by Richard Beam of the Center for Pennsylvania German Studies, Millersville State University. Further assistance was provided by the Lancaster County Historical Society, and its staff, led by Thomas R. Ryan, Ph.D.

Among those who agreed to be interviewed and consulted for this book were many people whose lives are forever attached to the community of

Hershey and the Hershey School. Included are Kathy Taylor, Ric Fouad, Bruce McKinney, John Halblieb, John O'Brien, Joseph Berning, Anthony Colistra, Tom Davis, Robert Vowler, and John Dunn.

Just as research requires the guidance of those who know the territory, writing cannot be done without the help of first readers and editors. In this case, David McCormick helped keep me on the path and editor Geoff Kloske provided just the right mix of warnings, encouragement, direction, and correction. Copy editor Trent Duffy went to extraordinary lengths to improve and clarify the manuscript line by line.

My support team for this project included my daughters Amy and Elizabeth and allies Brian Lipson, Ralph Adler, and B.D. Colen. Finally, credit for whatever original insight and understanding appears in this text must be shared by Toni Raiten-D'Antonio. Over the years I have learned from her how to recognize and appreciate the dreams, aspirations, conflict, and courage in the lives of others.

INDEX

ABOUT THE AUTHOR

Pulitzer Prize–winning journalist Michael D'Antonio is the author of many acclaimed books including *Atomic Harvest, Fall from Grace, Tin Cup Dreams, Mosquito,* and *The State Boys Rebellion.* His work has also appeared in *Esquire, The New York Times Magazine, The Los Angeles Times Magazine,* and many other publications.